GREAT VIOLINISTS
IN
PERFORMANCE

GREAT VIOLINISTS IN PERFORMANCE

Critical Evaluations of Over 100 Twentieth-Century Virtuosi

by Henry Roth

PANJANDRUM BOOKS
Los Angeles

First Printing.

Library of Congress Cataloging-in-Publication Data

Roth, Henry, 1916 -
    Great violinists in performance.

    Bibliography: p.
    Includes index.
    1. Violinists--Biography.   I. Title.
ML398.R68   1986   787.1'092'2   [B]   86-21248
ISBN 0-915572-85-0
ISBN 0-915572-84-2 (pbk.)

By the same author:

Master Violinists in Performance, Paganiniana/T.F.H. Publications, Inc. (Neptune City, NJ, 1982).

The Way They Play (Vol. 5-12), (Samuel Applebaum, co-author), Paganiniana/T.F.H. Publications, Inc. (Neptune City, NJ, 1978-1983).

Panjandrum Books, 11321 Iowa Ave., Suite 1, Los Angeles, CA 90025

Manufactured in the United States of America.

ACKNOWLEDGMENTS

I wish to express my profound appreciation to Professor Josef Gingold for his invaluable advice and suggestions. His constant encouragement and interest contributed significantly to the fulfillment of what has been a long and arduous, but eminently rewarding task.

To my wife Esther, for her myriad constructive criticisms and many months of editing and typing; to Laurie Dechery for her expert professional assistance in preparing the manuscript; and to Samuel Fordis for his numerous services in behalf of this enterprise, I offer thanks.

The rare photos in this volume appear through the generosity of my San Francisco friends Joseph Gold, Kenway Lee and I. MonDragon, as well as Zino and Yolanda Francescatti, Pavel Kogan, Lawrence Sommers, Mrs. Gregor Piatigorsky, Morris Victor, Ben Berzinsky, Jill Spalding, and Louis and Annette Kaufman. Photos of contemporary artists appear through the courtesy of Columbia Artists Management, IMG Artists, International Artists Management, Maxim Gershunoff Attractions, Gurtman and Murtha Associates, and several of the violinists cited herein.

Special recognition must be given to the *The Strad* of London for granting permission to reprint excerpts from some of my published articles, and James Creighton for his indispensable *Discopaedia of the Violin*.

Richard Greene provided the data on country and western violinists.

English spellings of Chinese names were kindly supplied by Professor Situ Hua-Cheng, Chairman of the Society of Performing Arts at the Central Conservatory of Music in Beijing.

To all the above I express my gratitude.

H.R.

TABLE OF CONTENTS

Fritz Kreisler (1875 - 1962)

One of the most individualistic performers in the annals of violin art, the beloved Kreisler opened new vistas of sound, expressiveness, charm, elegance and nobility of style. Both as composer and as instrumentalist, he expanded significantly the lexicon of violin playing. Includes brief illustrations of how he produced some of his uniquely personalized expressive effects.

Zino Francescatti (b. 1902)

The ultimate embodiment of the Gallic ethos in violin art, he combines a flair for Paganiniana gymnastics with a consistently glowing tone and cultivated musicality in an extensive repertoire. Francescatti's rise to stardom was slow and arduous, but he has long since won the right to be included among the foremost violinists of the twentieth century.

Nathan Milstein (b. 1904)

He is the incarnation of violinistic longevity. Both Milstein's professional colleagues and the public revere the subtle mechanics of his fabulous instrumental mastery, together with the virility, vigor and audacity of his interpretations. Contains a detailed comparison of Milstein and Heifetz.

David Oistrakh (1908 - 1974)

A transcendental artist, violinist and human being, his superlative expressive powers, a natural extension of his personality, touched the heartstrings of his listeners. Included is a candid analysis of his performance, his teaching philosophies and his relationship to the Soviet hierarchy.

FOREWORD

I have closely and carefully followed the development of violin art and the performance of its noted practitioners throughout my life—a subject that has always fascinated me in all its myriad aspects. As a devoted student of our beloved "fiddle," I found *Great Violinists in Performance* an ideal companion to Henry Roth's *Master Violinists in Performance*, which was so enthusiastically received by professional violinists and lay readers alike. Both are certainly among the very best works I have ever read dealing with our great violinists of the past and present.

Excellently written and meticulously attentive to detail, it never fails to sustain interest, and is a far more personalized account than most other books in its field. Roth's encyclopedic knowledge, profound powers of evaluation, uncompromising honesty and boundless enthusiasm place him among the top writers dealing with the art of violin playing.

My heartiest congratulations to the author for enriching all of us with this splendid volume.

Josef Gingold

PREFACE

Great Violinists in Performance, a companion volume to my *Master Violinists in Performance*, consists of comprehensive evaluations of master violinists and their musical backgrounds. For readers who have not yet encountered my previous book, allow me to clarify my violinistic and musical philosophies, as well as the intent of this book. After a lifetime as a professional violinist and nearly a quarter of a century as a regularly published music critic, I still regard the violin primarily as an instrument of song. As the instrument closest to the human voice, beauty and individual character of tone remain among the cardinal components of violin art. Furthermore, I hold that the element of personality in performance is the principal factor that separates truly great artists from superb instrumentalists . This point of view is stressed throughout these pages.

The judgment of every concert-goer, professional critic or lay auditor, is subjective, based upon aesthetic preferences and cumulative experience. However, in attempting to analyze a performer's equipment and artistic priorities, it is imperative to be objective as far as human frailty will permit. One may admire greatly the performances of given artists, yet find them alien to one's own temperament, tastes and sensibilities. Nevertheless, these artists should be given their full due.

In making evaluations, mere clinical examinations and quotes from past critical reviews are not sufficient. The ultimate determinant in assessing and characterizing an artist is to place him in historical perspective—that is, in relation to his predecessors, contemporaries, immediate successors, and general development of the art of violin playing. This is the approach which *Great Violinists in Performance* adopts. It is only natural that the reader will disagree with some of my observations and statements. But if this volume can provoke that reader to further independent investigation and thought on this subject, the cause of violin art will have been furthered, and the purpose of this book fulfilled.

Violinists can be categorized in many ways: by nationality, birth date, status, national "school," pedagogical lineage, or even alphabetically, and it is certain that whichever procedure is chosen, it will be unsatisfactory to one or another commentator or reader. Realizing that one cannot please everybody in all things, I have again employed several methods of presentation, and hope the reader will find this acceptable.

Although I have heard nearly all the violinists cited here in live concert, and in most instances on numerous occasions and under a diversity of performance conditions, recordings must neccessarily play a key role in appraising the degree of their artistry. For example, how else can we realistically assess deceased artists if we have not heard them in live performance? However, I admit that one must be wary of forming hard-and-fast opinions on the basis of recordings alone. This is particularly true of those manufactured in the modern era, for which scientific editing and engineering sound manipulation have become standard procedure. Even if one hears these recordings as taken from live performances, there is no guarantee that the playing has not been mechanically "purified" and the sonority enhanced. Meticulously edited specimens can be notably superior to a violinist's live performance, especially in the case of violinists ranking in the second and third categories. Quite often it is much easier to make an accurate evaluation from the "one-take," minimally-spliced recording of the teens, twenties and thirties, provided they are not too primitively produced and are in reasonably good condition.

For better or worse, once an artist is deceased and his playing is beyond living memory, recordings represent the only testament of his performance. Thankfully we have recourse to this priceless source that enables us to hear a myriad of violinists, from Joachim and Sarasate to the contemporary scene. Granted, the pre-1925 recordings contain all manner of inadequacies and flaws. Yet without them we would be completely dependent on conflicting "ear-witness" accounts, many by observers lacking intimate professional knowledge of the various levels, specifics, and nuances of violin art. Thus I feel that a survey of an artist's recordings in consort with live concert evaluations, must be an integral part of this volume. After all, the thousands of recordings of both live and deceased artists are readily available only to collectors and connoisseurs, not to the general violin fancier. In preparation for this book I carefully relistened to more than 300 works recorded by David Oistrakh, large and small, and a comparative percentage of the body of recordings by all of the artists mentioned.

When making evaluations, it must be taken into consideration that some major artists are more convincing in showpieces or vignettes than heavyweight concerti; others in bravura gymnastics rather than introspective, or even patently romantic sonatas. But there is a place for all in our wondrous pantheon of violin art!

Since this is a treatise pertaining specifically to solo violin performance, not pedagogy, I have elected to include only those teachers who have enjoyed careers as soloists on an important level. The complex matter of violin pedagogy in all its ramifications is a subject for another volume, or series of volumes. No disrespect whatsoever is intended to those eminent and worthy pedagogues not named.

In the period from the maturity of Kreisler at the turn of the century to today, many aspects of violin art—its standards of musicianship, the content of programs, concepts of what constitutes top-level tone quality, and a multitude of related matters—have radically altered. Revolutionary advances in technical mastery and tonal production, and expanded repertorial demands have taken place. Selection and application (or omission) of left-hand expressive devices remain key points of contention between opposing schools of thought. The "new" continues to struggle against the "old," and surprisingly, at times they even contribute significantly to each other. The phenomenon of international, national and local competitions has taken on an incredible importance, unprecedented opportunities (plus many an inequity and injustice) for young violinists. With the entry of the Asiatic nations into the field, violin art, for the first time in history has become truly internationalized. The ensuing chapters touch upon all of these points.

GREAT VIOLINISTS IN PERFORMANCE does not purport to be an encyclopedia of violinists. Unfortunately many fine violinists deserving recognition are not included for sheer lack of space. To these respected colleagues, I offer my apologies.

To Esther, my beloved wife—the
most sensitive, compassionate,
generous and humane person I
have ever known.

Fritz Kreisler, the personification of violinistic elegance, charm, bewitching sound and uniquely personalized style

CHAPTER ONE

Fritz Kreisler

B
Y THE TURN OF THE CENTURY, the art of violin playing had entered the flood tide of romanticism, and came to be dominated by the heightened standards of overt emotionalism as personified by the immortal Belgian Eugène Ysaÿe (1858 - 1931). The lofty academicism of Joseph Joachim (1831 - 1907) and the cool, glittering virtuosity of Pablo de Sarasate (1844 - 1908), while still held in universal esteem, were being displaced by new concepts of sound and interpretive style. Giants though they were, each in his own individual manner represented violinistic modes that belonged to the late nineteenth century, already declining. Vestiges of their influence could be heard among violinists in the concert halls of Europe and America for some time after their demise, but the changing tastes of audiences demanded playing that expressly emphasized "feeling." In the inevitable struggle between old and new the "sensual" players of tonal opulence were destined to triumph.

If Ysaÿe can be thought of as having linked the violin art of the nineteenth and twentieth centuries and as being the catalyst and artistic inspiration of a legion of younger hyperromantic musicians throughout the world, it was Fritz Kreisler (1875 - 1962) who became his direct heir. Kreisler's hegemony spanned half a century. By the end of the second decade of the twentieth century he had prevailed over Mischa Elman in their contention for public favor, and not even the awesome feats of the young Heifetz could diminish Kreisler's popularity with the mass audience and with the critics. In fact, many listeners who acknowledged and revered the peerless mastery of Heifetz continued to maintain that they derived more aesthetic satisfaction from Kreisler's playing. It would be difficult to name a violinist more beloved by his public and colleagues alike. As one of the most individualistic performers in the annals of violin art, Kreisler opened up new vistas of sound, expressiveness, charm, elegance and nobility of style. Both as composer and as instrumentalist, he expanded significantly the lexicon of violin art.

Freidrich-Max ("Fritz") Kreisler was born in Vienna on February 2, 1875 (Jascha Heifetz was born on the same date twenty-six years later). His father, Samuel Kreisler, was a physician and had come to Vienna from Krakow. In Kreisler's younger days, his Jewish origin was common knowledge in Europe, and was often cited in print, as in *My Memories*, the autobiography of the Belgian virtuoso Ovide Musin. Later, when the Nazis came to power, his stupendous career in Germany was brought to an abrupt end. Kreisler never participated in Jewish activities, however, whether religious, social or philanthropic, and like so many Austrian Jews of the period, he gravitiated easily toward Catholicism, especially after his marriage to Harriet Lies, a Catholic-American. His mother, Anna, a housewife and mother of five who displayed no musical talent, played an important role in Fritz's life. Although in poor health, she accompanied Fritz to Paris for his final two years of violin study.

Kreisler was given a miniature violin at age four, and when he evinced precocity, his father, an amateur violinist, soon bought him a better instrument and proceeded to give him lessons. His first professional teacher was Jacques Aubert, a theatre concertmaster. At age seven he was admitted to the Vienna Conservatory, the first student under ten ever to be accepted. Here he became the pupil of Joseph Hellmesberger, Jr., and had harmony and music theory classes with Anton Bruckner. He also studied the piano, for which he had an exceptional talent. At ten, the boy won the gold medal for violinists at the conservatory, an unprecedented honor for one so young.

A group of friends presented the young Kreisler with a three-quarter size Amati and insisted he be sent to study in Paris. This represented a financial hardship for Dr. Kreisler. After auditioning before a jury of eminent professors at the Paris Conservatoire he was admitted to the class of the venerable Joseph Lambert Massart, a former teacher of Henri Wieniawski, and had lessons in composition with Leo Delibes. At twelve, the boy once again received an unprecedented honor by winning the Conservatoire's *Premier Premier Prix*.

Kreisler never received formal violin instruction after the age of twelve; his further development was dependent upon his genius and keen powers of observation. Heard by the famed pianist Moritz Rosenthal, he was engaged as an assistant artist for fifty concerts, including many in America, and was paid $50 per appearance. His playing evoked contradictory evaluations. In Boston, Howard Malcolm Tichnor of the *Daily Globe* wrote: "the lad ... accomplished his task creditably but gave no evidence of remarkable talent or remarkable training ... He plays like a nice, studious boy who has a rather musical nature ... but cannot be ranked among prodigies or geniuses." Louis C. Elson of the *Daily Advertiser* (known for his pocket-size music dictionary) disagreed, writing: "young Master Kreisler is a genius who has yet something to learn...He is, I think, destined to become a very great artist if he does not disdain further study."

In his 1888 debut with the Boston Symphony under Walter Damrosch the thirteen-year-old played the Mendelssohn Concerto in E-minor and Ernst's *Hungarian Airs*. Kreisler's biographer, Louis Lochner, states that the following year in his debut with the Chicago Symphony under Hans Balatka, the boy performed Wieniawski's *Faust Fantasy* on a program which starred the pianist Rosenthal. (Actually the official Chicago Symphony was not founded until 1891). From the *Chicago Times*: "If his bowing were as good as his left hand work, he would now be one of the most remarkable players of the day." In contradiction, the *Chicago Tribune* reported: "His performance was crude and frequently out of tune."

Returning home rich in experience but in economic straits, he spent the next two years studying scholastic subjects at the Piariste Gymnasium in Vienna, a school directed by Catholic laymen of the Piarist order; he then spent two years in medical school. It is said that during these years he did not touch the violin.

At twenty, after joining the army, he played intermittently for the soldiers; it was about this time that he composed his monumental cadenzas for the Beethoven concerto.

Following his two years of army service, educated and ready to face life, he decided to make music his career. He spent eight weeks practicing assiduously to regain his technique. Hearing of a vacancy for the second desk in the Vienna Hofoper orchestra, he auditioned—and was turned down by no less a judge than the well-known Arnold Rosé, concertmaster and founder of the Rosé String Quartet. The verdict alleged that Kreisler was "no good at sight reading." This was a patently ridiculous statement, since the young man was already a thorough musician and was known to be extraordinary at learning and mastering new scores. Doubtless Rosé was bewildered by the vivid vibrance of Kreisler's tone in contrast to his own old-fashioned, dry sound, and was possibly tainted by professional jealousy. Nevertheless, Rosé was no different from many other observers and critics of the day who tended to look backward in performance standards. Even the great Joachim, who considered the young Franz von Vecsey a peerless prodigy, was not at all enamored of Kreisler's playing. It took many years for Kreisler's then-unorthodox sound and style to win mass audience acceptance, particularly in Central Europe. Even in his home town of Vienna, many listeners preferred the comparatively dry sound of Huberman.

Undaunted by his failure with the Hofoper orchestra he managed to obtain various solo engagements with the assistance of influential friends who were impressed by his highly personable manner, as well as by his great talent. In Constantinople his playing delighted the Sultan, and during a Russian tour he played the Tchaikovsky concerto with much success. A second Russian tour was interrupted by a madcap decision to run off to Finland for a romantic interlude with a Finnish girl he had met in Warsaw. Later, in Paris, he pawned his violin to buy expensive presents for a girl with whom he was temporarily infatuated. It was during this profligate period that he began to compose his vignettes.

Meanwhile, his reputation as an artist was burgeoning. He won the approval of the eminent critic Eduard Hanslick for his playing of the Bruch Concerto No. 2 with Hans Richter and the Vienna Philharmonic. But it took him far longer to gain wide public favor in his own home town than in the United States and England. In December, 1899, a golden opportunity presented itself when he was invited to play the Mendelssohn concerto with the redoubtable maestro Artur Nikisch and the Berlin Philharmonic. At the conclusion of the performance, Ysaÿe, who was in the audience, stood up ostentatiously and applauded.

As early as 1901 Kreisler played trio concerts with Josef Hofmann and Jean Gerardy, often to very small audiences; before that he had given sonata concerts in a tour with Harold Bauer. It was during this period that he also barnstormed through the English provinces in joint recitals with tenor John McCormack. Often the box office receipts netted them only ten or twelve pounds together, from which Kreisler's pianist was guaranteed three pounds a concert. Their largest fee was sixty pounds.

Yet for all the warmth of his growing audience and critical reception, Kreisler's solo career was in serious danger of foundering. Like Paganini, Wieniawski, Ysaÿe and many another colossal talent before him, Kreisler was a hedonist, lacking direction and self-discipline.

Fortunately in 1902 he met, fell in love with and married Harriet Lies (Mrs. Fred Woerz), a wealthy American woman who uncompromisingly regulated and dominated his personal, social and professional lives, and was in effect responsible for the ultimate success of his career. Once Kreisler came under the sovereignty of this iron-willed, imperious lady, his days of wastrel frivolity were over. In later years she would declare characteristically: "I have made him," a true if not particularly modest statement. Because she was a divorcee, they were married in a civil ceremony: not until 1947 were they permitted to marry in a Catholic service. Next to his wife, his closest friend and associate was his manager Charles Foley.

In 1905 Kreisler received $400 for two appearances with the New York Philharmonic; by 1910 he earned $600 per concert while touring as a soloist with the Boston Symphony, and $800 for each of two recitals. By the mid-1920s he was earning $3,000 per concert, and in 1944 he received $5,000 for each of his first five broadcasts.

Fritz Kreisler at twelve when he won the
Conservatoire's **Premier Premier Prix**

Fritz Kreisler in mid-career

Nathan Milstein and Kreisler in 1943

Gradually he overcame nearly all of his opposition in the early 1900s and inured the mass audience to the sound and style that were so different from those of his predecessors and contemporaries. He began to make more and more recordings: by 1914 he was among the highest paid performers in the recording field. In 1910 he had accepted the preposterous sum of $1,000 for fifty of his arrangements and so-called transcriptions from the B. Schott music publishing company in Mainz, but later, of course, this was adjusted to be commensurate with his skyrocketing reputation.

During these years he greatly enlarged his repertoire. In 1910, Kreisler gave the premier performance of the massive Elgar concerto in London, which had been dedicated to him.

His success continued unabated until 1914 with the outbreak of World War I. Acting in accordance with the dictates of his conscience, Kreisler, an active reservist in the Austrian army and a devoted subject of the Austrian Kaiser, went to fight for his native land in August of that year. The Austrian government, which could have profitably employed such a world-renowned artist in any number of propaganda situations, displayed its abysmal stupidity by sending him into the trenches. After several weeks on the Russian front he was wounded in the leg and discharged as a "complete invalid." By November, 1914, he was already back in New York. The following year he wrote a small quasi-diary published in book form titled *Four Weeks in the Trenches (The War Story of a Violinist)*, a superficial if sincere account of his experiences. According to the book, it would seem that Kreisler fought strictly as a patriotic duty in "service to his fatherland" rather than for any deeply felt political or philosophical convictions. He did, however, help to support the families of some of his fallen comrades for many years, a humanitarian act typical of Kreisler.

At first, his wartime activities had no adverse effect upon his career. But as the war dragged on, stories of German atrocities became widely known and pro-Allied sympathies soared. When the United States entered the war, Kreisler's vast popularity, like that of other artists loyal to the German-dominated Central Powers, began to plummet. In the 1917 - 1918 period, many of his so-called friends deserted him, and he was forced to retire from the American concert stage. He reappeared in Carnegie Hall on October 27, 1919 amid continuing protests which forced him to cancel numerous proposed concerts. Even as late as 1924, Kreisler encountered protests in France which affected his performance schedule. However, by the 1920 - 1921 concert season in the United States, the public had forgiven his indiscretion and he quickly became once again an adored figure. This is the single episode in Kreisler's adult career during which he was not an idol of the mass audience. Unlike Elman, Thibaud, Kubelik, Huberman and other stellar violinists, Kreisler's unparalleled hold on the mass audience endured, as did the esteem of his colleagues and critics—right up to his last public concert on November 1, 1947.

After 1933 Kreisler no longer appeared in Germany because of his Jewish heritage (although the Lochner biography craftily evades the issue). In 1935 Kreisler was involved in a brouhaha with certain martinet critics concerning the spurious origin of some of his compositions, an incident which will be discussed below.

On April 27, 1941, he was struck and seriously injured by a delivery truck while crossing a New York street. The convalescent period required several months, and he did not perform publicly until January, 1942. He became an American citizen in 1943.

In his final years Kreisler's playing suffered from the usual violinistic infirmities brought on by old age. Fritz Kreisler died on January 29, 1962, shortly before his 87th birthday.

Kreisler has been the subject of countless articles and critiques, culminated by Louis Lochner's *Fritz Kreisler,* a volume which is obviously the officially sanctioned survey of his life. Although Kreisler himself remains a beloved figure, various colleagues who knew him personally are sharply critical of the book, not only because it is written with the roseate rhetoric of an utterly compliant press agent, but also because it is marked by the customary shortcomings of an observer who has not had intimate experience with the art about which he writes. Unfortunately, the book neither offers significant details of Kreisler's violinistic training, nor does it discuss the technical problems that he had to cope with and overcome during his early studies. Still, the biography contains a wealth of anecdotes, quotes and data of importance (and a certain number of contradictions). If one accepts the book strictly as a meticulously orchestrated account, it is well worth reading.

Lochner tells of Kreisler's love of collecting rare books and manuscripts. He also depicts him as a philosopher, linguist, intellectual and humanist of impeccable stature. The case for the final description is not strengthened by the violinist's warm friendship with the dictator Mussolini only a few short years before the Fascists began their cruel depredations against the people of Ethiopia, Spain and Italy. But at least Kreisler was not biased in his associations: he was also a good friend of Albert Einstein. Obviously his music-making endeared him to almost everyone on the personal level. And what is even more important, he remained an exceptionally kind, benevolent man all the days of his life, ever generous to his colleagues in every respect.

Kreisler was often referred to as "The King of Violinists," a sobriquet which fit his platform image and general deportment as well as his performance. His concerts exuded a special aura, and listeners often felt like privileged guests at a memorable royal function. Yet there was nothing pompous or affected in the man. He would walk out majestically, holding his violin by the scroll at arm's length, tune up quickly without fuss, and begin. While playing, his stance was relaxed and his body gestures natural. The only sign of tension was his habit of repeatedly tensing his cheeks, a mannerism that always reminded me of a chipmunk busily munching a nut. One invariably felt about Kreisler, the artist, the same way one felt about Einstein, the scientist-humanist. His speech always retained a Teutonic accent, but the ad-lib address he gave at his seventy-fifth birthday fete was testimony to his eloquence in English. He spoke with a lisp. He had an intrinsic sense of humor which he exercised freely in his younger years, yet dignity gradually pervaded his public image as he grew older. His penchant for humor was often evident in his private relationships and, of course in many of his compositions. But he never would play the fool at a concert in order to evoke titters from the audience. He was the king of all he surveyed, not the court jester.

There was nothing extraordinary about the size or shape of his hands: they were strong, yet pliant. His fourth finger was comparatively short, and while he used it without stint in technical passages, he almost always preferred using his third finger in vibrant lyric playing.

Kreisler's reflexes were magnificent. Though never a gymnast of the fingerboard, the sheer velocity and clarity of his filigree passage work and trills surpassed those of most specialists in Paganinian bravura; his finger articulation was almost in a class by itself; his superb penchant for trills and finger tremolos is vividly manifest in his unique cadenza for Tartini's *Devil's Trill* Sonata which, unfortunately, he never recorded. With the exception of a few sensational technicians who were infinitely inferior to him as tonalists and artists, Kreisler's technical equipment compared favorably with any of his colleagues of the pre-Heifetz era.

Much is made of the fact that Kreisler was opposed to long hours of practice; that he actually practiced little; and that he would walk onstage and perform with little or no warm-up. But it must be remarked that because of this, the first fifteen or twenty minutes of his playing could be extremely rough and untidy, and not until he was thoroughly warmed up and acclimated to his surroundings did he sound like "Kreisler." He stated: "I never practice before a concert. The reason is that practice benumbs the brain, renders the imagination less acute, and deadens the sense of alertness that every artist must possess. Before a concert I merely dip my fingers in hot water for a few seconds." He did not specify what he did when hot water was unavailable. Of course, audiences accepted inconsistency from artists in bygone days, even from those who practiced incessantly. Perfection had yet to become a fetish. Even in Kreisler's finest playing, there were apt to be minor blemishes, but when he finally reached full stride, he played so gloriously one could forgive him anything. And though his career carried over into the era of new technical standards (initiated by Heifetz), audiences tended to overlook his less elevated moments and to dote upon those that were irresistible and inimitable.

Kreisler's bowing included certain unorthodoxies. Whereas some violinists (Zimbalist, for example) took pride in their ability to negotiate the "long bow" (i.e. using a single stroke for an extreme length of time in cantilena passages), Kreisler was actually extravagant in his constant bow changes. He sought and achieved robustness and resonance of sound at all times, in every type of passage, and preferred to use strong modern bows screwed to inordinate tension. Thus, the separation of bow hair from stick was outsized; one never heard the "stick" in his playing, only the hair in full contact with the string. His bows took a beating; fortunately they were not the old, irreplaceable French masterpieces. It is safe to say that no great violinist in memory changed bows as often as Kreisler. His bowing was an integral element in one of the cornerstones of his art—the distinctive rhythmic pulse that characterized everything he played, masterwork or miniature. A key factor of his superlative rhythmic faculties was his rubato phrasing, a cardinal feature of his playing. Kreisler, like Ysaÿe before him, possessed a gift for rubato which enabled him to take rhythmic liberties without sabotaging the natural beat inherent in the music. When he elected to either push or hold back in the rhythm for expressive purposes, and he did so often, he instinctively compensated for it. One of his most beguiling tricks was using the upper part of his bow to accentuate, individually, a group of notes in a subtle phrase ending with rubato.

In matters of tempo, Kreisler greatly preferred deliberation to haste. He was never a player who rushed from climax to climax, leaving prosaic sections between. Every note and bar was precious to him; nothing was ever wasted and, in general, his tempi were slower than those of today's violinists; in many instances, considerably slower.

The Kreisler tone was magical in its effect, different from any other; bewitching, yet virile; fragrantly sweet but never cloying. The tactile impact of his left hand fingers was amazingly articulative, yet the tonal texture was "meaty," without a trace of lean linear sound.

Accounts of his playing, both written and "ear-witness," constantly emphasize that he was the first to use the continous vibrato. Flesch cites his "extraordinary intensive vibrato." These statements are true, but they do not encompass the entire subject. As far back as Wieniawski (1835 - 1880) (who is said to have taught it to Vieuxtemps), and somewhat before, romantically inclined violinists used some degree of vibrato for expressive purposes, as opposed to the classically oriented academicians who shunned vibrato as an abhorrent aberration. The latter played in a manner we

Kreisler in New York, 1948

Zino Francescatti and Kreisler in the former's New York home, 1954

would consider impossibly "dry," especially those trained in the German school. Kreisler sustained a semblance of vibrato even in technical passages in a manner that was far in advance of even his most romantically inclined colleagues and competitors. However, it is necessary to understand that other violinists, either by design or in emulation of Kreisler, could "shake their arms off" and not approximate the Kreisler sound. That is because his vibrato was not only continuous and singularly intense, but was produced differently. Where others used a wrist or arm vibrato, or a combination of the two, or a tense fingertip vibrato (especially prevalent among French violinists) which tended to be taut and often unpleasant, Kreisler used what I have chosen to call a "reflex" vibrato. One never saw Kreisler indulge in furious hand or arm "flapping" when vibrating; rather his vibrato was generated from some point "within" the arm to the oscillating fingertip, which had an extremely narrow point of contact. The result might be likened to an electric current enlivening each note he played to whatever degree he chose. Others had fast vibratos that were tense rather than intense; studied, overt appendages to their technical arsenals. Kreisler's vibrato was as natural to him as is swimming to a fish. A significant advantage offered by his unique vibrato was an ability to make lyrical passages of doublestops sound like two separate voices blended in mutual song in a manner unexcelled, and perhaps unmatched, by anyone. At no time did he indulge in the currently widespread habit of vibrating on some notes and playing other with "dead" fingers in a single lyric expressive passage. Kreisler's tone and vibrato are all the more remarkable inasmuch as they were honed in an era that still looked askance at intense vibrato and "sound for sound's sake."

Together with the phenomenon of his vibrato, Kreisler had yet another expressive weapon of devastating import—his vast array of seductive slides, portamentos and position changes. The scope of these devices was perhaps more extensive and diversified than that of any other elite twentieth-century violinist. One cannot claim that some of these devices were not also used by his colleagues, great and lesser, but the results of those who tried to imitate the entire gamut of these embellishments—who had not his prodigious vibrato, temperament and unfailing elegance of taste (and who did?)—were usually nothing but pale mimicry. It should be recognized, however, that more than a few of the older-generation players profitably incorporated elements of Kreisler's expressive devices in their performance and even reflected a modicum of the radiance of Kreisler's elegant musicality. In his book *The Principles of Violin Fingering*, the Soviet pedagogue I.M. Yampolsky states: "The Kreisler portamento is based mainly on the *sliding of one finger*" (his italics). This is substantially incorrect. A great many of Kreisler's unique expressive slides and position changes involved *two* fingers—the "bridging" note and the "landing" note.

A vital component of his uniqueness in this area was his ability to articulate the "landing" note of his position changes with an instantaneous rapid vibrato that never required "getting set." Admittedly, some of Kreisler's expressive artifices may sound dated or overdone to modern ears, but whatever his excesses, they were part and parcel of his violinistic way of life, and contributed enormously to the individuality and allure of his playing.

Any attempt to make an encyclopedic survey of Kreisler's expressive contrivances could scarcely fulfill its purpose. The finger connections could be fast or slow, blatantly emphasized or exquisitely subtle. His ability to sustain "life" in position changes was transcendent. Many consisted of "bridging" effects in combination with non-primary fingers; others were employed in changes from one string to another, or were simplistic up or down one-finger slides. On occasion he even used an effect similar to the famous "Heifetz slide," gliding up the string with the "landing" finger and hitting the note with instantaneous intense vibrato. I have provided a few few random examples for the interest of professionals and students, but efforts to describe them on paper can hardly be satisfactory. They must be demonstrated in the flesh. As we know, expressive slides, portamentos and position changes of all types are now "out of style," and only Perlman (and, to a lesser extent, a few others) among contemporary violinists uses them to any considerable degree and, it might be added, with astounding success.

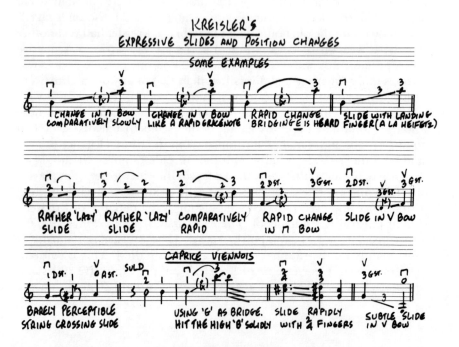

CAPRICE VIENNOIS

INDIAN LAMENT

FAIRLY HEAVY SLIDE IN ⊓ BOW

SLIDE RAPIDLY WITH 1ST FINGER IN ⊓ BOW

SLIDE WITH 2ND FINGER

SLIDE IN V BOW

SLIDE ON D & A STRINGS

SCHUBERT SONATA (DUO) IN A MAJOR, OP. 162

A SUBTLE 'HEIFETZ' SLIDE

EST.

THE CHANGE FROM A ST. TO E ST. IS INAUDIBLE

VALLE MUSIC PAPERS 12441 Riverside Drive
Phone 762-0615 No. Hollywood Ca 91607

GRIEG SONATA IN C MINOR, OP. 45

ALLEGRETTO ESPRESSIVO ALLA ROMANZA

3 GST.

SLIDE IN V BOW

HEIFETZ TYPE SLIDE

SUBTLE SLIDE

SLIDE WITH 3RD FINGER TO 4TH FINGER

2 DST.

3

SLIDE IN V BOW

SLIDE IN ⊓ BOW

BEETHOVEN CONCERTO - LARGHETTO

D ST.

4 A ST.

SUBTLE SLIDE IN V BOW

POSITION CHANGE IS SUBTLY ELEGANT, BUT DEFINITIVE

For all its grace, elegance and nobility, Kreisler's playing was pure sensuality. Each note was negotiated with an ear for beauty and expressed a great *joie de vivre*. No violinist ever played more liltingly. His was a seething temperament, albeit one governed by patrician instincts. He consistently sought to charm his listeners, and every facet of his playing was oriented toward that end. But for all the sensual nuances of his art, his spiritual qualities were celestial.

Nonetheless, it would be unrealistic to say that he did not have detractors, especially in the early part of his career, and even in later years. These observers considered Kreisler a glorified salon player and a purveyor of kitsch. This was clearly unfair. Although it was true that he was supreme as a player of inconsequential ear-tickling bagatelles, and shrewdly used this marvelous skill in the aggrandizement of his career, Kreisler was also a superlative interpreter of the masterworks within the context of his time and aesthetic priorities. True, as one of the great personalities of the violin, his sound and style were emblazoned on every bar of his playing, in every type of work. Since the composer's text was so firmly wedded with Kreisler's unique violinistic personality, it was difficult to tell where one left off and the other began. Indeed, he freely transcribed numerous major violin works: the Tchaikovsky concerto, the first movement of the Paganini Concerto No. 1 and Corelli's *La Folia*. Many professionals, including myself, feel that far more often than not, the effects of these compositions were heightened substantially. And his piano and orchestral accompaniments were invariably superior to the originals. Kreisler was seldom less than respectful, but was in no way subservient to any composer's so-called intentions. He was never a favorite of die-hard academicians. His art was dedicated to "making music" for people in every walk of life to enjoy—and to the devil with dispassionate nominal "rules." At the same time, his infallible good taste prevented him from violating the essential spirit of any composition.

Kreisler's memory was extraordinary. Even with the score on a music stand he never really needed it. Apart from lifelong acquaintance with his recordings, I enjoyed the privilege of hearing Kreisler in live recitals and as a soloist with orchestras (as well as on radio broadcasts) over a period of many years. Each event was a memorable experience, even those in which he was flagrantly off form. His recording legacy is comparatively limited in repertorial scope, but his live performance repertoire was broad. Among those that stand out in my mind are his Viennese-tinted interpretation of the Tchaikovsky concerto with piano accompaniment, in which a constantly whistling open E string did not disturb his unflappable poise a whit; his feisty and ineffably lyric performance of his transcribed version of Paganini's Concerto No. 1 (first movement) when he was already in his sixties; the unforgettable nobility of his Beethoven concerto when in top form; the delicious exuberance of his Mozart Concerto No. 3 (with piano); the dazzling trill-tremolo batteries in his brilliant cadenza to Tartini's *Devil's Trill* Sonata; and the magical effect of his brief transcriptions and original compositions which, despite myriad performances, always sounded fresh and vital. One could go on and on.

The Kreisler discography consists of more than two hundred works, large and small (mostly the latter). Sadly, many of his prime performances of major works: the concerti of Elgar, Bach, Tchaikovsky, Mozart Nos. 3 and 5, Spohr No. 8, Vieuxtemps No. 2, Bruch No. 2, the Chausson *Poème*, the sonatas of Brahms, Mozart, Franck, and Debussy, and Bach's *Chaconne*, were never recorded. Nor were such choice smaller morsels as his *Praeludium and Allegro*, or his *Recitativo and Scherzo Caprice*, ever recorded—not, at least, on accredited labels.

As far back as 1904, his primitively engineered recording of the Bach-Wilhelmj *Air on the G String* shows him to be tonally and stylistically in advance of his competitors (with the exception of Ysaÿe). His 1908 Brahms-Joachim *Hungarian Dance No. 5* projects rich G string sound and dashing spirit.

However, the profusion of these pre-electric Kreisler vignette recordings that were destined to enchant the world began to appear around 1910. They ranged from about two to five minutes, tailored to fit the old ten-and twelve-inch 78 RPM discs, and included trifling settings of popular favorites: *The Rosary, Poor Butterfly, Old Folks at Home, Beautiful Ohio, On Miami Shore, Love Sends a Little Gift of Roses, A Kiss in the Dark, Blue Skies, The World is Waiting for the Sunrise,* and others. Kreisler's formula for these tidbits was simple: play the melody in the lower and upper register (or both), garnish it with doublestops and, when feasible, add the embellishments of those lacy, swift filigree passages that sounded as if they were improvised. Actually, it is said that he concocted these in an hour or two, and that often he went into the recording studio and polished the rough edges shortly before the "takes." This grouping was supplemented by brief Kreisler transcriptions and originals.

What can one say about these performances, slight imperfections and all, except once again to turn to that overused word (in Kreisler's case) "inimitable." Every expressive device in his lexicon was archly instilled into these miniature gems. If one concentrates on the "core" of the sound, Kreisler's eminence is readily apparent even in weather-beaten and scratchy recordings. Each listener familiar with these has his favorites, my own being the naively sentimental *From the Land of the Sky Blue Water* by Cadman, with its lascivious tone, ravishing rubatos and imaginative passagework; an unaccompanied version of Haydn's *God Save the Emperor*, the Austrian national anthem, set in a quasi-Bachian mode (one can almost visualize the uniformed Kreisler standing stiffly and reverently at attention as his adored Kaiser reviewed the troops). And how can one not include his early recordings of *Caprice Viennois* with its entrancing lilt and gorgeously vibrant doublestops, the exhilarating *Schön Rosmarin* and the bittersweet *Liebesleid*? These are only a few of the outstanding gems. Yes, it would be easy for a modern-day observer to question some of Kreisler's expressive ploys, as, for example, his three successive similiar slides in descending triplets in Massenet's *Meditation* from *Thais*. But despite the listener's better judgment he might well find himself accepting the exaggeration, because the entirety of the playing is so captivating.

A number of the early Kreisler brevities have been rereleased on long-playing records by companies specializing in this area, but the total is still comparatively small. If some major company were to decide upon making a monumental contribution to violin art (as did RCA with the six-volume, twenty-four disc *Heifetz Collection*), it could do no better than to include sixty or seventy of these mini-treasures with the later vignettes and a limited number of Kreisler masterwork recordings. Such a compilation would constitute an invaluable research and training bequest to the coming generations. This is not to imply that young artists should strive to imitate Kreisler. They could not do it convincingly no matter how hard they might try. The value would lie in their being able to imbibe those beauties of sound and style that enraptured millions of yesteryear listeners, and perhaps even to learn a thing or two along the way.

The post-electric recordings continue the output of stunning short-piece discs, some of them rerecordings. The 1925 through 1929 group retains all the wondrous freshness of the old acoustical discs under superior engineering conditions.

Gypsy Andante, the slow movement from Dohnanyi's *Ruralia Hungarica*, Op. 32c, is one of the magical performances of this era, though the two outer movements of the suite contain more than a permissible amount of untidiness. The Dvořák-Kreisler *Slavonic Dance No. 3 in G* is another of this exalted caliber, with vibrant doublestop lyric passages that sound as if two violins were playing. The Dvořák-Kreisler *Indian Lament* and *Humoresque*, (the latter a best-seller), Kreisler's *Chanson Louis XIII and Pavane, Gypsy Caprice, Tambourin Chinois* and *Old Refrain* are but a few of the more impressive in this genre.

The quality of Kreisler recordings remained high until the latter 1930s, but it is the opinion of many observers that his playing from about 1910 to the end of the 1920s represented his peak performance. Unfortunately, many people have heard only his recordings of short numbers made near the end of his career with Charles O'Connell and the Victor Symphony Orchestra, which are considerably below his finest playing. As Kreisler approached seventy, his hearing gradually deteriorated and he was increasingly subject to flatness of pitch, especially in the higher register of the E string. Throughout his career, when encountering temporary pitch problems, he tended idiosyncratically to play flat rather than sharp.

Before discussing Kreisler's major work recordings, mention should be made of several collaborations with other artists. His 1915 disc of Nevin's *Mighty Lak' a Rose* with Geraldine Farrar (and a murky orchestra) demonstrates how a violin obligato in his hands could enhance the entire character of a performance. With all due respect to Farrar, it is essentially Kreisler's record. Even more radiant are his pairings with the legendary John McCormack, one of the few artists who could participate with Kreisler on equal terms. Their 1914 recordings of Godard's *Lullaby* from *Jocelyn* (in which Kreisler plays a single incorrect note), and the 1920 Rachmaninoff *O Cease Thy Singing, Maiden Fair* and *When Night Descends* can only be described as sublime, and on a par with the Elman-Caruso vignette collaborations. One can only wonder how much (or more probably, how little) preparation Kreisler made for these heavenly duos. Infinitely less balanced artistically is the 1927 recording of his transcriptions of Bizet's *Intermezzo* from *L'Arlesienne* and Corelli's *Sanctissima* played with his cellist brother Hugo and pianist Michael Raucheisen. Nine years younger than Fritz, Hugo was a solid player of orchestra section caliber but simply no match for his brother.

An interesting pairing is the 1915 Bach Concerto for Two Violins in D-minor with Efrem Zimbalist and string quartet collaboration. As a duo effort it is not truly distinguished, despite the allegation in the L.P. rerelease program notes by the well-known New York critic Irving Kolodin, that their "two sounds might almost be the product of the same impulse, so well are they conciliated." This is simply not the case. Kreisler's vibrant tone clearly dominates Zimbalist's cool though pure sound throughout. Each of the artists sustains his own personal style (in slides, articulation etc.), and the two are quite disparate. The disc is significant as a historic testament, and both violinists play well, individually.

Kreisler's sonata recordings with Serge Rachmaninoff (1928) and his complete cycle of Beethoven's ten Sonatas for Violin and Piano with Franz Rupp (1935 - 1936) represent yet another pinnacle of his recording career. The Rachmaninoff association includes the Grieg Sonata in C-minor, a natural for the potent descriptive powers and glowing tone of Kreisler in a performance that, to my taste, has never been equalled. His novel slides and his sense of pacing and imagery are ideal for this music. Curiously, Rachmaninoff takes rhythmic liberties in the opening of the second movement (♪♪ ♩ instead of the printed ♪♪ ♩ which Kreisler plays) and elsewhere, but his third movement is boldly evocative; the melodic passages are compellingly ariose. Equally impressive is their Schubert Sonata No. 5, Op. 162, with its lissome elegance and charm. And Beethoven's Sonata No. 8 in G, Op. 30, No. 3, is the archetype of spontaneity, silkily smooth and refined. In these three sonatas, the Kreisler stylistic insignia is ever the paramount ingredient of the performances.

The union with Rupp is certainly one of the all-time elite sonata disc collections. Beethoven is thoroughly imbued with the lighthearted Viennese spirit by the violinist with the sensitive, sympathetic collaboration of Rupp, who discreetly avoids stressing his own personality in deference to that of Kreisler. A more ebullient, vivacious interpretation can scarely be imagined. The Sonata No. 5 (*Spring*) pulsates with youthful exuberance; No. 7 in C-minor is lightly dramatic, and the sound in the second movement, angelic; No. 3 in E-flat major, with its perky articulative challenges, is rhythmically superlative; in No. 10 in G-major, Op. 96, Kreisler never relaxes his expressive instincts no matter how unwieldy the passages, as in the thorny finale. The entire execution projects a disarming sense of ease. Of the ten, only No. 9 (*Kreutzer*) falls below his highest standards, with the opening a bit "wobbly." At times there is a bit of pitch flatness, and in general it is less spotless than the other sonatas, yet there is, especially in the second movement, some glorious playing. Taken collectively, had Kreisler never left us any other recordings than the Beethoven sonata cycle, his position among the immortals in the violin pantheon would be assured.

Like most of the great violinists, Kreisler played string quartets and related chamber music with his colleagues privately whenever possible. His own String Quartet in A, typically rich in string color and lustrous harmony, was recorded in 1935 by Kreisler with Thomas Petrie, William Primrose and Laurie Kennedy. This is an unjustly neglected opus, though admittedly it requires a first violinist with a distinct flair for the effervescent Kreisler style to give it full relevance. The second movement contains echoes of *Tambourin Chinois*, the fourth reflects a rhapsodic mood akin to those of *La Gitana* and *Gypsy Caprice*. One may find the totality of the work somewhat saccharine, but its unorthodox loveliness is difficult to resist, particularly when Kreisler is presiding at first violin with such excellent collaborators. This is a seamless performance of a quartet that deserves periodic resuscitation. Those organized ensembles that regularly incorporate one work of easily listenable romanticism and instrumental opulence in their programs would do well to learn Kreisler's quartet. There is nothing quite like it in the repertoire.

Apart from the so-called Vivaldi Concerto in C-major which is actually a Kreisler composition, he recorded only six concerti. The Beethoven, Brahms, Mendelssohn and Mozart No. 4 concerti were recorded twice.

The Beethoven, recorded with Leo Blech and the Orchester der Staatsoper Berlin, 1926, is more consistent in sound and technical detail than the 1936 version with Sir John Barbirolli and the London Philharmonic. The latter is still superb, and the orchestral sound is understandably superior in engineering. One can pinpoint an occasional exaggeration of slides, but the spirit of his interpretation is extraordinarily free, yet architecturally sound. And unlike so many modern violinists who smother the Beethoven with constant détaché bowing, Kreisler cannily alternates détachés with spiccatos and even staccatos. The third movement cadenza comprises a lesson in remarkable bow control, and the balletic opening of the movement recalls a resonant horn-like fanfare. The *Larghetto* is positively celestial. In all, the performance is the very personification of nobility in the most august sense.

The Brahms concerto recording of the 1920s, also with Blech and the Berliners, is a bit superior to the 1936 disc with Barbirolli and the London Philharmonic. Kreisler does not evince the unerring technical security of the best modern players, but his expressive powers are at play in every passage; there are no uneventful "valleys" between the "peaks." The *Adagio* is sovereign in its tonal color and nuance, and the slashing opening thirds of the *Allegro giocoso* erupt with scintillating vibrance. His Brahms cadenzas may be marginally less Olympian than those for the Beethoven, but they are nevertheless grandly conceived.

Although the orchestra's sound suffers from the recording's antiquated engineering, the 1927 Mendelssohn concerto (Blech, Berlin Staatsoper) is again a smidgen technically superior to the 1936 recording with Sir Landon Ronald and the London Philharmonic. The violin sound is riveting in its winsome purity. Both discs register Kreisler's artistic character to an extreme degree. In the 1927 version he plays a harmonic E in the opening passage, as opposed to a solid finger E in the later disc, an unimportant detail in itself, but proof that Kreisler was amenable to changes of fingering over the years. The *Andante* is played like an endearing vignette; the short section connecting the *Andante* and *Allegro molto vivace* stresses poetic repose. In the earlier disc the finale is meticulously clean and buoyant.

Kreisler's temperament was intimately attuned to the Mozartean ethos. This is markedly evident in his recording of Mozart's Concerto No. 4 in D, K. 218 with Malcolm Sargent made around 1936, the second of his two recordings of this work. Ever an individualistic interpreter, this is among the most personalized of Kreisler's major work performances. Following the so-called "military" opening the playing is exceptionally relaxed, though a sense of buoyancy is consistently sustained. Melodic themes are more legato than is usually heard, and the cadenzas of the first two movements (his own) are highly imaginative and rich in the use of doublestops; the end of the *Andante cantabile* is meltingly poetic. The *Rondeau* is unduly slow; in a lesser player the music might be hopelessly bogged down, but Kreisler's sound and grace impart relevance to the various tempi. Surprisingly, the final cadenza is disappointing and is insufficiently related to the thematic material. In all it is the kind of unorthodox performance that "grows" on the listener with repeated hearings.

One of Kreisler's lesser-known recordings (not issued officially) is the Bruch Concerto No. 1 in G-minor (with Eugene Goosens and the Royal Albert Hall Orchestra), made December 29 and 30, 1924, and January 2, 1925. He is in optimum form, and his opulent G string sound sparks a sumptuously lyrical interpretation.

Although Kreisler was never included among the Paganini specialists, his arrangements of Paganini compositions verify his respect and admiration for the Genoese genius. As a young man, Kreisler refurbished *I Palpiti, Le Streghe, Non Piu Mesta* and *La Clochette* with piano accompaniments far superior to the simplistic originals of Paganini, and added double harmonics, finger-twisting runs of lightning-speed fingered octaves and other intricate embellishments. I am not aware, however, of any performance of them by Kreisler in his maturity. He also renovated the *Moto Perpetuo* accompaniment, and provided accompaniments for Caprice Nos. 13, 20 and 24 (as well as a few minor structural changes). Indeed, the Kreisler piano part for the opening lyric section of Caprice No. 20 is instilled with harmonic magic.

Predominant among his Paganini transcriptions is Concerto No. 1 in D-major, Op. 6, for which he provided an original orchestration of heroic motif and lush harmonic contrivance. This comprises only the first movement, a tradition probably initiated by the German violinist August Wilhelmj (1845 - 1908), but constitutes a tour de force, almost eighteen minutes in length, of considerably more musical substance than the Paganini original. In our time, the concerto is played in its entirety in Paganini's own version except for the various individual cadenzas. It is unfortunate that the Kreisler version is no longer played, since his stylistic enhancement deserves to be retained in the repertoire.

In 1936, at age sixty-one, Kreisler recorded the concerto with Eugene Ormandy and the Philadelphia Orchestra. The performance is scrupulously clean technically, though some of the more strictly bravura passages are played at a more sober pace than is the wont of modern fingerboard gymnasts. Kreisler endows the work with a special flavor, Viennese, if you will, that is quite irresistible. The sheen of his tone, his lyric phrasing, and the uniqueness of his expressive devices add up to a memorable performance. (Alfredo Campoli has an admirable recording of this transcribed version.)

For many years Kreisler refused to perform in radio broadcasts, but he ultimately yielded to the lure of tremendous fees, and possibly to a desire to keep abreast of his younger colleagues. In addition to his recordings there are undoubtedly air-checks of some of his broadcasts. I once heard an air-check of a portion of Viotti's Concerto No. 22.

A key element in the success of Kreisler's compositions was his exceptional gifts as a pianist. In 1925 he recorded piano transcriptions of eight of his popular violin vignettes for Ampico player-piano reproduction, all executed in a manner closely akin to his violin playing.

His compositions and transcriptions were direct extensions of his musical personality and performance. How does Kreisler rank as a composer? He was a significant composer, albeit a minor one. It is true that except for his string quartet, operettas and a few individual songs, Kreisler was strictly a composer of violin music, and in that respect was extremely limited. But compared to the thousands of violin vignettes written by violinists of all categories, Kreisler's works were a landmark of novelty in construction, harmonic invention and inspiration. They represent a genre of music quite different from any other efforts in the field. Those who tried to imitate or emulate these compositions could not produce pieces of equal caliber, although certain transcriptions, in particular those of Heifetz, do contain positive elements of harmonic novelty, inventiveness and genuine talent. Kreisler, however, was not only a composer of charm and originality, and transcription stylist supreme, but was also personally responsible for elevating piano accompaniments for violin vignettes from the old, basic chordal patterns to a much higher level of harmonic diversity, color, nuance and imagination. These tantalizing exotic accompaniments often incorporate a novel use of fourths and fifths, in combination with a wide variety of other doublestop effects.

For the better part of a century, Kreisler originals and transcriptions dominated those sections of violin programs devoted to short pieces and encores. Their popularity and universality were further ensured in that many of them could be negotiated by lesser violinists or capable amateurs. When changing standards and critical snobbery rendered them out of fashion for modern recitals that had been transformed into chamber music sonata concerts, they lay idle for a couple decades and were not often included in major recitals. But recently we have been witnessing a Kreisler renaissance. Most of the best younger-generation violinists have produced all-Kreisler albums, and are including some of these pieces in their live programs. Frankly, in terms of sound and style, these performances, except in a few instances, are sorely lacking the kind of magic that can raise this type of music to its fullest potential. Nor can all of the echo chamber amplification and engineering artifices this side of heaven equate their individual sound with that of Kreisler. But at least the pieces are now approached more and more seriously and conscientiously, and less often with the sort of condescending attitude that "we play this trivia to please audiences whose artistic tastes are impoverished." The fact of the matter is that Kreisler's works are very difficult to play with top-level artistry. They demand tonal and interpretive powers considerably in advance of the more technical showpieces of Paganini, Vieuxtemps, Wieniawski, Sarasate, and their lesser counterparts. Many a facile finger-board practitioner who can sail brilliantly through Wieniawski's *Scherzo Tarantelle* or the *Original Variations*, Op. 15 will founder badly when faced with the prospect of playing the doublestops of *Caprice Viennois* with vibrant beauty and lilting musicality.

In 1935, the origin of fourteen of Kreisler's so-called classical manu-scripts were the subject of a heated exchange between the violinist and various music critics, specifically Ernest Newman, the noted British mu-sicologist. For over thirty years Kreisler had been playing and publishing these pieces. Printed on the sheet music was the statement: "They are, moreover, so freely treated that they constitute, in fact, original works." This cue should have prompted any alert critic to view them as Kreisler originals, a fact that had long been known to such musicians as Zimbalist, Spalding, Heifetz, Enesco, Persinger, Rupp, and Lamson, among others. After all, if *both* the violin and piano parts of the piece have been completely rewritten, what is left, save possibly a theme, or remnants of a theme?

But these compositions contained absolutely no thematic material from old classical masters (except for the first eight bars of *Chanson Louis XIII and Pavane*), and no one ever said they did. Instead, they were individ-ually subtitled "in the style of" individual old masters, some of whom were not necessarily "masters" at all. Yet, even this modest allegation is specious. Why? Because each of these compositions: *Praeludium and Allegro* (Pugnani), *Allegretto in G-minor* (Porpora), *La Chasse* (Cartier), *Menuet* (Porpora), *La Précieuse* (Couperin), *Scherzo* (Dittersdorf), *Sicil-ienne et Rigaudon* (Francoeur), *Study on a Chorale* (Stamitz), *Tempo di Minuetto* (Pugnani), *Chanson Louis XIII and Pavane* (Couperin) and Concerto in C-major (Vivaldi), *is pure Kreisler* in style *from first note to last*, except for the eight bars mentioned above. Any first-class critic should have noted this. At no time did Kreisler say or imply that these pieces were based on themes of these "old masters," as he did, for example, with his transcription Tartini's *Variation on a Theme of Corelli*.

Had Newman's ego been less pontifical, he would have taken the mild hoax in good humor, as did Olin Downes, the American critic. But even the latter erred in this friendly statement:

> It was undoubtedly to the great advantage of the compositions that they did not bear his name as a composer. Neither the public, nor the press, nor Mr. Kreisler's colleagues would have taken as kindly to these compositions had they been designated as being merely the creation of a living violinist.

Nonsense. His principal colleagues already knew of the innocent masquerade. The public would have adored these pieces regardless of who wrote them, especially as played by Kreisler. (Did they not continue to love them even after Kreisler admitted his authorship?). And had not Kreisler been a beloved international figure for more than three decades before the controversy, except for the World War I incident? And can anyone truly believe that had the words "in the style of" been deleted the critics would have attacked the pieces because they were "the creations of a living violinist?" More likely, many of them might have highly commended Kreisler for his obvious genius in this field!

A half-century has passed, and the "scandal" has long since been forgotten. The protagonists are no longer living. But Kreisler's delightful compositions still are published widely wherever the violin is played. One cannot say that all of these vignettes are of highest quality. *Syncopation, Marche Miniature Viennoise, Aloha Oe, The Volga Boatman* paraphrase and others are eminently forgettable, even in the capacity of miniatures. But such gems as *Praeludium and Allegro, Recitativo and Scherzo Caprice, Liebesleid, Caprice Viennois, Liebesfreud, La Gitana, Gypsy Caprice*, the Mozart *Rondo, Tambourin Chinois*, the Tartini-Kreisler Variations, *Schön Rosmarin*, the three Dvořák Slavonic Dances and a host of other Kreisler originals and transcriptions seem destined to outlive us all.

Another important facet of Kreisler's inventiveness was his cadenzas. Although they are far from being technically simple they are devised with such canny understanding of the violin that they tend to sound much more difficult than they are. Certainly his cadenzas for the Beethoven and Brahms concerti, and Tartini's *Devil's Trill* Sonata rank among the finest ever composed. In listening to post-Kreisler cadenzas, one can often feel his influence, even in cello concerto cadenzas.

Kreisler began at age four with a toy violin; at eight he was given a half-size Thir; at ten, a three-quarter size Amati, and for his Paris Conservatoire victory, won a gleaming red Gand-Bernadel, a gift from his father. He played on a Grancino for eight years, then a Nicolo Gagliano. During his Gagliano period he bought a Stradivarius he subsequently disliked, and then graduated to the "Hart" 1737 Joseph Guarnerius del Gesù. Later he purchased his favorite, a 1733 Guarnerius del Gesù. He bought and sold many instruments: a 1733 Strad, ultimately acquired by Huberman; the 1734 "Lord Amherst of Hackney" Strad; the "Greville" Strad; the "Earl of Plymouth" Strad; a Petrus Guarnerius of Mantua; a Carlo Bergonzi; a 1732 Guarnerius (from Tivadar Nachez); a 1720 Daniel Parker and a magnificent Vuillaume copy of a Guarnerius.

No doubt his finest violins played an important role in the quality of his sound, as with any other violinist. But blessed with a natural tone and vibrato of such seductive beauty, Kreisler would have sounded phenomenal even if he had played on the proverbial "cigar-box."

Kreisler owned a Tourte bow, but usually played with one of his several Hill bows or a Pfretschner, with the hair inordinately tightened. He shunned the use of shoulder pads, feeling that such appendages vitiated an instrument's tone.

In his "wunderkind" and early adult years, Kreisler's piano accompanist-collaborator was Dr. Bernhard Pollak and, in the early 1900s, André Benoist. Later, his European pianists include Michael Raucheisen, Franz Rupp, Erno Balogh, Hubert Geisen, Arpad Sandor and Otto Schulhoff. For concerts in the British Isles his pianists were Sir Hamilton Harty, Haddon Squire, Charleton Keith and Jorge Zulueta, though the British recorded Beethoven sonata cycle was performed with Rupp. His North American and Australian collaborator was Carl Lamson from 1912 to the end of his career, possibly a record for such a partnership. Kreisler was reportedly exceptionally kind and generous to his pianists (which cannot be said for all of the great violinists), and his relationship with Lamson was one of utter benevolence.

A man of his time, serialist music and avant-garde experimentation were an anathema to Kreisler's sense of musical form and beauty. The aesthetic and spiritual qualities of his playing embody values and standards vastly different from those of our day. He produced tonal, expressive and stylistic effects that are no longer heard or even sought after, and in his time he exerted a tremendous influence upon the performance of violinists everywhere. In that respect, he taught untold numbers of violinists, though he had only two "official" pupils, Samuel Dushkin, noted for introducing works of Stravinsky, and Louis Edlin, concertmaster of the Cleveland Symphony in the early 1920s.

The depersonalization of the computer age has somewhat dimmed the lustre of Kreislerian romanticism, but his spirit lives on through his infectious compositions. As an artist, he was a molder of phrases from which dreams are made, revered by audiences and critics alike; a true monarch of his realm who brought an incomparable state of grace to violin art that endured for half a century.

Kreisler (rt.) next to Beethoven's Monument in
Pershing Square, Los Angeles, circa 1939 - 40

Left: Kreisler's Guarnerius del Gesù
Right: Francescatti's "Hart" Stradivarius, 1727

Zino Francescatti, a truly noble artist, a scintillating technician and an elite representative of piquant, cultivated music making

CHAPTER TWO

Zino Francescatti

URING THE LATE 1930s the Great Depression was still raging. Kreisler, Heifetz, the young Menuhin, Szigeti and Milstein represented the topmost echelon of violinists in box office draw, followed by Elman, Huberman, Spalding, the young Ricci and Morini. Enesco had become deeply involved in composition and teaching, and Thibaud was no longer in significant contention, though he still concertized. The young Stern had already made his youthful debut, but was not yet ensconced among the leading mature artists or those ex-prodigies who had built mass audience followings in their childhood. Severe economic retrenchment represented an almost insurmountable barrier to new artists seeking to scale the heights, and in this period many outstanding talents were forced to enter the symphonic or commercial fields in order to earn a livelihood.

Many a European violinistic luminary had made an American debut during the Depression years, hoping for success. Despite everything, the United States was still the mecca for musical artists, in terms of financial reward. But a good many of those who won critical acclaim here were forced to return eventually to their places of origin, though some remained as political refugees. Gifted Americans, too, sought gold and glory with scant results. Among the aspirants were new young artists like Ossy Renardy (1920 - 1953), first to record all twenty-four of Paganini's caprices (with piano accompaniment) and Guila Bustabo (b. 1919), an intense, propulsive player with extraordinary facility and the first woman to record the Paganini-Wilhelmj Concerto No. 1, with the Sauret cadenza. Their bids for recognition were initially successful, but neither was destined to enter the "charmed circle." Indeed, only a violinist of the very highest qualifications—and one whose musical personality and character were in some measure different from those of the reigning elite—could hope to launch a top-level concertizing career.

Such an artist was René Charles (Zino) Francescatti. At thirty-seven, he was already a fully seasoned performer when he made his American debut in November, 1939, playing the Paganini Concerto No. 1 (complete version) with the New York Philharmonic. His rise to stardom had been long and arduous, but he was recognized eventually not only as the heir to Thibaud, once the "greatest French violinist," but also as one of the world's leading violinists.

Francescatti's date of birth has often been given as 1905 or 1903, but he himself states that he was born on August 9, 1902, in Marseilles. As the name suggests, his father, Fortunato Francescatti, originally from Verona, was of Italian lineage; his French mother, Ernesta Feraud, was from Marseilles. Both were trained violinists and teachers. Before their marriage she had been his pupil. They were wed when he was forty-six and she was seventeen. Zino had one younger brother, Raymond, who did not become a violinist. In Milan, his father had been a pupil of two noted virtuosi, Antonio Bazzini, composer of *La Ronde des lutins* and other bravura dazzlers, and Camillo Sivori, the only important pupil of the legendary Paganini. From Sivori he learned Paganini's unique methods of fingering.

At age five, Zino was given a tiny violin, more a toy than a legitimate instrument, and in the first lesson he cleanly negotiated a G-major scale. He is the only elite twentieth-century soloist to have been taught exclusively by his parents. His father gave him lessons "from time to time" (as Francescatti states), and his mother supervised his daily practice. With the three of them and their pupils, there was violin playing in progress in all parts of their large home, day and night.

The elder Francescatti, concertmaster of the Marseilles Symphony, was a stern, sometimes harsh taskmaster, who once kept his son working on a single scale for over an hour until it was absolutely perfect. The boy's mother, a violin soloist in her own right, was his champion and, at times, his protector. In her eighties she was still playing well. She died at age ninety-eight.

Zino was a willing pupil, and as a child practiced one hour before and one hour after school. In his early years he worked diligently at the various exercises of Ševčik and the études of Kreutzer and Gaviniès. He states that he relished every type of technical challenge: doublestops, trills and harmonics; that he had a natural vibrato ("My vibrato developed by itself, naturally") and staccato, and encountered no particular difficulty in developing facility in either hand. From his tenth to his fifteenth year he was enrolled in a private school to enable him to practice at least four hours daily. During this period his working day often approximated sixteen hours; his practice began at 6:30 a.m. Like most boys, there was a time when he preferred playing ball to practicing, but this soon passed. At ten he performed the Beethoven concerto. Ysaÿe, Thibaud and Kreisler

Camillo Sivori, star pupil of Paganini, virtuoso and teacher of Fortunato Francescatti, Zino's father

Fortunato Francescatti

Francescatti at age fourteen, 1916

became his idols.

He made his formal debut at a Marseilles *Concert Classique* program at fifteen with the organist Marcel Dupré; the recital included the Wieniawski Concerto in D-minor and Bach's *Chaconne*. However, Francescatti was never touted as a child prodigy and never participated in a competition. His rise to renown progressed slowly, with illness disturbing the early part of his career.

Since Francescatti's father did not want him to play publicly, he continued to work intensely until he was twenty, at which time he went to Paris to make his way in the world. There he played the first movement of the Paganini concerto. Later he learned the entire concerto, and it became one of his musical hallmarks, though he was never limited to the role of a violinistic gymnast. At twenty-two he was granted an audition with Thibaud, who greatly encouraged the young man. Shortly afterward, he was engaged to accompany Maurice Ravel and the singer Maggie Teyte on a concert tour of England. As late as 1928 he worked for a living in the Straram Orchestra, at that time a leading orchestra in Paris. He was also presented as a duo soloist with that ensemble in Mozart's *Symphonie Concertante*. Over the years he doggedly climbed the ladder of success in Europe, and in 1938 made a triumphant Western Hemisphere debut in Buenos Aires, playing the Paganini Concerto No. 1 under José Iturbi. After each of several performances at the Teatro Colon in Buenos Aires, the police had to escort him from the auditorium to protect him from the congratulatory crowds. Once in Detriot, after a performance of Paganini's *I Palpiti*, the audience cheered for seventeen minutes.

Francescatti gave first performances in Paris of Szymanowski's Concerto No. 2, Respighi's *Concerto Gregoriano* and Witkowski's *Dances*; in Philadelphia, of Milhaud's *Suite*; in New York, the Casadesus *Sonata*. His repertoire of contemporary works includes major compositions by Prokofiev, Walton, Ben-Haim, Hindemith, Stravinsky and Leonard Bernstein.

Francescatti married another violinist, Yolanda Potel de la Brière of Paris, whom he met when he was concertmaster and she was a member of the Gaston Poulet Orchestra. They had one child, who did not survive.

In 1975, after a brilliant career, he decided to retire at age seventy-three. He states: "I had enough of this life of travel. It was becoming tiring, and I wanted to enjoy the last part of my life quietly, doing what I enjoy. I finished my concert career in fine form, and no one can say that I retired because I was playing poorly."

Zino Francescatti has never sought the limelight by means of extramusical exploits or publicity feats. He is a quiet, modest person, whose deportment and social graces are as polished and refined as his playing. Though universally celebrated as a French violinist, he is a direct vio-

The Francescattis in their former New York home

Francescatti (far right) with Mr. & Mrs. Robert Casadesus
and Mr. & Mrs. Albert Spalding

linistic descendant of Paganini through his father and Sivori. No other
living or recent violinist of eminence can claim such a heritage. "Sivori
initiated my father into the secrets of the violin, and father later imparted
to me the knowledge gained from the virtuoso," said the violinist. His
playing possesses the purity of line and statement attributed to the pre-
Paganini Italian school and not an iota of Paganini's sensationalist
excesses. But it also reflects an aura which is ineffably French. It has been
said that if Paris is "The City of Light," the art of Francescatti is its
embodiment—radiant, lustrous, perfumed, graceful, utterly felicitous
and, at times, cloyingly sweet. His sound is striking in its brightness and
clarity. It is twentieth-century playing, smartly disciplined, free of interpretive exaggerations.

Whereas Thibaud was essentially a stylist with perhaps the most limited repertoire among international-level violinists, Francescatti expanded
tremendously the so-called French violinistic horizons as represented by
his predecessor, not only in repertorial scope, but also in technical
achievement. Former French violinists such as Emile Sauret (1852 - 1919)
and Henri Marteau (1874·- 1934) were credited with having more sheer
fingerboard facility than Thibaud (1880 - 1953), but he surpassed them by
far in tonal beauty, sophistication of style and overall artistry. In turn,
Francescatti, though listed as only one year younger than Heifetz (whose
birth date of 1901 is generally accepted), came to maturity after the
awesome new Heifetz standards of instrumental command had already
been established. Although he had been greatly impressed and, to a sizable
degree, influenced by Ysaÿe, Kreisler and Thibaud, he belongs to a later
generation of artists.

Francescatti describes his musical priorities and approach, and touches
upon the differences between himself and the players preceding him in
the following article from *LISTEN* magazine, April, 1945:

> It is self-evident that quite different demands are made today upon
> the violin virtuoso. When I stand on the concert stage in front of a
> large audience I am fully aware that I have to give not only my best all
> through the evening, but that I have to transmit the spirit of the
> composition as faithfully to the public as I possibly can, without any
> distortion or interpretative conditions beyond the scope of the work.
>
> The great Belgian master of the violin, Eugène Ysaÿe, once gave a
> concert in Bordeaux. He was not feeling too secure as a result of
> excessive drinking on the previous night. The audience jeered at first,
> but later in the evening the virtuoso collected his wits and delivered
> one of his inimitable performances that carried the public to the
> limits of frenzy and enthusiasm. In one evening he brought forth the
> gamut of emotions from jeers to delirious applause. But today an
> artist must be at the top of his form from the first note to the last; the
> level can never fluctuate....... The honest and sincere artist of today is

Francescatti, his wife Yolanda and his mother
Mrs. Ernesta Francescatti, in Monterey, Massachusetts

Casadesus (left) and Francescatti, 1965

a professional man who loves his profession but does not endow it with any mysterious qualities in order to attract people eager for out-of-the-way sensations. How ludicrous it would be today to influence an audience by telling it that the virtuoso is in league with the devil or is a secret Casanova. And while it may have been more glamorous to be touched by people on the street who wanted to see whether one is made of flesh and blood (as happened to Paganini in London), it is certainly more satisfying to see the thousands of grateful people to whom the modern artist has opened the true world of genuine music.

One cannot assert that Francescatti's musical aura is as striking or explicit as that of Ysaÿe, Kreisler, Elman, Heifetz or the young Menuhin. Nevertheless, there is a special character, a vitality and a savoir faire to his playing that set him apart from a host of gifted virtuosi who possess vibrant sound and creditable musicianship. In hearing Francescatti at his best, the first adjective that may come to mind is—enchanté. Indeed, one can become so mesmerized by the total effusiveness of his musicality and the affectionate charm of his tone that such matters as spiritual sublimity and musical introspection are temporarily banished from the mind. He is never less than the impeccable gentleman of the violin.

As a bravura technician, Francescatti belongs in the first rank. In addition to his splendid live and recorded performances of the Paganini Concerto No. 1 in D-major, he plays and has recorded Paganini's *God Save the King, The Carnival of Venice Variations, I Palpiti* (with his own original, brilliant finale) and eight of the Paganini caprices. And what is more important—he never sacrifices beauty of sound or sincerity of purpose in the interest of technical exhibitionism. He constantly seeks out and stresses the Italianate lyricism and musical blandishments of these works, as opposed to single-mindedly executing fingerboard gymnastics. His coordination between right and left hands is of the highest order. His immaculately manicured fingers are of no more than average length, and the span of his hands and breadth of his fingertips are not at all unusual in comparison with, for example, the massive hands of Perlman. But his fingerboard facility is superbly flexible.

The Francescatti tone, though ever ear-titillating, is quite soft-grained and tends to be rather single-dimensional, a quality which places certain limitations on his art, lending a veneer of "sameness," a lack of diversity to his sound. The root cause of this lies in his vibrato, which is produced by the wrist and arm and has a widish oscillation. True, he produces degrees of variance in its speed, but not to any great extent. Its speed may approach rapidity but not the ultimate in intensity, though it reflects no vestige whatsoever of the stiff, tense fingertip vibrato once widely associated with French-trained violinists. His interpretations are piquant, amiable, infectious, sleek and elegant, rather than probing or emotionally profound. Thus, his most convincing performances are of works that are bright, buoyant and brilliant. Sombre or cerebral music is not really his forte, though he plays it with commanding instrumental authority and provocative sound.

The Francescatti bow arm is honed in the general manner of the so-called French-Belgian school (though I prefer to consider the Belgian school as related to, but separate from, the French). His crisp spiccatos are neatly controlled, his flying staccatos scintillate and his on-the-string staccato is sturdy, though he does not employ the extremely rapid stiff-arm variety. And his sustained, cantilena bowings, seamless in delivery, are mellow in texture.

In the area of expressive finger slides and position changes, Francescatti stands somewhere between artists such as Kreisler and Heifetz who were lavish in their use, and current violinists who employ them little or not at all (though Perlman employs them liberally). Strong in the influence of Kreisler, Francescatti's slides occasionally recall those of his older colleague, but are in no way imitative; most are distinctly his own, and he uses them sparingly and with patrician discrimination. Generally he favors the use of "bridging" fingers in expressive position changes, rather than direct "fleshy" slides to a climactic lyric note. And the selection of these expressive devices is tastefully governed by the style of music he is performing. His music-making constantly sings, and tenderness, an element in serious decline in current playing, is one of his most endearing qualities. Some observers feel that this tenderness has a feminine tinge, in the positive sense, but this should by no means imply that there is either physical weakness or effeminate frailty in Francescatti's playing. His tone can become almost hypnotic in its uniformity and, at times, the "perfume" can become too intoxicating. However, it is a decidedly masculine perfume, calculated to seduce the listener.

Francescatti's musical temperament is ever ardent and lightly sensuous, but not intensely voluptuous. Nor are dramatic utterance and tension hallmarks of his art. Yet his playing possesses a constant glow even when his vibrato is minimal or not being used; he is one of the few whose music-making "smiles."

According to his own statement, he never practiced an "enormous" amount during the mature years of his career, nor did he ever use a tape recorder when practicing. Overpractice, he feels, can be harmful and detracts from the freshness and spontaneity of playing, though he is definitely opposed to the theory of little or no practice as ascribed to Kreisler. He does suffer from pre-concert nervousness, but once onstage keeps matters under firm control. Before a concert he warms up with scales and Ševčík exercises rather than passages from the works he is to perform. He eats little before a concert, perhaps only buttered bread, and drinks coffee, which he also drinks at intermission.

Francescatti vigorously recommends strong finger pressure on the strings, especially in soft passages: "That is what gives it a beautiful tone." He continuously strives to improve his fingerings. "After each public performance you analyze those passages that have been awkward, and proceed to make changes." Stressing the need for different bowings when concertos are played with orchestra as opposed to concerto performances with piano, he states: "Twice as much power is required when one is being accompanied by an orchestra. Orchestral sound resounds far more than that of the piano. In many passages I use two bow strokes with orchestra as opposed to one with piano."

He derives much pleasure from playing chamber music privately. Publicly he has performed trios with pianist Cutner Solomon and cellist Pierre Fournier at the Edinburgh Festival, and his longtime partnership with pianist Robert Casadesus has produced some of the more felicitous live and recorded sonata playing of their era.

The recordings of Francescatti number about 110 compositions, large and small, including the multiple recordings, comparable to the 120 of Milstein. (Similarly in 1950, when both were in mid-career, Francescatti's fee for three appearances with the New York Philharmonic was $3,600; Milstein's, for the same stint, $3,800). From the mid-1940s to the mid-1950s many of his finest major work recordings were made in mono and early stereo. His sound is especially well-suited for the microphone, and it can be said that his recorded art is at least equal to that of his live performance, if not actually superior in sonority and projection. In *The Way They Play*, Volume 1, p. 35, by Samuel and Sada Applebaum, Francescatti states:

> The nuance problem is solved in a different manner when making recordings than when playing in public. The dynamic markings must be handled in a different way. When making a crescendo from piano to forte, the range must not be so great, or rather let me put it this way, play forte most of the time. If you wish to get softer, become only marginally softer. If you wish to make a crescendo, get only slightly louder, since there must not be a wide range of dynamic expression . . . . . In a concert hall, of course, there are no such limitations. When making recordings, it is very easy to overdo. While playing in the manner I prescribe for recording, it may sound dull to the human ear, but the microphone picks up the subtle, tiny nuances.

One of the most impressive and widely known of his recordings is that of the Paganini Concerto No. 1 in D-major (with Eugene Ormandy and the Philadelphia Orchestra). At the time, the Francescatti version represented the antithesis of the heaven-storming drama and operatic thrust of the 1934 recording by Menuhin at eighteen, which was the only recording of the entire version for quite a few years. Francescatti's interpretation, less sensuous, is nonetheless charged with bravado, exquisitely lyric and technically impeccable. It compares to the Menuhin performance as does a superlative lyric soprano to an equally great dramatic soprano. His flying-staccatos sparkle. A section of the last movement is omitted, perhaps in the interest of record space limitations prevalent at that time. Through the years this recording still ranks among the finest in style and individuality. (Francescatti states that he used both his own cadenza and that of Carl Flesch in his performances; the one used in the recording is that of Flesch.)

Another of his most renowned recordings is the Saint-Saëns Concerto No. 3 in B-minor (Mitropoulos, New York Philharmonic), an ideally polished interpretation that embodies the Gallic spirit of the music with unsurpassed lustre. His expressive portamentos are never overdone. The opening movement is taken at a propulsive rate, but not so fast as to distort the lyric flow. The *Andantino*, though lovely, would perhaps have benefited from a bit more repose; the finale is played *Allegro non troppo* as indicated, and avoids undue haste. In subtlety, color and nuance, it remains a model for works of its kind.

Lalo's *Symphonie Espagnole*, without the *Intermezzo* (Mitropoulos, New York Philharmonic), is as dashing as D'Artagnan and suavely etched, perhaps the most desirable of Francescatti's three recordings of the work. The *Scherzando* is enriched by many intelligently placed expressive slides; the languorous triplet theme midway through the finale represents some of his most sensuous playing. The charm of this performance recalls Thibaud; somewhat less individualized, but far more disciplined musically, and digitally perfect.

In this category belongs the Vieuxtemps Concerto No. 4 (Ormandy, Philadelphia Orchestra), a recording that, together with those of Perlman and Menuhin, is just a notch below the peerless Heifetz recording; technically cleaner than that of Menuhin, if a bit less forceful and spontaneous. Overall it is superlative bravura playing.

Bruch's Concerto No. 1 in G-minor (Schippers, New York Philharmonic) is warm and affectionate rather than dramatic, and does not project the ultimate tension, but in the Mendelssohn Concerto Op. 64, Francescatti's penchant for lightly amorous, vivacious utterance is at its zenith. Mozart's Concerto No. 5 in A-major and No. 2 in D-major (de Stoutz, Zurich Chamber Orchestra), Tartini's Concerto in D-minor (deftly orchestrated and conducted by Francescatti, Zurich Chamber Orchestra) and the Bach Concerto in E-major (Szell, Columbia Symphony), mirror the multiple virtues of the Mendelssohn. The Mozart No. 3 in G-major and No. 4 in D-major (Walter, Columbia Symphony) are pure and straightforward performances, though in the latter there are glimmers of airy sound in the *Andante*. Chausson's Concerto for Piano, Violin and String Quartet, Op. 21 (with Casadesus, Guilet Quartet), commemorating the 1955 centenary of the composer's birth, is ineffably polished in the traditional French manner; the *Sicilienne* in particular is exquisitely wrought.

Among more contemporary major works, his Walton concerto recording (Ormandy, Philadelphia Orchestra) is eloquently lyric, as is his superbly expressive rendition of Prokofiev's Concerto No. 2 in G-minor (Mitropoulos, New York Philharmonic), which is climaxed by a finale of exciting articulation and drive. The recording of Leonard Bernstein's Serenade for Violin, String Orchestra, Harp and Percussion (Bernstein, New York Philharmonic), compares favorably with Stern's.

Francescatti handles the stratospheric challenges of the Beethoven concerto with noble artistry (Walter, Columbia Symphony). It is not an interpretation that consistently digs deeply below the surface of the music, but his sound is always beautiful, and his phrasing, lovingly expressed. Walter's relaxed, reflective accompaniment adds much to the whole. Kreisler's cadenzas are tossed off with lithe virtuosity, and only a fleck or two of spotty intonation at the close of the *Adagio* mars an otherwise immaculate performance. Such a blemish would be summarily edited out in a current recording.

Although Francescatti plays the heavier-textured Romantic concerti with complete authority, the inherent incandescence of his tone and his harmonious temperament are less than ideally suited to their performance. His recording of the Brahms concerto, for example (Ormandy, Philadelphia Orchestra), while containing a sensitive *Adagio* and a brash, gutsy finale, and while seemingly larger-scaled than his live performance, does not convey the requisite darkness of sound and spirit in the most expressive and introspective passages. The same dichotomy marks his spirited recording of the Tchaikovsky concerto, (in which he surprisingly inserts the Auer-inspired D-major scale in thirds like a rapier thrust into the cadenza); effulgence rather than impassioned utterance is the distinctive feature of this interpretation. The Sibelius concerto (Bernstein, New York Philharmonic) also possesses strengths and short-comings similar to those of the Brahms and Tchaikovsky.

In Brahms's Concerto for Violin and Cello, with Pierre Fournier (Walter, Columbia Symphony), the violin dominates, as the cellist plays rather placidly and reticently; the entire performance registers insufficient tonal intensity for this weighty music, and there are minor lapses of ensemble detail between the solo instruments.

One of Francescatti's important virtues is his ability to play violin-piano sonatas meaningfully, an accomplishment that is by no means shared by all eminent violinists, especially those who emphasize works of bravura gymnastics. In their chosen repertoire, his collaboration with Robert Casadesus constitutes one of the best-integrated violin-piano duos recorded for posterity. Aside from the instrumental and musical factors involved, their performance reflects a kindred artistic ethos and a single-ness of purpose that are encountered only rarely.

Prominent among their sonata recordings are those of French origin, such as the popular Fauré No. 1 in A-major and the lesser-known No. 2 in E-minor, an intensely songful but rambling work that requires a team of the Francescatti-Casadesus caliber to give it relevance. The Franck and Debussy sonatas, too, are strikingly French in character.

Their recording of the complete Beethoven sonatas unfailingly communicates a sense of exhilaration and spirit. In No. 5 (*Spring*), Francescatti's radiant tone is ideally suited to the season. The ticklish passages from the *Allegro con spirito* of No. 3 in E-flat major are gracefully negotiated; the *Adagio*, alert to climactic surges, misses a bit of dark quality in the more wistful passages; the *Rondo* finale scampers merrily. The No. 7 in C-minor, sometimes dubbed *Winter*, mirrors a glistening snowy landscape more than a gusty hiemal tempest; the *Allegro* finale is exceptionally zestful. The sharp changes of mood in the knotty No. 10 in G-major are deftly delineated in a sensitively etched interpretation; the last sections of the *Poco allegretto* finale are articulated adroitly. The introduction and opening movement of No. 9 in A-major (*Kreutzer*) enjoy optimum clarity of line; in the *Andante con variazioni*, Francescatti sustains interest even in those variations in which the piano is dominant. There is never a feeling of prosaic academicism; the *Presto* finale is propulsive without mindless haste, and the few lyric passages receive their full due. The remaining sonatas of their Beethoven cycle are comparable in blithe artistry.

In his recording of the Ravel sonata, with Artur Balsam at the piano, their approach to the opening *Allegretto* is rather aggressive. The *Blues* movement, unexpectedly schmaltzy for a player of Francescatti's gentility, undulates impudently; the *Perpetuum mobile*, a technical tour de force, noticeably faster than Oistrakh's recording, is spotlessly clean. The violinist joins pianist Eugenio Bagnoli in Schubert's Sonatina Nos. 1 and 3, Op. 137, and the massive *Grand Fantasy*, Op. 159. The ungainly passages of the latter are handled with a sense of ease, and all is superbly polished, though the violin's presence is slightly undercut in the engineering. It is among the few best recordings of this thorny work.

Francescatti's recordings of the Bach Solo Partita No. 2 in D-minor and No. 3 in E-major accentuate songfulness. Although a sense of baroque refinement is ever present, he does not patently minimize his vibrato, and if a "meaty" position change suits his musical purpose, he utilizes it.

Obviously he is neither dominated nor hampered by any of the various current theories about Bach performance. His aim is to render it pleasing to the ear. Except for *Menuetto No. 2* of Partita No. 3, in which he deliberately stops his vibrato in the opening bars and then turns it on (to no apparent musical advantage), his playing is never mannered or arty. The *Chaconne* is organ-like. In four-string chords he will lash back from the higher strings to emphasize a lower thematic note, but not in every instance. Those movements that are ancient dance forms are played very rhythmically; his *Gigue* is joyous, his *Saraband*, stately, his *Courante*, a straightforward Italianate dance. Studied overintellectualization is not a component of Francescatti's art.

Medium-length works of stylish bravura are among his most superb performances. Saint-Saëns' *Introduction and Rondo Capriccioso* exudes a typically French bonhomie; the *Havanaise* is lightly amorous and languorous. Ravel's *Tzigane*, recorded with pianist Artur Balsam and again with Bernstein and the New York Philharmonic, is both gloriously rich in sound and crystal-clear, more French in spirit than rhapsodically Magyar. The composer, his longtime friend, preferred it played in that context. Chausson's *Poème* is another of his choice renditions, lustrous in tone and sophisticated. Sarasate's *Zigeunerweisen*, the historic predecessor of Ravel's *Tzigane*, is spicy and colorful both in the piano version with M. Fauré and with the orchestra (Smith, Columbia Symphony). Two versions of the Vitali-Charlier *Chaconne*, one with pianist Balsam, the other with de Stoutz and the Zurich Chamber Orchestra (somewhat thickly orchestrated by Francescatti), find the variations admirably diverse in mood and elegantly stated, with the heroic thematic octaves of the final section vibrantly alive. One can appreciate all the more the stature of Francescatti's playing by comparing these performances with the mediocre recording of Viktor Tretyakov, gold medalist of the Tchaikovsky Competition. In Paganini's *I Palpiti*, tastefully orchestrated by Francescatti, he captures the work's pure Italianate flavor while disposing of the devilish technical challenges with complete aplomb; the double harmonic passages are pellucid (de Stoutz, Zurich Chamber Orchestra).

Like his greatest colleagues, Francescatti is a master of the art of the vignette. A partial survey of these disc performances, all with pianist Balsam, finds Ravel's *Pièce en forme d'Habanera* as exquisite as a fragment of the finest Castilian lace, and the Poulenc-Heifetz *Presto in B-flat major*, an outstanding transcription, is stunningly facile. Villa-Lobos' *Black Swan* is visually allusive;Massenet's *Meditation* from *Thais* artfully captures the anguish of the repentant courtesan. Eight of Paganini's Caprices, Nos. 9, 13, 14, 15, 20, 21, 22 and 24, with piano accompaniments composed by Pilati, patently accentuate the lyric, but are technically superb. Ravel's *Kaddisch*, underplayed, with scant vibrato, is quite "un-

Jewish;" only the final bars register some of the poignance of a kaddish.

His recordings of a group of Kreisler originals and transcriptions recall the impeccable taste of their creator, though of course Francescatti's comparatively slow vibrato fails to approximate the magical tonal vibrance of Kreisler. Nor does he strive to imitate the unique expressive slides and position changes of Kreisler. But the nobility of his style and his infallible finesse render the interpretations compelling, although one may wish to debate minor details of the performances. *Allegretto* and *Minuet*, both purportedly "in the style of Porpora," *Caprice Viennois*, *Tambourin Chinois* and *Schön Rosmarin* are among the most winning. In *Praeludium and Allegro*, the speed of the prelude dissipates a measure of the segment's grandeur, but the *Allegro* portion is delightfully expressive and not at all played like a technical exercise. *Londonderry Air* is heartfelt and poignant, but the high E string repetition of the theme, unaccountably played in harmonics, lessens the intensity of the climax. *Liebesleid* sings tenderly, but just misses the bittersweet essence of the music. *Rondino on a Theme of Beethoven* is a bit too slow for optimum charm, and *Liebesfreud* begins with brio, but surprisingly, some of the variations are omitted. Deserving positive mention is Tartini's *Variations on a Theme of Corelli* (from *L'arte del arco*), played with delicate, cultured virtuosity, supported by de Stoutz and the Zurich Chamber Orchestra, in a fastidious Francescatti orchestral setting.

Most of the Francescatti recordings should be reissued. Such new exposure could provide many a valuable lesson to our younger generation violinists, as well as immense listening pleasure to all. It is but rarely that one hears a French violinist (or one of any nationality) playing in a manner so expressive of the Gallic ethos.

Francescatti is a competent pianist, speaks French, English and "very little Italian," and is a chain smoker. He believes that "Violin contests are good. They develop interest for the instrument and give opportunities to young violinists." In keeping with this conviction, he has served as a juror in the Queen Elisabeth, Thibaud, Flesch, Geneva and other competitions. Among the current generation of violinists he is particularly partial to Perlman, which is easily understandable, since Perlman so definitively carries on the direct traditions of the romantic, post-Ysaÿe era, in which Francescatti himself was a leading figure.

The violinist still possesses his magnificent "Hart" Stradivarius, and the Sanctus Serafin on which he played his historic performances of the Paganini Concerto No. 1. He also had an Andreas Guarnerius and a Scamparelli which he presented to pupils, and several modern instruments were donated to the Galamian Foundation. Among his collection of a dozen bows, his favorites are those by Peccatte, Lamy and Voirin. He preferred lightweight bows and used different bows for different works.

For Brahms and Sibelius he used the Lamy.

Francescatti has made a major contribution to violin pedagogy by editing a considerable portion of the standard violin repertoire for the International Music Company, which has also issued two of his original compositions: *Aria* and *Polka*. He has had several transcriptions published by Mills, and has written various other violin pieces and some preludes for piano, all as yet unpublished.

In 1928 and 1929 Francescatti taught pupils at the École Normale de Paris, but did not teach during his long career as a touring soloist. Later he conducted some master classes in Montreux. Since his retirement, many young violinists have come to him for advice and coaching, among whom he names Ayla Erduran, Regis Pasquier, Marie-Annick Nicolas, a Tchaikovsky Competition laureate, and Nina Bodnar, winner of the Thibaud Competition. Francescatti coaches only those young people he feels are uncommonly gifted, and once accepted, he gives of his time and energy without stint. Young artists from all over the world continue to seek his guidance. He advises pupils to listen to recordings of the works they are studying, but vehemently warns against any tendency to imitate the interpretations. Live concerts, he feels, can be immensely helpful to those students who are wise enough to treat each violin concert as an invaluable lesson from a master rather than an occasion for superficial criticism. He has never (except in his impecunious youth) accepted payment for his lessons, which run a minimum of two hours. And he does not speak kindly of "prestige" teachers whose outrageous prices for lessons are out of reach of many deserving students.

Because he has chosen to keep a low profile, Francescatti does not always receive the approbation he deserves, yet professional violinists hold him in very high esteem. Kreisler considered him "one of the finest representatives of violin playing that we have," and Francescatti has been cited as a *Commandeur de la Legion d'Honneur*, a *Commandeur de l'ordre de Leopold de Belgique*, and in August, 1985, a *Grand Officier de l'ordre National du Merite*.

Among his many touring experiences was a trip to Israel at the time of the 1956 military campaign. When other artists might have fled the country to avoid the dangers of war (as did the Jewish Erich Leinsdorf in 1973, deserting the Israel Philharmonic without notice), the non-Jewish Francescatti insisted upon remaining and continuing his numerous concerts under any and all performance conditions. At one point he played in a Jerusalem hall that was only a few hundred yards from the Arab gun emplacements. In appreciation, the Israeli government presented him with *The Sword of Solomon* Award.

Intimates of Francescatti speak glowingly of his philanthropic assistance to deserving pupils, which has always been conferred privately, as he seeks no recognition for such gestures.

Concerning the status of current violin performance, Francescatti states in the March 1986 issue of *Strad* magazine:

> The art of violin playing is progressing in *quantity* not in quality. It is a good thing that more young people are studying the violin. But we no longer produce great musical personalities. The training of young musicians today is much more rounded than in my day. Pupils are immersed in study of solfeggio, harmony, theory, chamber music playing, orchestral rehearsals etc. This is excellent for producing teachers, career orchestra players and "team" players in general, but not necessarily for solo artists. Virtuoso command of the violin must be acquired while one is still young, and the hand and finger muscles are at their most supple, that is, if the violinist has aspirations of becoming a soloist. After about twenty it is too late to acquire this degree of technical prowess! Mastery of the great concertos and show-pieces must come early in life, the sooner, the better. Once this is accomplished, the young musician has an entire lifetime to read about music history and take pleasure in playing chamber music. I am referring, of course, only to the most *gifted* youngsters who realistically have a potential for a solo career. With this approach, the young violinist's musical personality, assuming he or she has some latent measure of individuality, can best be encouraged and developed. We have many young players today who play marvelously, but one is not very much different from the other in terms of personalized musicality. Another problem is the emphasis on "competition" repertoire. One hears of students who wander from one competition to another slaving away at the same compositions year after year.

At this writing the Francescattis live in La Ciotat, France. In the same issue of *Strad*, the eighty-three-year-old violinist states:

> At last I can do exactly what I want. I am privileged to live in a quiet little town near Marseilles where the climate is exceptionally good. I look at my garden and receive my friends at lunch or in the afternoon. I enjoy good food. I listen to young violinists when they come to play for me. From time to time I attend concerts, listen regularly to recordings and radio broadcasts and watch television. My hobbies are chess and my stamp collection.

Francescatti, recovering from a serious 1983 illness, no longer touches the violin. In 1987, a Francescatti International Violin Competition, to be held every two years, is scheduled to be inaugurated in Aix-en-Provence. To ensure its high artistic level, only laureates of other major competitions will be permitted to compete, and awards will be commensurate with the stature of the event. This competition will alternate every other year with the Casadesus Piano Competition currently held in Cleveland.

A truly noble artist, Francescatti, is a fount of tasteful, cultivated musicality, who has long since won the right to be included among the foremost violinists of the twentieth century.

Nathan Milstein, a shining symbol of stunning virtuosity, dashing, ever-vital musicality and incredible career longevity

CHAPTER THREE

Nathan Milstein

WHEN NATHAN MILSTEIN made his American debut on October 17, 1929, Kreisler was still charming his adoring international audiences. Heifetz had long since vanquished a legion of outstanding players and established his awesome new violinistic standards. The boy Menuhin was the phenomenal prodigy of the time, packing concert halls everywhere. Szigeti, with his crusading intellect, continued to attract listeners who sought lofty, unpretentious musicianship. Such stellar artists as Elman, Seidel and Zimbalist had already been comparatively downgraded. It seemed impossible that another Russian-Jewish violinist whose formal training had been attributed mainly to Stolyarsky and Auer, could launch a major career, particularly in the colossal shadow of Heifetz. However, a virtuoso of Milstein's caliber was simply not to be denied. He has succeeded in surviving all of his former competitors, and his brilliant career has become the longest in the annals of violin art. Indeed, if anyone has ever discovered the violinistic equivalent of the legendary "Fountain of Youth," it is he.

Milstein was born in Odessa, Russia, on December 31, 1904, one of seven children. (Odessa colleagues allege that he was born two years earlier). Neither of his parents was a musician and he states: "I started to play the violin not because I was drawn to it, but because my mother forced me to. She sensed my affinity for music. But only when I progressed far enough to feel the music itself did I practice willingly and eagerly."

At age seven, after a brief unsatisfactory period with a local teacher, he went to the renowned Odessa pedagogue, Pyotr Stolyarsky, who was David Oistrakh's only teacher. Milstein remarks, "I studied with Stolyarsky at the Odessa Music School for about three years. We were with him twice a week, and eight or ten pupils would come to the lesson. We would learn from each other." Stolyarsky never played for his pupils at lessons; all his teaching was done by explanation. In 1915 the boy went to St. Petersburg and studied with Auer until the master left for Norway in

1917. It is not clear who brought him to the capitol, or how and under what circumstances he was accepted into Auer's class.

Milstein is not at all charitable toward his teachers. Among other derogatory statements he has said, "Some of what you hear about the great teachers amount to no more than myths. Stolyarsky used to eat an egg when we played for him in Odessa, and Auer was no teacher at all—he picked only pupils who didn't need him." In another interview he said, "I don't feel that Professor Auer had a great influence on me. It was the surroundings and the atmosphere in the class where we worked, because there were so many very gifted young people playing from whom you learned more than from the teacher. In the class of fifty to sixty pupils, only two or three played." Milstein is not specifically mentioned in Auer's autobiography, nor even, oddly enough, in the comprehensive Flesch memoirs.

Taken at face value these remarks might lead one to conclude that the child Milstein learned the rudiments of violin playing strictly on his own. And there can be no doubt that on the whole, Milstein was Milstein's teacher—but someone somewhere must have shown him how to hold the violin and bow properly, how to place his fingers on the strings correctly, how to draw a bow tone resonantly, how to vibrate, and the many other purely technical details that every serious violinist must master. Even the young Heifetz had his father, a competent violinist, to help him in daily practice. Elman's father, too, assisted his son. Milstein, however, in the years during which he was still too young to navigate violinistically by himself, claims that he had no one but his mother, who was not a musician, and his teachers, whom he censures. All this makes no sense, and we can only hope that one day Milstein himself will tell the story of his early development with candor. Was it perhaps Stolyarsky, well-known for his ability to teach the rudiments of violin playing, who was actually responsible?

Unlike many of the finest violinists, Milstein was never a child prodigy. In any event, like Huberman, Elman and Szigeti, Milstein was on his own as a violinist at a ridiculously young age (in his instance, at thirteen). Nor does he appear to have had a mature artist of any type as his overall musical and artistic mentor. His general scholastic education was sacrificed in behalf of incessant violin practice, and it was only in later years that he "filled in the gap and did a great deal of studying."

When next we hear of Milstein in 1921, he is not yet seventeen and is giving four concerts at the Kiev Conservatory with the pianist (in later years the noted pedagogue) Sergei Tarnowsky. Here he was heard by Vladimir Horowitz, his senior by one year, and they became fast friends. In fact, the violinist moved into the Horowitz ménage, where he was treated like a member of the family for three years. During this period he

Milstein at age seven

Vladimir Horowitz, Alexander
Glazunov and Nathan Milstein
in Leningrad circa 1920

From the left: Alexander Merovitch, manager of the trio, Milstein,
Gregor Piatigorsky, Vladimir Horowitz and unidentified man arriving in
New York on the S.S. Leviathan for their 1932 - 1933 American tour.

performed in numerous concerts with Vladimir as co-soloist on a single program, usually with Genya, the pianist's sister, serving as Milstein's accompanist.

Sponsored by the new Soviet government and publicized as "children of the Soviet revolution," they were presented throughout the country in clubs, factories, political gatherings and concert halls, and before every conceivable type of audience. Shortly they were joined by the even younger cellist, Raya Garbousova. It was the post-revolutionary period of near-famine. Often they received chocolate for payment when they would have preferred "bread and salami." Touring conditions were abominable. In 1924 Szigeti heard Milstein at the home of Nadine Auer, daughter of Leopold, in the USSR, and described him as "a fabulously gifted young man who seemed diffident about his impending first trip across the borders to Berlin."

It was their manager Alexander Merovitch who sparked the emigration of Milstein and Horowitz from the beleaguered Soviet Union in 1925. Sent abroad officially to represent and herald the cultural status of the new state, they never returned. Merovitch proceeded to introduce them to European audiences and to build their careers. That of Horowitz burgeoned rapidly, whereas the rise of Milstein progressed at a much slower pace.

In 1926 Milstein went to Eugène Ysaÿe as a prospective pupil, but the Belgian master remarked: "Go, there is nothing I can teach you." Their association was very brief, and Milstein can in no way be considered either a bona fide pupil or disciple of Ysaÿe. Yet despite his Russian origin and background, one can perceive stong influences of both the old Russian school and the Belgian school in his playing.

About this time he met the cellist Gregor Piatigorsky, and the pair, taking an instant liking to each other, subsequently teamed up with Horowitz to form a trio, though each was primarily interested in furthering his solo career.

Piatigorsky, in his book, *Cellist*, p. 163, describes Milstein as he was then:

> His quick movements, lively eyes and shiny black hair, and his strong medium-sized frame suggested youth that would stay with him forever. It didn't take long to realize that he stood squarely on the ground and was equal to any situation he might encounter... So spontaneous and harmless was he that one hated to be critical of anything he said... His violin belonged to his body no less than his arms and legs... Nathan could be only what he was, a marvelous violinist... He was self-sufficient, unperturbed and always neat; his friends, his surroundings, his violin, his exquisite cashmere sweaters, all existed to augment his pleasures.

Milstein in 1930

Milstein and Piatigorsky

Of Milstein's playing habits Piatigorsky adds:

> I never caught him practicing scales or any other exercises. In fact, he did not give an impression of practicing at all. He just played on the fiddle and with the fiddle. I only rarely found him without the violin in his hands. As long as he had his violin, no one could disturb him... Occasionally he imitated other violinists, but when I asked him to impersonate one he particularly admired, he said: " It's dangerous, for if I succeed in playing like him, I would not want to play like myself ever again.

The cellist once told me privately that even when Milstein shaved, the violin was perched on a nearby chair in case he should think of a new fingering or bowing to try out. It is said that an important part of his technical development resulted from practicing difficult passages from Chopin's piano music.

He became an American citizen after his first American tour in 1929. In 1931 the illustrious trio, sometimes referred to as *The Three Musketeers*, gave some concerts with but limited success. Only Piatigorsky of the three had had any comprehensive chamber music experience, and apparently while each played his own part impressively, the "musketeers" were often prone to shoot at different musical targets in terms of ensemble, and their individual sounds did not blend. They did not make a single chamber music recording as a group.

Milstein has been one of the least publicized of the twentieth-century elite virtuosi. Yet for the past five decades most observers have consistently included him among the first half-dozen leading violinists. The sheer brilliance of his playing has sustained his career with no assistance whatsoever from notoriety garnered through "extracurricular" social, political or philanthropic activities, such as have involved certain of his famed colleagues.

Like the few most illustrious violinists, his tone has several different facets of color as opposed to those outstanding players who possess only a one-dimensional wrist vibrato sweetness of sound. His tone can be fervent, but is never quite voluptuous. Its quality might best be described as "silvery." Its power of penetration is superb, and it possesses extraordinary solidity and toughness of fiber without becoming hard-edged. His intonation vies with that of Heifetz in immaculate accuracy.

Milstein's vibrato is that of a "classicist." His style ranges from no vibrato to a sweetly lyric "medium" and thence to a fast, ardent, closely-knit vibrato in which the top joint of the finger plays a significant role. It does not, however, attain the ultimate opulence of sound. He uses his vibrato as a "coloring" agent rather than as a device to titillate the ear, and the fact that he is often sparing in his use of vibrato tends to make his climaxes all the more intense when he "turns it all on." This use of

Family photo, 1950; rear: Milstein; front left: Jill Spalding (Milstein's step-daughter), daughter, Maria, and wife Thérèse

Thérèse Milstein playing Liszt's piano in Count Cini's palace with adoring husband looking on, circa 1954

Nathan Milstein in 1956

Jill Spalding, Nathan, and Thérèse Milstein, circa 1958

vibrato also has its negative side, in that his subdued lyric passages are at times comparatively underplayed. Throughout most of his career Milstein has manifested a vibrato idiosyncrasy by often beginning a lyric note without vibrato and starting vibration at some point during the note. But in his late years this habit has been eliminated, to a large extent. Though Milstein frequently alternates non-vibrato notes with vibrant ones, he does not approximate the irritating and vitiating practice of "hot and cold" vibrato in a single singing phrase that has become so prevalent among violinists in the last two or three decades.

Milstein's playing encompasses many moods. He can intone with chaste, almost detached sobriety, or generate the propulsion of a jungle cat. The spirit of his art is eternally youthful as is the aura of the man himself. It is perhaps his *intensity of spirit* that is the dominating characteristic of his performance. His playing is ignited by an impellent drive that can border on fury. Conversely, it does not reflect an exceptional degree of poetic imagery. Purity of line and refinement of taste, rather than graceful elegance, are important components of his musicality. A single, short work can reflect both brashness and modesty.

Milstein's interpretations are deeply felt and always well-ordered, though not profoundly cerebral. His art eschews heart-on-sleeve emotionalism, and while he often plays with abandon, it is not a wayward abandon. He is adept in the use of subtle, suave slides and position changes for expressive purposes, but in a manner less pronounced than that of Ysaÿe, Kreisler, Heifetz, Menuhin, or even David Oistrakh.

There is nothing unusual in the physical structure of Milstein's hands; they are remarkably supple and flexible. The coordination between his hands is astounding, and accounts not only for the speed and clarity of his rapid passagework, but also for its inordinate smoothness and fluency. One may attend a Menuhin, Stern or Ricci concert that is well below their highest standard, but Milstein's consistency seldom falters. A "live" Milstein recital is almost always a memorable event. Although many of his recordings are superb, the ebullient Milstein vitality, thrust and propulsion are at their communicative best in the concert hall. Milstein's audiences, like those of Heifetz, instinctively feel the artist is in complete control. Hence they are relaxed and at ease, subject only to the music itself. His instrumental control is phenomenal; his knowledge of the instrument, encyclopedic.

Milstein has stated: "The shoulder should play an important part in the equalization of the (bow) tone. I object to too much wrist and lower forearm. Most times I use very little wrist. I change bow from the shoulder rather than the wrist." This somewhat unorthodox shoulder application can be noted easily. He uses no shoulder pad or cushion.

It is often pointed out that having a good staccato is not essential, and that a violinist can enjoy a brilliant career without ever using staccato. Milstein is the living example of this view. For all his marvelous technical skill in both hands, he does not possess a reliable staccato, or if he does, he chooses not to use it in public. Even such passages as the scales in the first page of the *Rondo Capriccioso* section of Saint-Saëns' *Introduction and Rondo Capriccioso*, traditionally played in staccato, are negotiated in spiccato by Milstein. As if in compensation for his avoidance of staccato, he has a spiccato of which the crispness, articulation and control are of breathtaking perfection. And in detonative bowing passages, his explosive yet crystal-clear impact is unsurpassed.

The late celebrated violist William Primrose, in his book *Walk on the North Side*, p. 153, said of Milstein:

> Once he starts playing (in private) he is difficult to stop, I am happy to relate . . . His pragmatic knowledge of violin playing is vast, and I hope he will teach regularly someday . . . It is well known that since this writing he has established himself as one of the violin's most outstanding teachers . . . He believes in taking a common sense approach to everything, doesn't make anything mysterious.

In discussing Milstein, Piatigorsky told me:

> Nathan is at his very best when he plays by himself, as in the Bach solo sonatas or Paganini caprices. Here he is in entire command without the need to deal with another personality. He is next best when in collaboration with a pianist, though he is very hard on and demanding of his piano accompanists. With conductors he is generally uncomfortable, and tends to regard them as the enemy, sometimes with good cause.

I had occasion to verify this last statement, and described such an incident in a 1965 review:

> In more than forty years of concertizing, Nathan Milstein has earned and sustained a reputation as a paragon of violin consistency in addition to his status as an invariably brilliant technician. Indeed, in these areas he has but few peers. Thus, it came as a rude shock to hear Mr. Milstein hack and race his way through the Brahms D-major Concerto with a disdain for clarity and phrasing that bordered on the flippant. What should have been a masterful performance turned out to be a hollow caricature of the celebrated Milstein art at his Friday afternoon Music Center appearance with Zubin Mehta and the Los Angeles Philharmonic Orchestra. And if Messrs. Milstein and Mehta were on speaking terms it was not particularly evidenced in their musical rapport. In fact, at one point in the third movement the gentlemen were perilously close to musical fisticuffs. The entire affair had best be forgotten.

Yet two days later on Sunday at a UCLA recital with pianist Leon Pommers, I was able to write, "Nathan Milstein came to town. He is now sixty years of age and looks fifteen years younger—and he combined the ebullient enthusiasm of a youth making a debut with a seasoned artistry that was, if possible, greater than ever. He was, in a word, magnificent!"

The Milstein public performance repertoire is neither as broad in scope nor as large in size as that of Heifetz, D. Oistrakh, Menuhin, Stern, Szeryng or Ricci. Szymanowski and Prokofiev represent the limits of his contemporary music, though he has, on occasion, played the Stravinsky concerto and speaks of his desire to one day play the Berg concerto which he calls "glorious." He insists upon playing only those works for which he has affinity and affection, and is decidedly not a pioneer of new music. However, the continual repetition of his chosen repertory has never resulted in a loss of freshness or inspiration, as he invariably seeks and finds new musical insights in these works, constantly modifying fingerings and bowings to suit his changing ideas. Even in the standard repertoire one could compile a long list of familiar works he does not play in public and has not recorded, including the concertos of Sibelius, Elgar (he is purported to have studied it in Russia), Paganini, Bruch (Concerto No. 2 and the *Scottish Fantasy*), Bartók, Walton and Vieuxtemps, along with numerous sonatas and concert showpieces. But by and large, most of the important masterworks are part of his active repertoire.

The Milstein discography consists of some 120 different works, large and small, several of which have been recorded as many as three or four times. The Tchaikovsky concerto has always represented some of Milstein's most effective playing, and he has recorded it four times. All are dashing performances, but my favorite is the version made around 1948 with Frederick Stock and the Chicago Symphony, because it is the most personalized. Milstein uses some, but not all of the Auer alterations, though his interpretation, freely limned, is not particularly of the so-called Russian school. It is intense in character yet not conspicuously emotive; the *Canzonetta* is played simply and unaffectedly, and the final section of the third movement is propelled at an astonishing rate that is, believe it or not decidedly faster that the 1937 Heifetz recording!

His Brahms concerto, although lacking intellectual profundity, is violinistically superb and viscerally expressive, particularly in the section following the first movement cadenza, and in the *Adagio*, where he is generous in the use of suave slides and position changes. The finale is a typical Milstein tour de force. The cadenza, written by him, is exceedingly brilliant and not overtly imitative. Of his three recordings I prefer the vigor and unassuming musicality of the one with Anatole Fistoulari and the Philharmonia Orchestra.

The straightforward, respectful Milstein approach to the Beethoven concerto is not conducive to sensitive introspection, although his performance is instrumentally impeccable. For example, there is no variety in the repetition of phrases, especially in the *Larghetto*. All is crystalline in sound and earnestly wrought, but the phrasing is scarcely Olympian. Nor does he take many risks in pursuit of personalized nuances. His three original cadenzas sparkle, but again their merits are more technical than creative. Recordings with Erich Leinsdorf and the Philharmonia Orchestra, and with William Steinberg and the Pittsburgh Symphony are about on a par.

Milstein's Mendelssohn concerto with Steinberg and the Pittsburgh Orchestra is the best engineered of his three recordings, but the old mono version (Bruno Walter, New York Philharmonic) is perhaps a bit superior in terms of spontaneity. It is one of the most personalized of his performances: propulsive, ardent and immaculate.

His Bruch Concerto No. 1 contains much dramatic intensity; the final G-minor scale at the end of the first movement (in the recording with Steinberg and the Pittsburgh Symphony) is "beefed-up" with octaves in the top notes. The opening of the *Adagio* is somewhat reticent, but the climaxes soar, and the finale is highly charged. This is perhaps the most bouyant of the three Bruch discs.

Milstein chose to be his own conductor in recordings with the Philharmonia Orchestra of Mozart Concerto Nos. 4 and 5, resulting in readings that are more metronomic than they should be. As violin playing, they scintillate, but lack the ultimate in charm and amiability. Somehow the music does not seem to be in complete rapport with his temperament, though many a passage is rendered piquant by his remarkable spiccato. He has written all the cadenzas, of which the one for the first movement of Concerto No. 4 is, while rather predictable, the most inventive.

Two of his finest discs are the Dvořák concerto (Frühbeck, New Philharmonia Orchestra), a perennial favorite among professional violinists, and the Saint-Saëns Concerto No. 3 (Fistoulari, Philharmonia Orchestra), a stylish, spirited performance, if not a tonally opulent one. The Glazunov concerto, his United States debut vehicle with the Philadelphia Orchestra under Stokowski, is neatly lyric and ineffably polished, but lacking in tonal richness, at least in comparison to the peerless Heifetz performance.

The dashing Iberian motifs of Lalo's *Symphonie Espagnole* (Ormandy, Philadelphia Orchestra), without the third movement, habitually omitted by the Auer pupils, contain some of Milstein's most sensuous playing. Several of the more songful episodes could profit from a heightened sense of languor, but on the whole this is a debonair, electrically charged interpretation, and the tension he generates in the *Andante* is extraordinary.

The Prokofiev Concerto No. 1 (Carlo Maria Giulini, Philharmonia Orchestra) is played with consummate agility and silken smoothness, but lacks the acerbic attack of the memorable Szigeti disc. Concerto No. 2 (Frühbeck, Philharmonia Orchestra) is a dutiful performance somewhat wanting in affection; the lovely second movement is quite pallid.

Beethoven's two *Romances* (Harry Blech, Philharmonia Orchestra) are played purely and literally without inspiration, as are the Bach A-minor and E-major Concerti which he performs with an unnamed string and cembalo troup. The celestial slow movements project little subtlety. In two albums comprising eight of Vivaldi's nondescript concerti with a small baroque ensemble of American musicians, poor engineering diminishes Milstein's solo role. The results are dullish both in sound and style. However, the Vivaldi Concerto Nos. 28 (P. 258) and 39 (P. 229), recorded with the Bach concerti and realistically engineered, offer batteries of détaché bowings that are glitteringly executed, and show the violinist to his advantage.

One of Milstein's recorded gems is the Goldmark concerto (Blech, Philharmonia Orchestra), a stunning exhibition of virtuosity that once again demonstrates why Milstein ranks among the greatest violinists of this era. This recording of the Goldmark was unchallenged for many years until the appearance of the Perlman recording (though Bronislav Gimpel also made an excellent recording).

Milstein's collaborations with artists other than his piano partners or orchestras are few in number. A two-violin album with Erica Morini comprising Bach's familiar Concerto in D-minor, BWV 1043, and Sonata in C-major, BWV 1037, and Vivaldi's Concerto in D-Minor for Two Violins, Cello and Strings (Op. 3 *L'estro armonico*, No. 11) is quite unconvincing. Though Milstein appears to be striving for musical camaraderie with Morini, his more robust tone and articulation clearly dominate her thinner sound and fragile violinistic presence. The chaste performances are lackluster.

However, recordings with his old comrades, one with Piatigorsky, the other with Horowitz, are outstanding. In the Brahms Concerto in A-minor, Op. 102 (Fritz Reiner, Robin Hood Dell Orchestra, 1951), the Milstein tone, possibly inspired by the sumptuous Piatigorsky cello sound, is at its most intense. Their ensemble is excellent, and the overall performance is rugged and invigorating.

The 1950 recording with Horowitz of the Brahms Sonata No. 3 ·in D-minor, Op. 108, is surprising well-disciplined considering the propensity for individualism of each artist. Horowitz succeeds in projecting his famed "orchestral" sound without overpowering the violinist, and the duo's general restraint provides leeway for many subtleties.

Three Mozart Sonatas, C-major, K. 296, E-minor, K. 304, and G-major, K. 301, with pianist Leon Pommers, are performed with propriety and brio, but somehow Milstein does not "get under the skin" of the music.

The same might be said of Beethoven's Sonata in G-major, Op. 30, No. 3, and Sonata No. 9 in A-major, (*Kreutzer*), Op. 47 with pianist Artur Balsam. The outer movements are sprightly, though oddly, Milstein does not generate the excitement in the *Kreutzer* finale that he does in his live performances. The slow movements tend to be cool and fastidious, with but little probing below the surface. Truly transcendental interpretations of such movements require a greater degree of spiritual repose than Milstein seems to possess. Balsam's role is more that of an accompanist than that of an equal participant, although he plays with thorough efficiency.

The list of recorded Milstein showpieces and vignettes is extensive, and many of the performances are memorable. Heading the roster is his own *Paganiniana*, a hair-raising concoction of virtuosity for violin alone (about seven minutes in length), featuring refashioned themes from Paganini's Caprice Nos. 6, 14, 21 and 24, *Witches Dance* and the first movement of Concerto No. 1. Although the opus contains no double-harmonics or melodies accompanied by left-handed pizzicato, it is extremely difficult and demands the utmost in manual coordination. (In recent years Milstein has written another dazzler of the same genre based on Liszt's *Mephisto Waltz*, and playing it at age seventy-eight, he still scampered up and down the fingerboard with wonderful agility.)

Milstein's other superlative recordings include Szymanowski's *Nocturne and Tarantella*, Op. 28, in which the glacial misterioso of the *Nocturne* and the meteoric propulsion of the *Tarantella* are equally compelling; the impetuous dexterity of the Paganini-Kreisler *La Campanella* (the only Paganini opus aside from his own derivative *Paganiniana* that Milstein has recorded); the amazing speed and articulation of Suk's *Burleska*, though the haste of the middle section slightly militates against the work's innate Czechish "rollick;" the sustained excitement of Wieniawski's *Polonaise* No. 1 in D-major; the lissome gracefulness of Tchaikovsky's *Valse-Scherzo*; the Rimsky-Korsakoff-Hartmann *Flight of the Bumble Bee*, unhurried, with buzzing ponticello effects and an artful usage of open A and E strings to simulate "bee-stings;" the heady abandon of Wieniawski's *Scherzo Tarantelle* (the version with Balsam); the zesty, fervent, but not quite sensuous recording of Sarasate's *Romanza Andaluza* (with Balsam); and the striking nimbleness and "dead-shot" intonation of the *Perpetuum Mobiles* by Ries and Nováček.

Among his best lyric-oriented recordings are his own tasteful transcriptions of Chopin's Nocturne in C-sharp minor, the *Larghetto* in A-major from Nardini's Sonata in D-major, Massenet's *Meditation* from *Thais* and the Brahms Waltz in A-major, all reflecting a cool, gem-like luster and inner tension, but not calculated to bring a tear to the eye. In terms of charm, Milstein's most convincing vignette disc is perhaps the Leclair-

Kreisler *Tambourin*.

Not all of his short piece recordings are impressive. The Bach-Wilhelmj *Air on the G string* has insufficient richness of sound; Kreisler's *Rondino* and *Sicilienne et Rigaudon*, though seamlessly fluent, are neither very subtle nor elegant; Handel's *Larghetto* is uneven in vibrato and quite colorless; his Debussy *La Fille aux cheveux de lin* personates a bland, rather unaffectionate young lady.

A Milstein concert frequently includes a Bach solo sonata or partita, or a movement from one; the last is often presented as an encore, even after he has played a concerto with orchestra. He has recorded the entire cycle twice, once in 1957 and again in 1975. Milstein's solo Bach is immensely respected by most professionals and critics. The clarity of his sound and phrasing, his obvious sincerity of purpose, and the aura of virtuosity that pervades his playing are compelling. Some listeners may prefer their Bach more intellectualized, but both sets of Milstein's recordings of Bach rank high in competition with those of other elite artists, and are widely preferred to the extremely personalized set of Heifetz.

It is interesting to compare the solo Bach playing of Milstein at age fifty-three with that at age seventy-one. The 1957 performances are more vibrant and propulsive, the engineering more candid. The 1975 version is broader in concept, contains more minor rhythmic liberties and reveals certain changes in phrasing and choice of bow strokes. The expressive portamentos are fewer and less prominent in the later recordings. Milstein's tempi are in no way metronomic, but, for example, the basic tempo in the 1957 G-minor *Presto* hovers around 170 as against 148 in the 1975 version; the *Double* (Presto) in Partita No. 1, 152 as against 132; the C-major *Allegro Assai* is 136 as opposed to 126 in 1975; and the same tempo variance occurs in the E-major *Preludio*. All of the 1975 fugues are slower and more staid in character. Milstein has said: "In my Bach playing I stress the bass and middle voices separately, with particular emphasis on the bass almost as a separate entity." To an extent, Milstein has mellowed with age; his interpretations are more relaxed, and in some instances slower in tempo, owing perhaps to a desire for deeper musical introspection, or to the encroachment of age, or both.

The question is raised sometimes as to why Milstein's career, for all its eminence, has not attained the international success of the Heifetz phenomenon. One can pinpoint similarities in their masterful platform poise and ease of execution. But leaving aside their respective qualities of acquired musicianship and technical achievement, they are utterly unlike in temperament and musical perspective. True, Heifetz was established earlier, but this alone cannot account for his supremacy since the history of violin art contains many instances in which well-known artists, still in their prime, have been superseded by newcomers. The number of Heifetz recordings is at least triple that of Milstein's. And the fact that impresarios regulate the fees of artists on their ability to fill halls and sell records (as, for example, in 1950 the New York Philharmonic management paid Heifetz $9,500 for three concerts as against $3,800 for three Milstein concerts), is as good a barometer as any to judge their comparative mass audience popularity and box office draw.

The essence of the matter is that Milstein, for all his wonderful elan and boldness of thrust, is a classical violinist in the tradition of the old masters, whereas the unique Heifetz style, which is more readily identifiable, somehow epitomizes the sophistication and immediacy of the twentieth century. Heifetz's playing is, as Kreisler's was, decidedly "commercial"—Milstein's is not. Milstein's instrumental powers are prodigious, but those of Heifetz are even more so, particularly in the realm of tonal production and expressive nuances. This merely means that Heifetz's playing is more readily accessible to the mass public, just as those great violinists of the twentieth century with the most sensuality of sound (Kreisler, Elman, Heifetz, Menuhin, Stern, Perlman), have reaped larger monetary rewards than their colleagues.

Although Milstein is a strong violinistic personality, his individuality is not nearly as overpowering as that of Heifetz. And while his tone is appealing, it is nowhere near as recognizable as the singular Heifetz sound. One can hardly imagine Milstein playing *Bess, You is My Woman Now*, *Alt Wien*, *Hora Staccato* or *White Christmas*, or for that matter the concerti of Gruenberg, Walton, Korngold and Elgar. The ability to play these compositions ravishingly may not be of marked significance to musical aesthetics, but these are the pieces that "sell." Thus it is much more than just a "strange quirk of fate" (as Boris Schwartz stated in his recent book on violinists) that has determined the comparative magnitude of these two careers.

The very absence of such "commercial" qualities endears Milstein to a sizable segment of violin enthusiasts. He enjoys the utmost respect of professional violinists because he never upsets their sense of propriety, while at the same time offering artistry of virility, vigor and virtuosity of the highest order. Professionals understand the subtle mechanics involved in Milstein's fabulous instrumental mastery. Yet if they were given the choice, it is a fair wager that most would prefer to play like Heifetz.

Milstein's career has not attained the renown of that of Menuhin or Stern, either. One reason is that he has not generated publicity by indulging in extramusical activities. And his playing does not reflect Menuhin's profundity of spirit or Stern's intellectual authority and earthiness. But Milstein is superior to both on a purely instrumental level.

Milstein's transcriptions are not numerous. His *Paganiniana* and *Mephisto Waltz* arrangements are artfully conceived in the violinistic sense, as are the best of his cadenzas and encore type pieces. His knowledge of the instrument is rivalled by few. However, his cadenzas are not likely to be taken up by other violinists, as were those of Kreisler and Joachim.

At one time he played on the 1710 "Dancla" Stradivarius, but since 1945 he has performed on the 1716 "Goldman" Strad which he renamed the "Marie-Thérèse," after his wife and daughter.

Little has been published about his personal life. His hobbies have been painting and tennis ("when one plays correctly from the shoulder, it is the same as bowing"). For many years he refused to fly, but he finally reversed this policy. Milstein received the *Cross of Honor*, First Class in 1966 from the Austrian Ministry of Culture, holds decorations from Italy and Belgium, and is an officer of the French Legion of Honor.

At this writing he lives and teaches in London. On teaching, he has said: "What I feel I can offer these young musicians is simply what I have learned myself through experience. I try...not to impose my way on them, not to teach them to play, even, but to help teach them to think" (from "A Conversation with Nathan Milstein," Richard D. Freed, Bach Sonata Album (1975), program notes booklet).

Nathan Milstein has achieved a distinction unique in the history of modern violin art. At well past eighty, he is still concertizing, performing the great concerti and masterworks as well as such technical feats as his *Mephisto Waltz* and *Paganiniana* transcriptions. Even Heifetz was forced to retire at about seventy-three because of arm problems, and the playing of most of the elite violinists has begun to fray in their late sixties, if not before. Joachim and Elman played publicly until their mid-seventies, but their performances were more nostalgic than impressive. It would be unrealistic to assert that Milstein's violinistic equipment is as formidable as it once was. The intensity of his vibrato and his general tone production are clearly less consistent, as is the overall fluency of his playing. But the caliber of his performance is still incredibly high on his best days, and he has established a new age standard for violinists everywhere. Those who begin to find excuses for waning powers at sixty-five can look to Milstein. Such violinistic longevity can doubtless be attributed to a selfless dedication to his art which has shunned potentially debilitating distractions, to the lofty status of his basic technical powers, and to his excellent physical condition.

In the lexicon of violin art, the name of Milstein will be forever a shining symbol of violinistic virtuosity and mastery.

David Oistrakh, an embodiment of impeccable instrumental authority, lofty musicianship and heartwarming expressiveness

David Oistrakh

THE EMIGRATION FROM RUSSIA of Leopold Auer and his star pupils during or after the 1917 revolution was followed by that of numerous important violinists and pedagogues from Eastern and Central Europe. After the Nazi persecutions the main centers of violin art were located in Western Europe and the United States. Little was known in the West about violinistic developments in the USSR, which was beset by widespread famine, counterrevolution and, during the 1930s, sanguinary political strife

But in 1935, at the Wieniawski Competition in Warsaw, it became apparent from the strong showing of the two Russian contestants that violin art was still flourishing in that country. And in 1937 the Western world was astounded and shaken by the sensational success of Soviet violinists, who won five of the first six prizes in the prestigious International Ysaÿe Competition in Brussels. The gold medalist in that unprecedented triumph was David Oistrakh, not yet twenty-nine and a seasoned concertizing artist destined to become one of the elite instrumentalists of the century. Since that time, Soviet violinists have played a significant, sometimes dominant role in every major competition in which they have appeared.

The Soviet phenomenon, temporarily isolated by World War II and the hardships of the immediate post-war period, did not fully establish international status until the mid-1950s. Yet Oistrakh's reputation, based on European performances and his early recordings, had burgeoned through the years. His debuts in London, 1954 and in New York, 1955, merely served to validate what the international grapevine had been insisting— that Oistrakh was an artist on the highest level, both as violinist and as musician.

David Fedorovich Oistrakh was born on September 30, 1908, in Odessa. It is said that his biological father's name was Kolker, but the violinist always considered his stepfather as his real father. His mother sang professionally in the Odessa opera chorus; his stepfather, a shopkeeper, was devoted to music and played several instruments semiprofessionally. Captured by the Germans during World War I, he became a member of the Russian prisoners orchestra.

At age three and a half David was given a toy violin, and at five, a real one-eighth size instrument. He was one of the few eminent violinists who studied with only one teacher, Pyotr Stolyarsky, whose roster of pupils included many of the finest violinists in the USSR. Stolyarsky possessed an unusual ability to recognize those children who had extraordinary gifts.

In early childhood little "Dodi" was anything but an incessantly toiling prodigy. On the contrary, according to his son Igor, "he would make incisions on his violin strings and bow hair to avoid having to practice on Saturday and Sunday," a heavy burden for a family that could ill afford to replace them. However, he soon responded favorably to the excellent Stolyarsky system which, while taking great care to emphasize fundamentals, abstained from boring young pupils with dry exercises. The pedagogue won their good will and interest by introducing them to group and orchestral playing as quickly as possible. Though never exploited as a prodigy, Oistrakh began to thrive under this regimen.

In 1914, the child, not yet six, appeared in his first concert on a program which concluded with the graduation performance of Nathan Milstein. At fifteen he played Bach's A-minor Concerto with the Odessa Conservatory String Orchestra, and the next year in his first solo recital, the same concerto was included, together with several virtuoso-type pieces. In 1926 he was graduated from the conservatory in viola as well as violin. Anton Rubinstein's Sonata for Viola and Piano was incorporated into his valedictory program that also comprised Prokofiev's Concerto No. 1, the *Devil's Trill* Sonata and Handel's *Passacaglia* (the last two with string accompaniment). For all his skill as a violist, Oistrakh once stated: "the instrument didn't sit well in my hands." His graduation concluded his formal violin training.

In the following year he had occasion to play the *Scherzo* of the Prokofiev Concerto No. 1 for the composer, who reprimanded him publicly for performing it incorrectly. It was a disaster for the eighteen-year-old. Years later, after having attained world recognition, Oistrakh reminded Prokofiev, who had become a close friend, of the incident. The composer was visibly embarrassed.

A few months after the Prokofiev setback, he was invited to play the Glazunov concerto in Kiev under the composer's direction, after which they performed it in Odessa. At the behest of the conductor Nicolai Malko, Oistrakh made his Leningrad debut on October 10, 1928, with the Tchaikovsky concerto. Despite being forced to play on a poor instrument,

Oistrakh at age five and a half

Oistrakh at age eleven

David and Tamara Oistrakh

the violinist deemed his performance a success. But he was treated shab-
bily after having the misfortune of being ten minutes late to the first
rehearsal. The orchestra musicians seemed to resent the appearance of this
young upstart from the provinces.

By 1928 he had moved from Odessa to Moscow, where he was little
known and unaffiliated with the Moscow Conservatory. It was suggested
that he go to work as first violinist in the Bolshoi ballet orchestra, a
dreary, unacceptable way of life for Oistrakh's temperament. The concert
functionaries ignored him, and he earned his daily bread by playing in
popular entertainment "concert brigades."

During these years, Oistrakh performed in open-air concerts in freezing
weather, played background music for popular singers and dancers, and
traveled from town to town in horsecabs, spending the nights in railway
stations.

In 1930 he was married to Tamara Ivanovna Rotareva, an Odessa girl of
Bulgarian descent who had graduated from the Conservatory as a pianist.
The same year he took first prize at the All-Ukrainian Violin Competition
in Kharkov, a victory that added to his slowly rising prominence. In 1933
a break came when he was engaged to play solos for the film *The
Petersburg Night*, in which the main character was a violinist. The highly
emotional score was by Kabalevsky. Oistrakh dubbed the violin playing
offscreen, thereby contributing significantly to the film's success. In the
same year he performed the concerti of Mozart, Mendelssohn and Tchaikovsky on a single program. He was appointed assistant violin professor
at the Moscow Conservatory in 1934.

Standing head and shoulders above all the other contestants, he won the
first prize at the 1935 Second National Competition of Instrumentalists in
Leningrad. Soon after he was designated to compete in the First International Wieniawski Competition in Warsaw, an event that proved to be
his first step toward international renown.

The demands of the Warsaw competition were lower than those of
present-day major international contests: a maximum of twelve minutes
of Bach, three Wieniawski pieces, one romantic or contemporary work no
longer than ten minutes and, if one reached the finals, two movements
from a Wieniawski concerto.

It is well known that the atmosphere in Poland was virulently anti-
Soviet and anti-Semitic. The awards were presented by none other than
Jozef Beck, the Polish Foreign Minister who was a consort of Hitler. Yet
despite this handicap, five of the first nine laureates were Jewish, a fact
viciously excoriated by a writer in the *Warsaw Gazette*, who even assailed
the Jewish ancestry of Wieniawski. Oistrakh was awarded second place.
Ginette Neveu, a blazing talent of only fifteen or sixteen at the time, took
first prize. For all Neveu's admitted gifts, one must wonder how, as a

Laureates of the 1937
International Ysaÿe Competition:

Standing, from the left:
David Oistrakh, Boris Goldstein

Sitting, from the left:
Elizabeth Gilels, Professor Pyotr
Stolyarsky, Mikhail Fikhtengolts

David Oistrakh, Queen
Elisabeth of Belgium and
Pablo Casals at the Casals'
Festival in Prades, 1961

The Oistrakhs: Tamara, David and
Igor at their summer Dacha in 1938

teenager, she could be declared superior to the seasoned twenty-six-year-old Oistrakh in prime form, one of the supreme violinistic talents of the twentieth century. One can only conjecture as to the competence of a jury which placed the talented seven-year-old (or eleven, according to the Groves Dictionary) Ida Haendel ahead of the twenty-four-year-old Bronislav Gimpel, another considerable talent who had a substantial amount of concertizing behind him. Were they awarding current accomplishment, or what they thought was potential? For insight into Oistrakh's mental processes and depth of character, one can do no better than to read his touching letters to his wife written during the 1935 and 1937 competitions, as presented in Yakov Soroker's stimulating book *David Oistrakh*.

The Soviet establishment was extremely gratified by Oistrakh's Warsaw success. Following several concerts in Poland, the violinist was permitted to tour Vienna, Budapest and Istanbul. After winning the gold medal in the 1937 Ysaÿe Competition in Brussels, his career skyrocketed. He was now the acknowledged leader among Soviet violinists, respected all over Europe, and in a position to obtain the most attractive assignments. Though he was not able to make his London debut for another seventeen years, he did visit the city in 1937 and heard a concert by the sixty-two-year-old Kreisler, a revelatory experience that made a lifelong impression. In 1955 Kreisler attended Oistrakh's American debut, which the older master praised unstintingly.

Oistrakh's son Igor was born in Odessa on April 27, 1931, and David became the first elite violinist whose son was to become an internationally known violinist in his own right. Later, Leonid Kogan and his son Pavel shared this distinction, and still later, Dimitri Sitkovetsky, son of Julian, became an international violin competition winner.

Although it was Stolyarsky who, with the assistance of Valeria Merenblum, set Igor on the right path, his father contributed immensely to his training and career development and strongly influenced his playing style. One can only imagine the psychological problems that Igor encountered as the son of the great David Oistrakh. The elder was a conscientious and caring parent, but rumors concerning tension between the adult Igor and his mother, and eventually his father, were rife in Soviet music circles. Father and son, however, began to play duets publicly while Igor was still in his teens in 1947, and their fruitful musical collaboration continued until David's death.

As his fame soared and his influence in the Soviet music establishment increased, it was only natural that Oistrakh became a Communist party member in 1942. Now a ranking artist and public figure, he was often "on the spot" between government policy and his personal feelings. On many issues he was compelled to bob and weave artfully against the fluctuations of the official political line, though he was ever a staunchly patriotic

**David Oistrakh conducting Igor in
the Big Hall at the Moscow Conservatory**

**Zino Francescatti and David Oistrakh
in the former's New York home**

Soviet citizen. He supported his friend Shostakovich courageously throughout the composer's vicissitudes with the powers that be, while managing
to maintain his own artistic and personal integrity.

Oistrakh was a vociferous champion of Shostakovich's works, several of
which were dedicated to him. It is interesting to note the firmness of his
artistic views in the case of Prokofiev's Solo Sonata for Violin. Despite his
intimate friendship with the composer, despite the fact that he was renowned as an interpreter of Prokofiev's music, he steadfastly refused to
perform the work because he felt it to be inferior. Even more difficult and
sensitive was his position in relation to the growing anti-Israel and anti-
Semitic sentiment in the USSR. Irrespective of his beliefs (and they were
certainly pro-Jewish), he carefully avoided public martyrdom on the
issue, even taking an occasional small step backward in the interest of
survival. Yet after the 1967 "Six-Day" war, he bravely refused to sign the
anti-Zionist, anti-Israel document circulated by the government on the
breaking of relations between the USSR and Israel. When I stayed at the
Israel Philharmonic's artists' guest house in Tel-Aviv in 1974, Oistrakh's
photograph was hanging on the wall in the office, the only musician so
represented there at that time. He also refused to sign a document at-
tacking the "formalism" of Shostakovich and Prokofiev.

In 1939 he was made a full professor at the Moscow Conservatory, and
in 1941 he formed his trio with pianist Lev Oborin and cellist Svyatoslav
Knushevitsky. Following the outbreak of World War II he played innumerable concerts at the front, behind the lines and during the siege of
Leningrad.

Oistrakh's life after his rise to eminence was one of constant work, as a
performing artist, teacher and public figure. He contributed many cogent
articles on a wide variety of musical subjects. His schedule left scarcely a
moment for any significant relaxation; nonetheless, he always managed
to keep abreast of cultural, political and social happenings. Unlike many
excellent musicians whose interests are mostly limited to their art, he was
an extremely intelligent man with an intensely humanistic spirit and
outlook. No violinist since Kreisler has been so universally idolized as a
person. Whether the state of relations between the USSR and the West was
one of brinkmanship or détente, people readily sensed the special qualities of Oistrakh as they did of Kreisler during the anti-German atmosphere of World War I. For the most part they tended to exempt him from
anti-Soviet prejudice. He never required a public relations network to
keep his name in the news, as have at least two of his noted colleagues.

As he sped from triumph to triumph, his almost constant fatigue, later
aggravated by obesity, continued to take its physical toll. In 1964 he had
his first heart attack during a performance of Prokofiev's Concerto No. 2
in Leningrad. After a comparatively brief respite he was once more im-

mersed in work. Again in 1973 he spent many months in the hospital. One is tempted to blame the arbiters of the Soviet establishment for not taking direct measures to preserve so invaluable a national resource, since they closely police the work and activities of their artists. Had they ordered him to curtail his schedule by half, they would have been justified. But it is perhaps unfair to censure them, since Oistrakh's life-style was one he preferred, thrived upon and refused to mitigate. In 1960 he had assumed yet another responsibility, that of conductor, making his podium debut in Moscow: his heart must have failed under the cumulative strain.

On October 24, 1974, David Oistrakh died in Amsterdam. His widow Tamara, unable to overcome her deep depression after his death, took her life in 1978.

Oistrakh's merits as an artist are myriad; he was one of the most all-embracing violinist-musicians of the century. His British and American debuts were made in an era of comparative détente between East and West. However, even as the leading violinistic emissary of the Soviet Union, his career could easily not have taken off were he not so supreme an artist. There was always a plethora of observers and commentators ready to denounce the Soviet "School" as being old-fashioned and retrogressive. As is the case with all artists, there were some who were genuinely dissatisfied with certain aspects of his performance. But no one could deny that Oistrakh's emergence from Russia heralded something different in violin art, as did the appearance on the scene of Auer's pupils several decades earlier.

The key element in Oistrakh's artistry was his marvelous ability to move his listeners. This power enabled him to surpass many superb violinists and place him at the forefront as the chief rival of Heifetz, his violinistic and musical antithesis. His natural expressive abilities were incredible, and he represented a style of personalized playing that was different from that of any other artist. Many fine violinists mold phrases; Oistrakh caressed them lovingly. He was a wonderful storyteller. Though always controlled and in exquisite taste, sentiment was an essential component of his playing. He was a visceral player of sensuality; one of those elite violinists who can truly be called a poet. Few players are able, as Oistrakh was, to transform a mood of tenderness into dramatic intensity in a single bar. In addition to his finesse, precision, and intelligent, meticulously disciplined musicianship, there was always an aura of mystical Hasidic charm pervading his playing; a unique synthesis of bittersweet atavistic yearnings with the intense love of life so typical of the Jewish people.

His short, stout figure radiated a glow of healthy simplicity and rugged inner strength. Onstage he avoided all physical mannerisms. The texture of his tone was soft-grained. Occasionally in relaxed passages it was even airy, quite the opposite of the electrically charged sound of Heifetz. Oistrakh's technical command was prodigious. He could read and play at sight many of the most complex compositions such as Shostakovich's Concerto No. 2 and his violin-piano sonatas, unlike, for example, Szigeti, who required incessant toil in mastering any unfamiliar work. And probably as a legacy from his difficult early days in Russia playing under a variety of adverse conditions, his hands required little warm-up. Like Kreisler, his digital reflexes were the epitome of suppleness. His playing gained considerably in warmth, introspection and discipline through the years.

Oistrakh's vibrato was never extremely fast, and especially in his later years often ranged from medium speed to slow. But his fingertips were well padded and his basic sound was always rounded, even when his vibrato was at its slowest. Surprisingly, the comparative slowing down of his vibrato did not notably effect his emotional impact. In contrast to players like Kreisler, Elman and Heifetz, the intensity of his vibrato was not a prime factor in his tonal communication. Nonetheless, in impassioned passages, his double-stops sang uninhibitedly. His trill, too, was not of the greatest velocity, but he employed it so cleverly that in the trill-laden Kreisler cadenza for Tartini's *Devil's Trill* Sonata, it is impressive.

On the purely technical level he could play as fast as anyone, but he never made speed a preoccupation, or substituted sheer brilliance of execution for musical probity and insight. Clarity of statement was ever a priority. His sense of rhythm was unwavering, and the bowing articulation of his passagework, of great incisiveness. The Oistrakh bow arm was smooth, molded more in the Belgian tradition than in the old Russian manner of Auer. As a colorist of the highest order (in contrast to many superb violinists whose playing is essentially one-dimensional), his artful bowing and the canny variance of his vibrato played key roles in the spectrum of his sound. His bow strokes ranged from near the bridge to the area near the fingerboard, investing his playing with a diversity and subtlety rarely equalled.

Like Ysaÿe, Kreisler and Heifetz (though perhaps to a slightly lesser degree), Oistrakh had a highly individualized system of expressive slides and position changes that enabled knowledgeable observers to readily identify his playing. To a large extent these were based on one-finger slides, and especially down the fingerboard usually with the first or second finger. This he was able to negotiate with hypersensitive grace. For portamento effect he employed "bridging notes," some fairly overt, others barely perceptible. His use of these devices in the playing of his middle period, roughly from 1945 to 1960, was prolific, and in certain instances a bit overdone. However, in his later period he employed them less often, possibly as result of his continued exposure to Western playing, which had begun to frown upon such embellishments.

In discussing Oistrakh's equipment and style of delivery, it is necessary to stress one of his idiosyncrasies, a tendency that has a deleterious influence upon many violinists, some of outstanding achievement. I refer to the habit of using vibrato in lyrical phrases in an "on-and-off" manner which has no relationship to the development or expressivity of the phrase. Among violinists this digression is often resorted to either as an aid for intonation or general technical security, thoughtless indulgence, or an acquired mannerism. For many violinists it has become a musical way of life which blatantly detracts from the singing propensities of an interpretation. It is so prevalent that critics and commentators who would mercilessly lambast a singer were he or she to do this, seem not to notice the distortion in a violin performance.

One could not rightly blame Oistrakh for this epidemic, although many Soviet (and now other) violinists who consciously or unconsciously strove to imitate his style, succumbed to the infection. Curiously, the overall performance of Oistrakh himself was not seriously undermined even if the listener, on occasion, wished he would do it less frequently. His expressiveness was so natural that he surmounted the aberration. Unfortunately, his emulators are not endowed with such prodigious gifts. The uniqueness of Oistrakh's sound came from within the man.

His repertoire was very extensive. There were but few works of substance he did not play. Oddly, he never stressed the solo works of Bach in his programs or recordings as did, for example, Milstein, though he often performed the Bach sonatas for violin and piano (originally harpsichord), and recorded them all with harpsichord. Beginning with the compositions of Locatelli, Leclair and Tartini, his repertoire extended through the great classical and romantic masterpieces to the concerti of Stravinsky, Hindemith (but not the *Kammermusik* No. 4), Bartók No. 1, Prokofiev and Shostakovich, and many Soviet concerti not often played in the West, such as those of Miaskovsky and Rakov, and Taneyev's *Concert Suite*, Op. 28. It is said that he also performed the concerti of Elgar and Walton in the USSR. He did not publicly perform much of Paganini's music aside from the *Moses Fantasy* and a few of the caprices, but he valued his music highly, particularly the caprices. Oistrakh wrote:

> Paganini's music is a handbook for every violinist; it is wonderfully expressive and reaches any audience; filled with passion, it evokes ardent response in the listener's heart...the caprices are as fresh harmonically as if they were written yesterday...I believe that had Paganini created nothing but these caprices he could have entered the history of music just because of them. (Yakov Soroker, *David Oistrakh*, p. 59).

But as a balancing factor he also stated to young people:

> Strive to know more. Narrow-mindedness, limited range of interests
> may cripple any talent no matter how strong. Avoid prejudice in your
> repertoire. Do not let the brilliance of virtuoso pieces blind you to the
> many treasures of musical thought, often less spectacularly attired.
> (Soroker, *Oistrakh*, p. 105)

And on interpretation, he never regarded the printed score as inviolate
gospel, and often said: "Don't be afraid to argue with the composer, and
you will find what is your own." (Soroker, *Oistrakh*, p. 110) Only a few of
Kreisler's bonbons were incorporated into his programs, but he often
played such bravura pieces as Sarasates's *Carmen Fantasy*, the Saint-
Saëns-Ysaÿe *Valse-Caprice*, Zarzycki's *Mazurka* and Tchaikovsky's *Valse-
Scherzo*. One need only hear his recordings of Wieniawski's Three Etudes,
Caprice Nos. 2, 4 and 5 (with Igor playing the simplistic second violin
role), to appreciate the scintillating virtuosity and digital surety of his
basic violinistic equipment. A recording of Sarasate's *Zapateado* made
around 1937 compares with those of Heifetz and Kogan in sheer propulsion and brilliance.

He considered sound production to be an instrumentalist's goal, and
wrote: "Technique is not only fluency, it is also intonation, rhythm and,
of course, as an ultimate expression, sound."

On the subject of fingering, the violinist stated in the preface of *The
Principles of Violin Fingering* by I.M. Yampolsky:

> Ease of execution is not necessarily the most important criterion in
> the choice of fingering, for this should always be subordinate to the
> musical content of the work. Often, the "rational" fingering proves to
> be not better, but positively worse in not producing the tone color
> needed, nor giving sufficient clarity to the musical phrase. In this
> sense one can talk of the aesthetics of fingering, for the failure to
> understand the "style" of fingering at times destroys the musical
> conception of the work.

Oistrakh was not immune to nervousness, saying: "If one plays less than
twice a month, it could crack anyone's nerves," and he recommended
constant public playing as the only sure antidote. He admitted: "In most
cases I feel a tremendous inner tension," but warned against the danger of
being "too calm." He always used a shoulder pad to relax his left shoulder,
and was convinced that the amount of tone sacrificed was negligible.

Oistrakh frequently berated the flagrant competition mania in the
USSR, though he served perennially as juror and functionary.

> We cannot accept as correct a situation where the whole artistic career
> of a beginning musician is tied up with his results at an international
> competition. It must be remembered that winning a prize at a contest
> does not always define the real worth of an artist. Cases are known of

international competition winners who, returning to their day studies at the conservatory, could not live up to their previous success and became mediocre students. We know also of unfortunate mistakes that have been made at times in the choice of candidates for this or that contest, not all and not always the most deserving were included. (Soroker, *Oistrakh*, p. 111).

Obviously Oistrakh felt deeply about the injustices inherent in the entire international competition syndrome, including those perpetrated in his own country.

His recordings, numbering some 350 compositions, rank him as one of the top three recording artists together with Heifetz and Menuhin. Perlman, is probably next in line. This total is all the more remarkable since he did not make commercial recordings in his youth as did the boy prodigies Heifetz and Menuhin. More than a few works were recorded several times. It is unfortunate that some of the finest performances of his prime period (1945 - 1954) were on poorly produced Soviet discs, many of which were (together with tapes of live concerts and radio air checks) either reproduced on license or pirated in the West. One particularly inferior recording of the Beethoven concerto on the British Egmont label lists him as Marcus Belayeff with Vassili Shiveski and the Odessa Philharmonic. Close scrutiny identifies the record as definitely played by Oistrakh early in his career. He never recorded the complete Bach solo works; his single disc effort is the Sonata No. 1 in G-minor. In terms of engineered sound, it must be borne in mind that those discs *originally* made in Western Europe and the USA are far superior to those recorded prior to about the mid-1960s in the USSR.

Among his concerto recordings, the Mendelssohn (with Eugene Ormandy and the Philadelphia Orchestra, 1955) is wonderfully spontaneous, fresh and sparkling, indelibly stamped with Oistrakh's personalization. His powers are at their zenith. As in all his playing there are vestiges of "on-and-off" vibrato, but overall his vibrato is beautiful and freely applied.

The Dvořák concerto (Kondrashin, State Orchestra of the USSR) is another gem. Oistrakh begins in a comparatively relaxed mood, ending the opening phrase with a soft high E harmonic. But the modulated repetition is climaxed by the topmost A on the E string hit solidly with dazzling vibrance. The entire interpretation is graced with a sort of homespun Czechish charm. The orchestra is competent, but not in the upper strata.

The Glazunov concerto, played with the same group, is a highly individualized performance. One can pinpoint an over-abundance of slides, but its sheer expressivity ranks the interpretation among the most compelling two or three Glazunov recordings. However, the hair-raising 1934

Heifetz recording is still the front-runner.

An off-beat work, Taneyev's five-movement *Suite de Concert*, Op. 28, the equivalent of a concerto (Malko, the Philharmonia Orchestra, in the mid-1950s) is long-winded, with many attractive passages, but not calculated to win wide audience reception outside of Eastern Europe. Oistrakh's performance is a stunning feat, highlighted by the exciting *Tarantella* finale.

Lalo's *Symphonie Espagnole* can be heard on many excellent recordings, but Oistrakh's (Martinon and the Philharmonia Orchestra, all five movements), again from the mid-1950s, is among the most stylish. Not only brilliant violinistically, it contains an abundance of subtleties not found in most of the other fine recordings of the work. His vibrato is at its fastest and the performance is permeated with Iberian fervor.

One of Oistrakh's exceptional accomplishments was his ability to create a mood and sound of *misterioso*, which was to a large degree produced by artful bowing near the fingerboard. This is employed to great advantage in the opening and final sections of the first movement of Prokofiev's Concerto No. 1, as well as the filigree passagework of the composer's Sonata No. 1 and the third movement of Sonata No. 2. The biting satire of this disc of the mid-1950s (von Matacic, London Symphony) compares favorably with that of the splendid Szigeti recording of the mid-1930s. The same combination performs Bruch's Concerto No. 1 with surpassing affection; the *Adagio* is especially heartfelt.

Two recordings of Khachaturian's concerto, one with Gauk and the USSR State Symphony, the other (in stereo) with the composer and the Moscow Radio Orchestra, are about equal in performance; the violinist lovingly communicates the Armenian folkishness of the work.

The 1962 Bruch *Scottish Fantasy* (Horenstein, the London Symphony) is played with winsome tenderness, in contrast to Heifetz's burning intensity. Oistrakh's vibrato idiosyncrasies are evident; nevertheless, it is a graphic interpretation, infinitely more sentient and poetic than the recordings of Grumiaux and Chung, and far superior in tonal color to that of Campoli. Nor has the excellent Rabin recording (clearly influenced by Heifetz), or that by Perlman, the individuality of Oistrakh's.

Three versions of the Brahms concerto reveal it as one of Oistrakh's most exalted interpretations. The first, from the mid-1950s (Konwitschny, the Saxon State Orchestra), with the Joachim cadenza, is perhaps the most masterful and brilliant, though a 1961 version (Klemperer, French National Radio Orchestra) runs it a close second. A later recording (Szell, Cleveland Orchestra) is easily the best engineered, though the performance, while still formidable, is less alive in sound and marginally less than perfect in execution. There is also an early recording with Kondrashin and the USSR State Symphony. In this work Oistrakh's introspective powers elevate his performance above those of his colleagues whose playing is limited to virtuosity and visceral application without intellectual force.

A similar mastery is evinced in his Beethoven concerto, especially in a mid-1950s recording (Ehrling, Stockholm Festival Orchestra) in which he plays all of Kreisler's brief second movement cadenza. Here he imbues the work with a celestial glow, and yet it is ineffably human, marked with elegant classical sentiment without excessive emoting. The third movement, played rather slowly, emphasizes lyricism. Overall, the performance is one of the most moving of this immortal opus. A version with Cluytens and the French National Radio Orchestra (with a truncated second movement cadenza) is comparable. The "Belayeff" Odessa recording is, as indicated earlier, inferior in every respect. A Russian recording with Gauk and the USSR State Symphony is good but the engineering is inferior.

Oistrakh's Tchaikovsky concerto is an infinitely personalized interpretation. Who else could play the turn embellishment in the first phrase of the *Canzonetta* with such angelic grace? He instills in it a certain Russian character that differs from performances of both Western performers and of the old Auer pupils. Even in medium-speed passages he projects a lyric aura where others play these as purely technical progressions. He recorded the work six times. The recording with Konwitschny and the Saxon State Orchestra of the mid-1950s is especially strong in emotional impact, although the Moscow Philharmonic in the 1968 version under Rozhdestvensky is instrumentally superior, as is the engineered sound. On the violinistic level there is not an appreciable difference among the six; however, the 1968 live recording commemorating his sixtieth birthday displays occasional flickers of fatigue.

Ordinarily, the Sibelius concerto is not a preferred work for violinists with soft-grained sound. But Oistrakh's exceptional virility and verve along with his penchant for wistful expressiveness add up to a superb performance at the opposite end of the spectrum from the sovereign, icily rugged, yet heroically impassioned Heifetz interpretation. Of his four recordings a mid-1950s version (Ehrling, Stockholm Festival Orchestra) is the most alive in sound, closely followed by the one with Ormandy and the Philadelphia Orchestra.

For all of Oistrakh's disciplined, tasteful musicianship, his Mozart was romantically inclined in keeping with his innate style and personalization. Many listeners, including myself, enjoy his warm buoyant Mozart performances. Others, such as the late American critic, B.H. Haggin, prefer Mozart to sound more classical and strait-laced. Haggin roundly criticized both Oistrakh's Mozart (No. 4 in D) and his Mendelssohn concerto recordings. The most satisfying of his Mozart discs are the 1955 No. 4 in D-major, K. 218 (Ormandy, Philadelphia Orchestra) and No. 7 in

D-major, K. 271, of disputed origin, (Kondrashin, National Philharmonic—probably a Soviet orchestra). The No. 7 Colosseum label recording from the early 1950s begins with the third movement and ends with the first! Concerto No. 3 in G-major, K. 216 (Barshai, Moscow Chamber Orchestra) is surprisingly lacking in subtlety. A 1972 set contains Mozart's five authenticated concerti and related shorter works, plus an admirably integrated performance as violist with Igor on violin of the *Symphonie Concertante* with the Berlin Phiharmonic. The concerti, with Oistrakh as violinist and conductor, are vitiated by that metronomic feeling which nearly always ensues when there is no independent conductor, and the artist and orchestra are not year-round collaborators. Oistrakh's mastery is always in evidence but it is not his most spontaneous playing.

Other concerto recordings of special merit are the two by Shostakovich: the sprawling, emotion-laden 47-minute No. 1 (Mitropoulos, New York Philharmonic, 1956), a work now being widely accepted into the standard repertoire; the darker, intensely dramatic 29-minute No. 2 (Kondrashin, Moscow Philharmonic), less popular but eminently worthy; the hauntingly beautiful Szymanowski No. 1 radiating imagery and instrumental colors (Sonderling, Leningrad Philharmonic); the eloquent Prokofiev No. 2 (Galliera, Philharmonia Orchestra, 1959); the impassioned 21-minute Bartók No. 1 (Rozhdestvensky, USSR State Symphony) in a performance noticeably more expressive than the Stern recording; (he never did record the popular No. 2); and the stately, charming Viotti No. 22 (Kondrashin, USSR State Orchestra), dully reproduced on a German tape from a 1948 Soviet performance. Also of interest is the intricate, at times unviolinistic concerto by the East German Ernst Hermann Meyer (Suitner, Staatskapelle Berlin,1965), a grim, agitated, heavily-orchestrated 35-minute work of wide rhythmic diversity, not calculated to win a mass audience. In a Stravinsky concerto recording (Haitink, Lamoureux Orchestra), Oistrakh sounds fatigued, and seems to be searching for a profundity that is not inherent in the work.

Oistrakh was a masterful sonata player, and unlike several of his eminent colleagues, never made mere "accompanists" of his piano collaborators. If he dominated the duo, musically, it was always out of sheer talent, never by royal command. He handled many styles equally well, from the gay, rollicking Leclair Sonata No. 3 in D and the austerly poetic Locatelli-Ysaÿe Sonata in F-minor (with pianist Vladimir Yampolsky), through Mozart, Beethoven and the romantics, to Prokofiev and Shostakovich.

Among his most memorable sonata recordings are Prokofiev's No. 1 (with Yampolsky), which constituted a model for Soviet players and others, including Perlman; Schubert's *Grand Fantasy* in C (with pianist Frieda Bauer), in which his amazing ability for coloristic variety makes a delightful experience of a work that in lesser hands can be dull; Szymanowski's Sonata No. 1 in D-minor, Op. 9 (with Yampolsky), a work of impassioned lyricism; Grieg's No. 1 in F-major, Op. 8 (with pianist Lev Oborin), light-hearted, intensely Nordic in mood, is somewhat superficial music played with the meticulous care, respect and affection of a truly great artist.

Other outstanding sonata recordings are those of Karen Khachaturian, No. 3 in G-minor (marked Op. 1 in the Heifetz recording) and Prokofiev No. 2 (Yampolsky), with the third movement properly played *misterioso*, an uncommon occurrence among other artists, and a finale that is not rushed; Tartini's *Devil's Trill* (with Bauer) is a bit breathy in the opening lyric section, but Oistrakh daringly takes the final notes of the first two phrases of the ensuing section on the G string, unlike many of his colleagues who opt for the easy low positions. He also imitates Kreisler's four grace note endings, played poetically, at the tip of the bow in the second bars of the second and third *Grave* sections.

Several of his later sonata recordings project a sense of fatigue. Tempi are slower, and so is his vibrato. Many of the Franck tempi are so slow that the pulse of the music is affected, and to a lesser degree this is the case with his Brahms No. 3 (both with Sviatoslav Richter, 1968). An earlier version with Yampolsky is marginally better in this respect. Brahms's No. 1 (Bauer) is also tinged with fatigue, but Oistrakh's sheer talent surmounts this shortcoming. Notably superior are the Brahms No. 2 (Richter, 1972) and Schubert, Op. 162 (Bauer). Although the latter work "belongs" to Kreisler, Oistrakh's performance, much less intense in sound, is thoroughly charming and exceptionally attentive to detail.

In Mozart's No. 15 in B-flat (Yampolsky) from the mid-1950s, the slow movement is approached with marked romanticism and has quite a few slides, but the overall interpretation is gracious and compelling. And in Mozart's Twelve Variations on the theme *La Bergère Célimène* and Six Variations on the theme *Hélas, j'ai perdu mon amant*, Oistrakh imparts an extraordinary relevance to the slight, convivial music (with Paul Badura-Skoda).

His complete recording of Beethoven sonatas, with the superb performance of Oborin on piano, is one of the few most intriguing cycles. The sonatas are pervaded by a spirit of intimacy and ingenuousness. All is leisurely in tempo and cogently proportioned. The lighter, bright works such as Nos. 1, 2, 5 and 8 are limned with affection. In introspective passages, as in Sonata No. 10 and the second movement variation of the *Kreutzer*, Oistrakh transforms passages that sometimes can be uninteresting into endearing musicality. The deceptively difficult No. 3 is archly delivered with ease. Collectively speaking, one can pinpoint an occasional trace of tonal blandness or "airy" sound, but Oistrakh's Beethoven has few rivals in subtlety of nuance and range of color.

Oistrakh also recorded the complete cycle of six Bach duo sonatas with harpsichordist Hans Pischner. This is solid, tasteful playing sparked by Sonatas No. 3 in E-major and No. 4 in C-minor.

Two other sonatas merit special mention. One is Shostakovich's Op. 134 (Richter, 1969), an arduous work that has yet to be discovered by most Western players. Like so many sonatas of the era, it lacks compelling lyric themes, which may deter its popularization. Oistrakh sounds somewhat tired but negotiates the brusque, fast movements with his customary incisive flair. The other is the now popular Ysaÿe *Ballade*, No. 3 (solo, 1953). Here he is at his peak and captures the work's poetic spirit, as opposed to so many (including Igor) who approach it as a purely technical tour de force.

Among medium-length concert pieces with orchestra are three from the early 1950s transcribed from Russian tapes; a stunning imaginative recording of Chausson's *Poème*, in which the high octave passages soar with deliberate grandeur; Ravel's *Tzigane*, in a dynamic interpretation that is diversified in mood; and Glazunov's *Mazurka-Oberek*, a trifle that he could only have recorded out of his deep affection for the composer. All are with the USSR State Orchestra (instrumentally mediocre); the first two with Kondrashin, the third with Yudin.

In those short pieces with piano that he favored, Oistrakh could conjure up a magical spell comparable to that of the most notable vignette players. He respected them fully, and imbued such brevities with every facet of his art. His early recording of the Chopin-Sarasate Nocturne in E-flat major (with Makarov), may well bring a tear to the eye, along with Suk's sensuous *Song of Love*, Sarasate's languorous *Zortzico*, Wagner's sentimental *Albumblatt* and Tchaikovsky's *Meditation*, an old meandering Russian favorite. One can particularly appreciate Oistrakh's expressive powers by comparing his version of the *Meditation* with that of Milstein in the Glazunov arrangement with orchestra.

One might add to this prime list Szymanowski's shimmering *Fountain of Arethusa*, the exquisite reverie of Debussy's *Clair de Lune*, the captivating narrative of Wieniawski's *Légende*, the almost Hebraic lilt of Vladigerov's *Song from the Bulgarian Suite*, the folkish high spirits of Kodály's *Dances from the Village of Kallo*, the superb viruosity of Zarzycki's slight but sparkling *Mazurka*, and the glittering Saint-Saëns-Ysaÿe *Valse-Caprice*. All except the Chopin are with Yampolsky. Many more deserve mention.

In his duo discs with Igor, David invariably plays first violin, and as with his duos with Stern, David Oistrakh's unique sound and style can be readily detected. As a chamber music player he was a generous partner, and while he tended to dominate his collaborators by virtue of his talent (as have all the elite violinists), his willingness to blend with them in sincere unity is easy to ascertain in recordings. His roster of worthy trio recordings with Oborin and Knushevitsky include those of Haydn, Beethoven, Chopin, Glinka, Dvořák, Mendelssohn, Schubert, Smetana, Rimsky-Korsakov and Rachmaninov, among other chamber works.

Many of the brightest violin talents in the USSR were assigned to study with Oistrakh as a finishing course after their preparation with other leading professors. As was to be expected, practically all became laureates of major competitions. Among the best known, in addition to his son Igor, are Valeri Klimov, Viktor Pikaisen, Gidon Kremer, Nina Beilina, Rosa Fain, Stefan Gheorgiu, Eduard Grach, Oleg Kagan, Mark Lubotsky, Viktor Danchenko, Stoika Milanova and Ion Voicu.

Oistrakh devoted much thought and care to his responsibilites as a teacher. Not only did he demonstrate his ideas with his violin, but as a man of superior intelligence he was able to write about pedagogical details with clear, penetrating thought. He did not have his pupils play scales at the lessons; rather he instructed them how to practice scales at home. Pyotr Bondarenko was his chief aide, who helped prepare the students. Other assistants were Igor, Viktor Pikaisen, Olga Kaverzneva and Solomon Snitkovsky. Often Oistrakh would ask a pupil to relate what he thought were his shortcomings, thus transforming him into his own critic. He strongly reprimanded pupils who played in a dull, over-careful manner, and would urge them sometimes to "lose their heads" or to play as they would act in a scene of anger. Beauty and distinctiveness of sound were all-important goals towards which he constantly exhorted his students. Concerning practice, he recommended that they "live with the violin all day, everyday." However, he thought that four hours of work in the morning was too much, and advised shorter sessions throughout the day and night, so that the mind could remain alert during practice.
He wrote:

> Youth is very sensitive. It watches carefully the work of its teachers, and one has to strive forward intensely and unremittingly not to be left behind. I believe that the growing of my performance since 1934 is due in a large extent to my teaching activity as well... The level of our young violinists is so high that one feels somehow elevated just by associating with them... The evolution of my creative art and my teaching activity merge together. Both the positive qualities of the pupil's performance and its weaknesses, the difficulties encountered, leave a useful imprint on an attentive teacher; one notices in a pupil what one misses in himself. Students' mistakes are an important warning, pupils' achievements make imagination work. (Soroker, *Oistrakh*, p. 101)

Oistrakh showed great appreciation of and consideration for his piano collaborators: chief among them were Abram Makarov, Lev Oborin, Vladimir Yampolsky, Frieda Bauer, Sviatoslav Richter and Paul Badura-Skoda.

His main instruments were a Stradivarius 1705, once the property of the

French violinist Martin Marsick, which he seemed to prefer in his later years, and another Stradivarius 1714, formerly owned by Jacques Thibaud. Queen Elisabeth of Belguim, herself a violinist and longtime friend of Oistrakh's, willed him her own Stradivarius, a family heirloom. The viola Oistrakh played over a long period was an Andreas Guarnerius. His bows, oddly, were neither Tourtes nor prime French bows but of German make. A biographer, Ernst Krause, states that his main bow for a good part of his career was a Nurnberger; the violinist himself affirmed that he owned German bows by Dolling and Hermann. Whether this was merely a gesture of goodwill to the East German makers or whether he actually used them in concert is not clear.

Oistrakh was not immune to the "conducting fever," and as so many instrumentalists have done, he turned to the podium for an extension of his artistic satisfaction in his early fifties. Like his ambitious colleagues, he had extensive musical knowledge and razor-sharp instincts, but precious little practice of the conducting technique that takes so many years of study and experience to master. He was wise enough to realize his deficiencies in this respect, and strove to learn all he could of his new venture. His recordings as a conductor, which are reasonably good, include several major works from the symphonic repertoire and collaborations with soloists. But he never reached the point where he could be regarded as a professional maestro. Had he lived longer, he might have attained this goal.

The honors bestowed upon Oistrakh were numerous. In the USSR he was awarded a Stalin prize, first degree in 1943, was given the title of "People's Artist" in 1953, and won a Lenin prize in 1960. Abroad, he received an *Honoris Causa* degree from Oxford University and citations from the London Royal Academy of Music, Santa Cecilia in Rome and the USA Academy of Arts and Sciences, among others.

I recall vividly my own meeting with Oistrakh. He had played six concerts in the previous seven days. Following the sixth concert, I was introduced to him backstage. After the long, arduous recital, he was obviously exhausted. However, he insisted on "talking violin" for the better part of an hour. I was embarassed, feeling that I was keeping this great artist from his deserved rest, but his zest and enthusiasm were all-consuming. Finally, and regretfully, he departed from his dressing room, stepped into his waiting limousine and left for his hotel.

Oistrakh's characteristic generosity and kindness are widely known and documented. Menuhin offers an example of this in his *Unfinished Journey* in relating how Oistrakh, in 1955, gave him a facsimile score of the then unperformed Shostakovich Concerto No. 1, so that both could introduce the work at the same time. Numerous testimonials from his colleagues corroborate his rare stature as a human being as well as that of an artist.

In the hierarchy of twentieth-century violinists and, indeed, in the history of violin art, Oistrakh sits on the topmost level. His superlative expressiveness, sensitivity, lofty musicianship and technical authority have seldom been equalled. All great violinists have their adulators and admirers, but David Oistrakh, truly beloved by so many, was a transcendental artist and personality.

David Oistrakh's memorial by sculptor L. Kerbel in the *Novodevichy* Cemetery in Moscow

Isaac Stern, a superbly gifted artist whose best playing embraces both impassioned utterance and profound musical introspection

CHAPTER FIVE

Isaac Stern

THE DECADE OF THE 1930s was graced by some of the best violin playing in the history of the art. It was nearly impossible for a new young artist to break into the hierarchy represented by Kreisler, Elman, Heifetz, Menuhin, Milstein, Szigeti, Ricci, and, by 1939, Francescatti. Yet as always, dauntless young hopefuls sought to try their wings in an effort to join the ranks of the masters.

One of these was Isaac Stern. His first bid for an international career took place in 1937 in New York. I recall his nationwide broadcast, which featured the final movement of Bruch's G-minor Concerto, played with heroic thrust and tonal opulence. At the time I felt that this young man possessed qualities of a top-level violinist and artist. But he was not destined to be a world-acclaimed boy prodigy as was Menuhin, or even Ricci. His brilliant Carnegie Hall recital in 1943 sparked what eventually blossomed into one of the most significant and widely publicized instrumental careers of the twentieth century.

Stern's official birthdate is given as July 21, 1920; the place, Kriminiecz, in the Soviet Ukraine, a town about 350 miles northwest of Odessa. However, his early teacher, Robert Pollak, in his article published in the *Tokyo Evening News*, September 1953, stated: "One day in the fall of 1926, a short time after I had been appointed head of the Violin Department at the San Francisco Conservatory of Music, a husky little boy of eight came to my class for an audition. Technically he was not very advanced, but I recognized immediately his outstanding talent." I knew Pollak to he a highly intelligent, honorable person, a man not likely to forget the year he received a respectable conservatory position. Nor does it appear probable that Stern's parents would represent him as being eight if he were only six. Gdal Saleski cites Stern as having taken piano lessons at age six, then switching to the violin at eight. Perhaps a Stern autobiography will one day settle the point.

Stern's father was a painter, and his mother studied singing at the

Imperial Conservatory in St. Petersburg. They emigrated to San Francisco before Isaac was one year old. For about four years the boy studied with Pollak, whose roots and musical background originated in Vienna. From ages twelve to sixteen he studied with Naoum Blinder, a former concert-master of the San Francisco Symphony and himself a pupil of Alexander Fidelman and Adolf Brodsky in Russia. Stern credits Blinder as his principal teacher who taught him, among other things, to teach himself. At fifteen he played the Bach Double Concerto with Blinder and the San Francisco Symphony. Veteran San Franciscans, however, report that he had appeared as a soloist with this orchestra under Willy Vandenburg several years earlier. He also studied for a brief period with Louis Persinger.

Through the years Stern has become a leading figure of violin art, a superlative instrumentalist and musician, sponsor and mentor of such younger talents as Perlman, Zukerman, Mintz and others, and a most provocative personality who has evoked both mass adoration and, in certain quarters, bitter animosity. As one of the most influential forces on the international music scene, he is a fiery, immensely convincing speaker and proponent of humanitarian and cultural causes, celebrated as the saviour of Carnegie Hall in 1960 and for his efforts toward establishing the National Endowment for the Arts in 1964. An intimate friend of many prominent political, social and economic leaders, Stern is an indefatigable champion of the welfare of Israel and is intensely proud of his Jewish heritage. He still refuses to play in Germany as a protest against the Holocaust. Together with his activities in support of many Israeli musical organizations, he has been the prime force behind the America-Israel Foundation, which continues to provide scholarships for talented young Israelis. In addition to his eminence as a soloist, Stern is a chamber music artist of prodigious stature, whose trio with pianist Eugene Istomin and cellist Leonard Rose performed with distinction for many years, both in concerts and recordings. He also participates often in chamber music events with his younger colleagues.

Stern appeared in the film *Tonight We Sing* (playing the role of Ysaÿe), based on the life of the impresario Sol Hurok, his longtime manager, and was heard as the soundtrack violinist in *Humoresque*, starring John Garfield and Joan Crawford, and in the *Fiddler on the Roof* film. The 1981 film *From Mao to Mozart*, a report of Stern's 1979 sojourn in China, won an Oscar for the best documentary.

Once married to the ballerina Nora Kaye, Stern now has been married for over thirty years to his present wife Vera, who is intimately involved in her husband's activities. They have three children, Shira, Michael and David. He plays alternately on a magnificent 1740 Guarnarius del Gesù, said to have belonged to Ysaÿe, and on the "Vicomte de Panette" del Gesù.

The young Stern

Stern in 1963

Stern's playing, at its best, combines the traditions of the pre-Soviet Russian School, with its emphasis on beauty of tone and fervent individuality of interpretation, with the lofty ideals of musical integrity as inherited from Joachim through Szigeti. His hands, while not comparable in immensity to those of Perlman, are large and fleshy, and the character of his sound is as solid and robust as his presence. It is a sound that hearkens back to the rapturous outpourings of Kreisler and Heifetz but is not as voluptuous and vibrant. However, in his younger years Stern could "turn on the heat" through his reflex-type vibrato to an extent that few of his colleagues could equal or surpass. It is a sound impelled genuinely by the fingertip, as opposed to the current prevalence of slower, wrist-motivated oscillations which tend to produce tone that is sweet and lovely but not eminently vital. Stern's tone, while powerful and rich, is not as highly personalized as that of Kreisler, Heifetz, Menuhin or Oistrakh, whose individual sounds can scarcely fail to be identified almost immediately by knowledgeable observers of violin performance. But by means of his masterful use and control of vibrato, Stern's range of tonal color surpasses that of all but a few of his colleagues and competitors. He uses vibrato not merely as a device to bewitch the ear, but as a means of instilling maximal diversity in his interpretations. Thus he is able to project the darker hues of Brahms and Bartók as readily as the lighter textures of Mendelssohn and Mozart. Even when his vibrato is not in force, his tone retains a sense of life, and is never subject to the "on-and-off" aberrations of Oistrakh's imitators. He takes scrupulous care to adjust the type and speed of his vibrato to whatever style of music he is performing.

Though Stern has more digital facility than some may think, he was never a bravura technician who publicly featured or specialized in the finger-twisting escapades of Paganini, Ernst or even Vieuxtemps. Nevertheless, in his rise to eminence he vanquished a long list of gifted young violinists, some of them far more accomplished in fingerboard gymnastics. None, however, had the overall intellectual force, perseverance and sheer will power of Stern; the authoritative virility of sound that is the hallmark of the truly sovereign violinists; or the mastery of the most musically significant styles which distinguishes the violinist-musician from the more limited violinist-virtuoso. Nor for that matter did they possess, as Stern does, those elusive ingredients of inherent musicality and spiritual elevation that separate a great violinist from a great artist. Throughout his adult career he has refused to force his hands into unnatural positions for the sake of performing gymnastic feats, choosing rather to develop into an interpretive artist. Consequently his handling of sonatas and music stressing introspection is decidedly more profound and satisfying than that of most violinists whose playing gravitates toward superficial tour de force exploits. Stern, if he wished, could play with a lush, heightened romanticism that Szigeti could never produce tonally, and yet could accommodate himself to the most exacting demands of musical and stylistic rectitude. But he became so enamored of "turning off the emotion" that many of his concerts, especially from 1960 to 1970, began to approximate cerebral musical seminars. This never failed to delight those of his listeners who equate dull, lustreless playing with good musicianship

However, one cannot but feel that Stern in the role of "Herr Professor" is to a large extent motivated by affectation. After all, he is inherently a theatrical personality who can propound convincingly whichever musical approach he chooses, even if it does not represent the ultimate realization of his talent and communicative powers. For that reason one may hear Stern in several successive matter-of-fact performances, and then suddenly be bowled over by the "real" Stern playing like the man of passion and lusty appetite that he is. Perhaps a bit goaded by the competition offered by his prodigies Perlman and Zukerman, he now seems less inclined to opt for the role of the quasi-ascetic, at least for an entire performance.

Stern's brawny, yet utterly flexible bow arm is one of the most dependable components of his violinistic arsenal, and functions sturdily even into his later years, producing large-scaled sonority. He possesses a crisp spiccato, and both the normal and stiff-arm staccato. The latter enabled him, in his younger years, to play Dinicu's *Hora Staccato* (which Heifetz had transcribed and popularized), and although his rapid-fire staccato was lighter and had less bite than that of Heifetz (or, for that matter, the late Michael Rabin), it was nonetheless impressive.

In sostenuto strokes Stern uses as much of the bow hair as possible, whether playing forte or pianissimo. His bow grip is centered on a circle of the middle finger and thumb, and is not dominated by the pressure and extension of the forefinger in the manner of the Russian Auer pupils. He describes his bow arm as "rather heavy," and does not keep it inordinately high.

Stern advocates strong finger pressure in the left hand for optimum tone production. His fingers can be heard hitting the finger board in many recordings. But his trill, though rapid, is soft in texture and neither hard in impact nor electric in speed. And while more than a few fine violinists are ill at ease in lyric octaves of first and fourth finger combination, Stern plays them easily, cleanly and resonantly. He uses a shoulder pad, which is unusual, considering the shortness of his neck. In memorizing, he has stated that he prefers to rely on a mental picture of the score, rather than on finger patterns learned by rote.

Expressive slides and position changes do not play as major a role in his performance as they do with Kreisler, Heifetz, Menuhin or Perlman, but he does employ them frequently in his most ardent playing in the romantic repertoire, and almost always with mastery. One may hear him deliver a Mozart or Bach concerto with scarcely a finger portamento and then be nonplussed when he plays the final bars of the Franck sonata *Recitativo-Fantasia* movement with two rather gross downward slides. However, his innate good taste has but rarely yielded to such abuses, and his use of expressive slides has generally declined in his later years.

Stern has been a prime force in the changes that have taken place in program building since the Kreisler-Elman-Heifetz era. In carrying on a trend toward "good" music as emphasized by Szigeti, his influence has helped to transform the all-embracing violin recital of yesteryear into violin-piano chamber music concerts. Whether he did this out of a musical conviction, for technical convenience (to avoid the drudgery of constant practice demanded by difficult showpieces), or for both reasons, the modern violin recital has lost a great deal of its luster, charm and sheer entertainment. Unfortunately, in order to conform to this trend, we hear many violin virtuosi programming sonata masterworks for which they are intellectually and musically unsuited. And all too often in these chamber music affairs (including Stern's), the duo sonatas are played one-sidely as violin solos, with a hired pianist who subjugates his own musical personality to that of his employer. Like most of the elite violinists, Stern candidly defers to the supremacy of Heifetz and has stated that the present time will be known historically as the Heifetz era. Yet he was never loath to compete with Heifetz in many of the choice Heifetz masterworks, and even in such showpieces as Sarasate's *Zigeunerweisen* and the Bizet-Waxman *Carmen Fantasy.*

Many listeners have preferred Stern's well-ordered, sagacious interpretations to the extreme individuality of the Heifetz sound and style, his super-speed and the aloofness of his personality. Or for that matter, they have preferred Stern's playing to the technical waywardness of the mature Menuhin; the mellifluous but rather restricted tonal pallette of Francescatti; the scintillating but scarely introspective virtuosity of Milstein; or the intellectual emphasis of Szigeti. And for all the precocity of Perlman and Zukerman, many feel that neither approximates the tonal virility or interpretive maturity of Stern. To them, Stern has represented the consummate violinist-musician who possesses some of the finest characteristics of each plus a definitive personality of his own. On the other hand, it has been frequently pointed out that Stern does not achieve the thrilling vibrance, hair-raising articulation and perfection of Heifetz; the daring, imagination and sponaneity of Menuhin (at his best); the heartfelt expressiveness of Oistrakh; the tonal seductiveness of Kreisler and Elman; or the amazing agility and manual coordination of Milstein. Be that as it may, Stern has fully earned his place among the elite. With the appearance of Oistrakh in the Western world, Stern's position as the leading competitor to Heifetz (after 1955) in mass popular acclaim was marginally sidetracked by the Soviet star's immense success, although the two became intimate friends and recorded duos together. The increasing inconsistency of Stern's concert playing, due to his aversion to daily practice (as opposed to Oistrakh's meticulous preparation), did not abet his critical reputation. Many, particularly knowledgeable professionals, resented Stern's instrumental laxity and felt it was unfair, or even dishonest, for a modern artist to misuse his public by offering an inferior performance at top box office prices.

With the passing of the years Stern's playing took on some new characteristics, some say as a result of his association with the aged Pablo Casals. The hot-blooded scion of the Russian-Jewish tradition, while always a disciplined artist, began to intellectualize to such a degree that his performances took on an aura of preciousness (i.e. underplaying), especially in music of the classical repertoire. In fact, at times one would think that he was hoarding his energy for the next concert, afraid of exhausting all his resources in a single appearance, a single work, or even a single movement of a work. This was tantamount to a form of sophistication bordering on the blasé. One of the deleterious side effects of this musical way of life has been its effect upon impressionable young players who do not possess Stern's strengths but are prone to emulate his musical mannerisms. For a violinist who probably was beset by instrumental or musical idiosyncrasies to a lesser extent than any of his colleagues, this trend represented a major turning point in his art. And when, following his tremendously publicized Carnegie Hall exploits, Stern the *violinist* became Stern the *institution*, the instrumental consistency of his performances began to decline.

Stern's career as a public figure and spokesman expanded enormously. An anecdote widely circulated runs as follows : A man meets a friend and says: "I heard Isaac Stern last night." "Yeah?" quips the friend, "What did he have to say?" But more seriously, during the last couple of decades when Stern comes to town for a concert, invariably the first thing a professional will ask is: "Has Isaac been practicing?" Professionals greatly respect Stern's best playing, but many no longer buy tickets to his performances. This is unfortunate, for it may be that Stern *did* take time to practice and played impressively. Of course, irrespective of what professionals do or think, a Stern appearance practically guarantees a capacity audience and a tumultuous ovation, whether he plays well or is shamefully off-form.

Unlike Menuhin, whose instrumental vicissitudes in his later years seem due to a complex of problems, Stern's basic instrumentalism, while not equal to that of his earlier years, is still potent in his best playing. His technical vagaries are generally the result of insufficient practice. In his younger years he prepared conscientiously for each appearance. But his lifestyle now precludes his being a slave to the instrument as are Heifetz and Milstein. Stern's extramusical activities have doubtless prevented him from realizing the fullest potential of his talent.

In contrast to nearly all of his colleagues and competitors who, at one time or another, have performed works for which they are technically, musically or temperamentally unsuited, Stern is careful to play only those compositions for which he has complete musical affinity and instrumental equipment. He has deviated rarely from this principle, hence he successfully and deservedly has avoided criticism in this regard. This repertorial discrimination naturally extends to his recordings. The low-keyed oversophistication that regularly vitiates, at least in part, even the best of his latterday concerts, is only minimally evident in his meticulously edited recordings. And unlike Oistrakh's recordings, many of which were produced under inferior Soviet engineering conditions (i.e. those early recordings of works that were never rerecorded in the West), the body of Stern's recordings, including the early 78 RPM and mono 33 RPM efforts, are well produced.

In the totally uncritical section on Stern in Boris Schwartz's *Great Masters of the Violin*, it is asserted that "His recorded repertoire is immense; there is hardly a piece in the violin literature that he has not put on a disc." This is clearly incorrect: Stern's disc inventory comprises about 160 works, large and small, including rerecordings and chamber music, considerably fewer than that of Heifetz, Menuhin, Oistrakh, and by now, Perlman and Ricci. Admittedly, his colleagues have recorded far more short and medium-length pieces to inflate the total. But what is really significant in rebutting Schwartz's claim is the fact that Stern had never (at the time of Schwartz's publication) recorded any of the Bach Solo Sonatas and Partitas, or a single Paganini caprice, which are essential components of basic violinistics, whether or not Stern finds them amenable to his tastes or technical convenience. Stern had recorded only one of the ten Beethoven violin-piano sonatas, and none of the Mozart sonatas. Now that Stern, in his mid-sixties, is scheduled to record the Bach and Beethoven cycles, it will scarcely represent his playing at its peak level. Nor has he recorded the concerti of Elgar, Walton, Vieuxtemps, Spohr (*Gesangsszene*), Bruch's *Scottish Fantasy* and Concerto No. 2, Glazunov, Bartók's Solo Sonata, Tartini's *Devil's Trill* Sonata, or many other short and medium-length items considered part and parcel of the standard repertoire. He has recorded only two Kreisler brevities, none of the sparkling showpieces of Wieniawski or Vieuxtemps and only two by Sarasate. Stern's latter-day programs, generally overweighted with sonatas,

From the left: Nathan Milstein, David Oistrakh,
Stern, and Eugene Ormandy and Sol Hurok

Stern vacationing at the Aspen Music Festival in 1975

do not often included Bach solo works, although I once heard him play a satisfactory large-scaled performance of the *Chaconne*, and recently, a spotty rendition of the Solo Sonata No. 1 in G-minor. Whereas Heifetz chose to record the Bach solo cycle and incurred much criticism for what many observers feel is an overpersonalized performance of music alien to his temperament, Stern avoided interpretive controversy or competition with his peers in these monumental works by simply choosing not to record them at all in his technically prime years.

Stern did not have the opportunity to record many short pieces in his youth, as did the boy prodigies Heifetz and Menuhin. But the best of those he recorded in maturity (which total about 40), are played with sublety, sincerity and affection, in the tradition of earlier artists. And when he chooses to include as encores such vignettes as the Wagner-Wilhelmj *Albumblatt* or Kriesler's *Liebesleid* and *Schön Rosmarin*, even into his mid-sixties, they are played with a tonal lustre and a charm unheard in the younger generation, except perhaps (and to a lesser degree) in Perlman. Some of his choice efforts in this genre were recorded fairly early in his career with pianist Alexander Zakin, and focus upon pieces he played habitually in his concerts. In addition to those named above, Sarasate's *Caprice Basque* (omitting the doublestop theme repetition we hear as on the old Elman disc) is both stylish and audacious; Novaček's *Perpetuum Mobile* is spotless; the Dvořák-Kreisler *Slavonic Dance* No. 2 in E-minor is relaxed in tonal intensity but amiably expressive; Milhaud's *Tijuca* from *Saudades do Brazil* lilts idiomatically; and the Prokofiev-Grunes (transcriber not credited) *Danse des jeunes Antillaises* is compellingly bittersweet and *Masques*, grandiloquently sprightly. In Bloch's *Nigun* from the *Baal Shem* Suite the climactic passages are fiery, dramatic and soulfully "Jewish."

Less successful is a 1963 vignette collection with Milton Katims and the Columbia Symphony, orchestral arrangements by Arthur Harris. The title piece, Tchaikovsky's *None But the Lonely Heart* is tonally inconsistant; the Brahms *Hungarian Dance* No. 5 finds the violin line cluttered by the orchestral setting, as are Copland's *Hoedown* from *Rodeo*, Benjamin's *Jamaican Rumba* and Dvořák's *Humoresque*, though the last is graced with some exceptional doublestop playing. His Rimsky-Korsakov *Flight of the Bumble Bee* is appreciably less clean than that of Heifetz and Milstein. Gershwin's *Bess, You is My Woman Now*, Foster's *Jeannie With the Light Brown Hair* (much like the Heifetz transcription), and a somewhat simplistic arrangement of Schubert's *Ave Maria* are all played with warmth and affection, but these pieces essentially belong to Heifetz and are best passed over by other violinists. The choice item of the group is a personalized interpretation of Kreisler's *Liebesleid*.

A 1973 brevity compilation with Frank Brieff and the Columbia Symphony, also with orchestral arrangements by Arthur Harris, finds most but not all of the settings less overblown than on the 1963 disc, and more amenable to the nature of the material. Tchaikovsky's *Serenade Melancholique* is heartfelt, with a sumptuous G string sound not equalled by the more sweet-toned, wrist vibrato artists. Borodin's *Nocturne* from his String Quartet No. 2, in an admirable setting, is also outstanding in tonal richness. A long-winded version of Schubert's *Serenade* benefits greatly from some singing high-position doublestops. Debussy's *La Fille aux cheveux de lin*, its inherent delicacy vitiated by a busy orchestration, is nonetheless played beautifully, and Wieniawski's *Romance* from Concerto No. 2, underplayed at the beginning, gradually takes on an impassioned air. An arrangement of Mendelssohn's *On Wings of Song* is merely a pale impersonation of the splendid Joseph Achron transcription. In Rachmaninoff's *Vocalise*, Stern plays with polished lyricism, but somehow fails to get under the skin of the music. Rubinstein's *Romance* is rather dry in sound and at times underplayed; the Chopin-Sarasate Nocturne in E-flat (with the ticklish, agile cadenza, just before the ending, omitted; Sarasate's name is not mentioned) is well phrased and tonally robust, but lacks the magic of the Heifetz, Elman and Oistrakh recordings. In retrospect, it is clear that Stern is potentially a superb vignette practitioner. But although in the twenty- to forty-minute masterworks emotional restraint can be an integral part of the music, deliberate underplaying in short emotion-oriented pieces, even in minimal dosage, can detract significantly from the total impact of the performance.

On the technical level there is not a great deal of difference between the earlier and later Stern concerto and sonata recordings, though this is not necessarily the case in comparing his earlier and later concerts. It is impossible, of course, to know the exact extent of editing in the later recordings. Technical considerations aside, the differences are mostly revealed in musical approach. At some point in his maturity, Stern apparently came to believe that slowing down or even stopping his vibrato in certain passages expanded the range of his expressive powers and could add what might be termed a celestial element to his interpretations. (This has nothing whatsoever to do with the widespread habit of "on-and-off" vibrato with a single lyric phrase discussed above.) This change was coupled with a lowering of his softer dynamic shadings to the point of whispering. Many, including myself, feel that this attitude has weakened rather than improved his music-making. His most convincing playing occurs when he lets his emotions speak, or at least plays with sustained warmth. Musical effeteness is essentially unnatural to Stern's temperament.

Although the majority of Stern's recordings of major works reflect his highest standards, some are particularly outstanding. Among these is the

Brahms D-major Concerto, recorded three times (Ormandy, Philadelphia Orchestra; Beecham, Royal Philharmonic; Mehta, New York Philharmonic), with the Joachim cadenza. The Ormandy version is perhaps the best of the three, with engineering superior to the earlier Beecham recording, but some may prefer the marginally superior tonal intensity and individuality of the latter. The 1979 Mehta recording, less consistently intense in sound and exhibiting a few mannerisms, is still formidable. The dramatic thrust and virility of Stern's Brahms easily place it among the best half-dozen ever recorded, and in terms of introspection and profundity, it decidedly outranks that of any of his younger colleagues to date.

The thrice-recorded Tchaikovsky concerto (Hilsberg, Philadelphia Orchestra; Ormandy, Philadelphia Orchestra; Rostropovich, National Symphony) is also most satisfactory in the Ormandy version. The opening is played leisurely, as it should be but too often is not. Solidity of tone, with no vestige of airiness, and lyricism mark the interpretation. In the finale, Stern captures the rustic peasant essence of the melodic phrases, a characteristic of the music that is seldom understood by many modern players who all too often race through it rather mindlessly.

The Mendelssohn Op. 64 concerto has always been among Stern's finest interpretations. There is little difference in performance caliber among his four recordings (two with Ormandy, Philadelphia Orchestra; one with Bernstein, Israel Philharmonic, and a 1976 version with Barenboim, New York Philharmonic), though my own favorite is the earlier Ormandy recording. Stern's fairyland is clearly terrestrial; his *Andante* favors serenity more than intensity of spirit, and there is a sense of strength even in the finale's impishness. Yet it sustains an aura of lightheartedness that unfailingly illuminates the fey music.

The Mozart Concerto No. 5 in A-major (Szell, Columbia Symphony) is among his most buoyant and sunny Mozart recordings. Concerto No. 2 in D-major is occasionally too low-keyed, while No. 4 in D-major, strengthened by a brilliant rendering of the first movement Joachim cadenza, is more consistent in lyric statement (both with A. Schneider, English Chamber Orchestra, 1979).

In the realm of fiery romanticism, Stern's early recording of Wieniawski's Concerto No. 2 in D-minor is second only to that of Heifetz. The sound is positively opulent, and he employs expressive slides to grand effect. The Ormandy, Philadelphia Orchestra recording is better engineered than the one with Kurtz and the New York Philharmonic. Another great success is Lalo's *Symphonie Espagnole* (Ormandy, Philadelphia Orchestra) in the complete version. The *Scherzando* is more subtle and languorous than piquant, and the opening of the *Rondo* lacks the optimum lilt. But the *Intermezzo* is dashing and impassioned. The G string

**Stern generously substituted for scheduled soloist Pinchas Zukerman
(whose father had died) at the Aspen Music Festival in 1975**

climaxes in the *Andante* are rich in sound, and the lyric triplet section of the finale is compellingly suave. In all, it is larger-scaled than many excellent competitive recordings. The Dvořák concerto (Ormandy, Philadelphia Orchestra) is also among the three or four finest recordings of the work. All is muscular, and Stern hits the climactic high E string notes of the opening with brash attack. The final movement may be less devilishly brilliant than that of Milstein, but the eloquent *Adagio* is more glowing in sound and spirit.

Bartók's Concerto No. 2 (Bernstein, New York Philharmonic), is an ideal vehicle for the rugged propensities of Stern's temperament. Some may feel that the Menuhin recording projects more pure feeling, but Stern's performance excels it in neatness of detail, and is equally large-scaled and stylistically alert. The Concerto No. 1 (Bernstein, New York Philharmonic, circa 1960) is less consistent violinistically and tonally, but offers many moments of fervent sound and incisive passagework. In Bartók Rhapsodies No. 1 and No. 2 (Bernstein, New York Philharmonic), works rendered more relevant by their exotic orchestrations than by the blustery, rather banal violin material, Stern actually raises the level of the music by virtue of his ability to project the quixotic Magyar spirit.

Stern's intellectual capacities and unerring instinct for order and cohesiveness are especially effective in the outer movements of the Beethoven D-major Concerto (Bernstein, New York Philharmonic; Barenboim, New York Philharmonic, 1976). The two performances are about equal, though the later disc, surprisingly, shows more life in the *Larghetto*. There are moments in this movement when Stern plays with such relaxation that it is almost musically noncommittal, yet the lyric portions of the *Rondo* are exceptionally expressive. Kreisler's cadenza, freely played, is used for the first movement only; the second cadenza consists merely of the Kreisler trill and a connecting passage; the third, not identified in either recording, is idiomatic and brief.

Any performance differences in the two Sibelius recordings (Beecham, Royal Philharmonic; Ormandy, Philadelphia Orchestra) are minor. The first movements are stalwart and ardent but not particularly imaginative, and the *Adagios* are somewhat underplayed, though the Ormandy version is a bit more intense. The finales are outstanding; Stern's marcatos crackle marvelously, and he does not insert any slurred bowings in the tempestuous opening passages, as does Heifetz. His staccatos, too, are exceptional. This movement contains some of Stern's most audacious playing.

His recording of the Prokofiev Concerto No. 1 is superb, quite different in sound and approach from those of Szigeti and Oistrakh, but comparable to either in flamboyance and satiric bite. Concerto No. 2, also a fine performance, ranks among the three or four best in the category, just below the peerless Heifetz recording (both Ormandy, Philadelphia Orchestra).

Stern's Bruch Concerto No. 1 lacks dramatic tension in the opening; the first two movements meander between rich expressiveness and underplaying; the finale is wonderfully vigorous, crowned by stunning G string opulence. In the Viotti Concerto No. 22, played with Joachim's cadenzas (with some cuts) and adhering fairly close to the Joachim alterations in the *Adagio*, Stern's performance is musically authoritative but scarcely exciting (both with Ormandy, Philadelphia Orchestra). Stravinsky's Concerto in D is played robustly, but is not the type of music that displays Stern's talents to their best advantage (Stravinsky, Columbia Symphony, 1962). The hyperromantic Berg concerto, with its highly charged lyricism is considerably better suited to Stern, and he imbues it with acute tension (Ormandy, Philadelphia Orchestra).

Saint-Saëns' Concerto No. 3 is fairly stylish, but inconsistent in tonal lustre, especially in the slow movement, and at times the orchestra overpowers the violin in the second and third movements (Barenboim, Orchestre de Paris). The Bach Concerto Nos. 1 and 2 are pure in sound and concept, but the slow movements are vitiated by too much repose, and remain earthbound. Samuel Barber's infectious concerto is affectionately played and consistent in lyric utterance. Ebullience and dynamic thrust mark the recording of the Hindemith concerto. All four works are with Bernstein and the New York Philharmonic.

One must admire and respect Stern for choosing to tackle, in his late fifties, such formidable challenges as the contemporary concerti of George Rochberg (Previn, Pittsburgh Symphony) and Krzysztof Penderecki (Skrowaczewski, Minnesota Orchestra), especially since his career was perfectly secure and there was no need for such exertion. Obviously he had to practice assiduously to master these arduous, complex works. Both recordings are decisive interpretations. The much more lyric Rochberg is a prime example of the mellowing of Stern's playing in his later years. And in his mid-sixties, Stern is slated to introduce concerti by Henri Dutilleux and Peter Maxwell Davies.

In the area of recorded medium-length showpieces, the early Waxman *Carmen Fantasy* (Waxman, unidentified orchestra) is a tremendously brilliant performance, comparable to the Kogan recording, both just below that of Heifetz. Saint-Saëns' *Introduction and Rondo Capriccioso* (Ormandy, Philadelphia Orchestra) displays Stern's consummate understanding of the jaunty Gallic essence of the *Rondo*, playing it at a much slower tempo than the bravura but scantly stylish sprintings of Perlman, Igor Oistrakh and the overwhelming majority of younger violinists. Yet he tosses off the final page as dexterously and rapidly as the best of the technicians. The *Introduction*, too, is suave, though not graced with the exquisite Heifetz sound.

Ravel's *Tzigane*, which so often has been performed excellently on recordings, is endowed by Stern with sensuous tone throughout, and easily takes a place among the finest half-dozen renderings (Ormandy, Philadelphia Orchestra). His impetuous approach is, of course, quite different from the less gypsy-like French styling of Francescatti. Chausson's *Poème* finds the violinist not in top form (Barenboim, Orchestre de Paris). The opening orchestral introduction is conducted so slowly that it threatens to grind to a halt, sabotaging the inherent pulse of the music. Technically, some of the difficult solo passages are insufficiently polished, and the playing is tonally inconsistent.

The individual listener may disagree with a Stern sonata interpretation, or may decry the frequent vacillations of his inspiration or tonal intensity. But the fact remains that he can be, at his best, a superlative sonata performer. Even when he plays below his highest standard, his superior musical intelligence readily communicates to audiences and critics. And since in his later years his appearances with piano have been mostly limited to violin-piano sonata programs, to the near exclusion of bravura type showpieces, his rare musicianship can guarantee the continuation of his career as long as he desires, despite the inevitable waning of his technical powers.

Nearly all of his sonatas are recorded with his longtime collaborator Alexander Zakin, an impeccable instrumentalist, who, like the pianists of most stellar violinists, scrupulously avoids emphasizing his own personality while performing with his employer. One always knows for certain which is the soloist and which is the faithful retainer, even in the most complex sonatas.

Among the most compelling of his sonata recordings with Zakin are the Bloch Sonata No 1, transcendentally opulent in sound, communicating the vehement passion of an Old Testament pronunciamento, the two versions of Bartók's brusque, craggy Sonata No. 1, and the marvelously Magyar (not Gypsy) convolutions of Sonata No. 2. The exotic Enesco Sonata No. 3 in the Rumanian style is another commanding Stern interpretation.

Prokofiev's Sonata No. 2 in D-major, Op. 94A is an outstanding recording, lyrical and dashingly spirited, though (as is so often the case) the third movement misses the mood of reverie implicit in the music. Sonata No. 1 in F-minor, Op. 80, is solidly etched, but does not capture the subtle air of mystery in the subdued episodes that marks Oistrakh's matchless performance. Hindemith's uncharacteristically blithe Sonata in C stands high among Stern's lyric interpretations, and Beethoven's Sonata No. 7 in C, an early recording, is consistently alive in sound, large-scaled and sinewy in articulation, and one of the finest performances of that work.

The earlier of two Franck Sonata in A-major recordings is the more vibrant and buoyant in a deeply felt interpretation. The Debussy sonata of the latter 1950s, musically unimpeachable, contains underplaying and dullish tone, and does not sustain the French disposition of the work. Brahms' four sonatas, No. 1 Op. 78 (mid-1970s), No. 2, Op. 100 (1973), No. 3, Op. 108, (1963), and the Clarinet Sonata in E-flat, Op. 120, No. 2, transcribed for violin by the composer, are all examples of astute musicianship, but intermittenly suffer from loss of tension, and understatement, and on occasion, from cerebral mannerisms.

Stern has recorded all of the Beethoven, Brahms and Schubert trios, the Mendelssohn No. 1, Op. 49 and several other chamber music masterworks with his perennial partners Leonard Rose and Eugene Istomin. Each is a model of prime musicianship, instrumental authority and faultless ensemble playing. Stern's sound and musical inclinations, less individualistic than those of Heifetz, do not unduly dominate his colleagues, but his soloistic instincts color the overall musicality of the group. Two recordings of Brahms's Double Concerto for Violin and Cello with Rose (Walter, New York Philharmonic; Ormandy, Philadelphia Orchestra) are about equal in performance, though the violin presence is stronger in the latter's stereo engineering, and the instrumental relationship is similar to that of the trios. Overall it is one of the four or five most satisfying recordings of the work. Mozart's *Symphonie Concertante*, K. 364 for Violin and Viola, one with William Primrose (Casals, Perpignan Festival Orchestra), another with Walter Trampler (Stern, London Symphony), a third with Pinchas Zukerman (Barenboim, English Chamber Orchestra), are played affectionately and with meticulous detail. Fortified by superior engineering (1972), the Zukerman recording's rich viola tone marks it as perhaps even more impressive than the one with Primrose, although both performances are exceptional. The Trampler version, lacking an independent conductor, reveals a distinct dichotomy of tonal intensity between violin and viola. Stern recorded duos with Oistrakh, trios with Myra Hess and Casals, and quartets with Jean-Pierre Rampal, Alexander Schneider and Rose, and his chamber music recordings will no doubt continue. For all the high level of his recordings, Stern, like Milstein, is even more impressive in live performance, where the force of his personality adds an extra dimension to his art.

Stern the musician can not be separated from Stern the enterprising, aggressive personality and concerned world citizen. Whereas Heifetz's lifestyle grew progressively more private, and almost austere, Stern has relished his status as a public figure, and thrives on publicity. He has been known to refer openly to music critics as "howling dogs," yet in our single meeting, when I was introduced to him as a music critic, he was most cordial and affable, and at his own initiative he discussed musical matters with me at length.

Regardless of one's assessment of Stern as artist and man, his willingness to express publicly his opinions about himself is a rare and admirable quality. The following quotation from the *New York Times*, (October 14, 1979, Stephen E. Rubin), is a revealing, refreshing case in point:

> I am honestly very doubtful of my primacy. That I can do certain things differently—I don't say better—that I accept, too. But I look at the enormous accomplishments of some of my older colleagues and the incredible talent of some of my younger ones, who gobble up the literature, and I cannot honestly put myself in a class apart and say I know more than all of them collectively. I don't think I am really the kind of complete success musically that I'd like to be. There are many things I don't do well. I couldn't play a Paganini étude the way Milstein does today—no way! And there are other things that I have not done enough of.
>
> I just hope that God will grant me time, in the next 15, 20 years of work, now that I have made my mistakes, and done my experimentation, to concentrate on the areas I think are important musically, which would be, let us say, my final musical statement.
>
> That means that out of many years of trying, I found the things which I think are right and are wrong, for better or for worse. They're my way. In the same sense, I have learned in life what I think is right and wrong, and therefore I must do what I think is right. Yes, there have been people I've hurt, people I've overlooked, moments I would rather not think about when I have been foolish, stupid, excessive, arrogant. Arrogant. Sometimes I have walked over a colleague in a rehearsal without waiting for him to have the opportunity to say something.
>
> I would do better if I lived more healthily, exercised more, ate less. I'm a hog. I love food and drink. I love tastes and textures. I think I could be called a sensualist. But that is the power source of my playing. When I'm caressing music, it is very sensual. I love feelings and I love gratifying the senses. I would find it difficult to be abstemious. What I am, I think, more than anything else, is a willing and capable catalyst. You see, I have ambivalence. I'll be approaching my 60th year—45 years of playing on stage. That's a helluva long time. The trouble is, I don't feel 60. I feel as if I'm about to launch on the major part of my career.

When Stern is not in form and having technical difficulties, he uses his vast experience and the utmost force of his imperial personality to distract his audience from the realities of the situation. For example, on one occasion, during a ragged performance of the Beethoven concerto, while awaiting the solo violin entrance in a long orchestral tutti, he surveyed the musicians and conductor with patriarchal hauteur, and perhaps even disapproval, as if they were somehow playing with insufficient expertise. Then he gazed at the audience with a "stern" look that seemed to say,

"How lucky you are. Isn't this the greatest Beethoven you ever heard?" All this was was but a prelude to the climatic moment, when Stern tossed his head wildly, jowls quivering, stamped his foot furiously and made his solo entrance a split second before the orchestra, a ploy calculated to establish himself as the undisputed ruler of the domain. It was one of the more comical charades of the contemporary concert stage, and except for a few musical misanthropes, the crowd of worshipful listeners savored the scene with uninhibited relish, thoroughly convinced of their idol's infallibility. On the other hand, when Stern has sufficiently prepared himself and is in full command of his violinistic resources, he is capable of giving a performance of the Beethoven that possesses a majesty and mature masculinity that only a few of his colleagues could or can approximate.

The late George Szell, a sometimes irascible maestro of impeccable musical credentials, once publicly berated Stern and refused to record the Tchaikovsky concerto with him unless he "got into shape." But even Szell was no match for the wiles of Stern, and they finally developed a modus vivendi. If it so happens that Stern finds himself at odds with a conductor, he merely turns his back to the podium and fiddles away, leaving the conductor to follow him. Stern with his reputation and box office magic can, of course, get away with much. But woe be it to any young or less eminent violinist who dares imitate him: the conductor could, and very likely would, maliciously sabotage the performance.

The story of Stern's indomitable leadership in saving Carnegie Hall from the wrecking crew in 1960 is now legendary. He cannot be praised too highly for his organizational efforts in this behalf. He was consequently named president of the nonprofit corporation which directs and controls the hall's musical and financial destiny. Vera Stern has been at his side in many of the pursuits connected to its affairs and welfare. In fact, they were once accused by James Wolfensohn, the executive board chairman, of running it "like a mom and pop store." A public brouhaha involving a large block of tickets for a Vladimir Horowitz recital caused more than a little embarrassment for the Sterns, though it was never clear exactly who was responsible for the discrepancies; former executive director Julius Bloom took the official blame.

Stern is hardly one not to take advantage of power once it is in his hands. His enormous influence in Carnegie Hall's musical scheduling, his former unlimited access to the managerial clout of the late Sol Hurok, the eminence of his violinistic reputation and the perpetual thrust of his dynamic personality have been utilized in the service of many a positive cause. Conversely, his detractors, some of whom bear him implacable animosity, if not downright hatred, are of a different opinion.

In a world in which only a handful of violinists, historically, have been able to attain full-time, lifelong careers as soloists, the competition is incredibly fierce. Today, even most of the major competition winners who succeed in obtaining a certain number of concerts, cannot generate top-echelon careers. The young aspirant must possess a God-given talent clearly superior to his competitors. Even with such talent and a pocketful of medals, his success is not assured. But given this talent, plus the sponsorship of Isaac Stern, a young violinist is well on the way to superstardom. Unlike Heifetz, who has never been known to use his stupendous reputation to assist a pupil or protégé gain a concert career, Stern will move mountains to assist a talent whom he recognizes as extraordinary.

As a rare violinistic talent himself, Stern is eminently qualified to evaluate the degrees of talent among younger generation hopefuls. And his intimate ties with Israel, a nation peopled with a race that has produced violinists of genius since the days of Ernst, Wieniawski and Joachim, have enabled Stern to guide the careers of the phenomenal Itzhak Perlman and Pinchas Zukerman. Without doubt, in these two instances, Stern has selected the utmost in current violinistic talent, and his efforts in behalf of other promising talents continue. In light of the ascendency of Perlman and Zukerman, certain other violinists of solo caliber have had to settle for lesser careers, just as the phenomenal success of the young Heifetz downgraded a host of excellent violinists.

Stern has made some comments from which aspiring violinists can profit greatly—"The violin is a continuation of the voice," he asserts. "You sing in your head and play what you hear." This is invaluable advice in an era in which the essential lyric qualities of the violin are being diminished in favor of such things as the depersonalization of sound and style, correct but sterile and colorless interpretations, and unmelodious percussive and/or sensationalist effects. He also points out that it is the milliseconds between notes; it is *how a violinist goes from one note to the other*, that makes great music. Actually, it is the lack of this instinctive ability which transforms the concerts of many an out-standing contemporary violinist into highly respectable, but easily for-gettable events.

Stern is steadfastly devoted to the welfare of Israel. In addition to being of great assistance in bringing Israeli talent to the world, he has played innumerable concerts in its desert army camps as well as its cities; engaged in endless fund-raising; pursued other artists to donate their services there; and even organized a musicians' boycott of UNESCO in protest of its 1974 cultural aid ban against Israel. This boycott, along with other organized protests, eventually ended the ban. He has been (and still is) in effect Israel's cultural ambassador. But never one to follow blindly, Stern, a profoundly political entity, has publicly criticized individual policies of the Israeli government.

Stern either speaks or understands six languages, plays tennis with a gusto quite in contradiction to his portly physique, and loves to play chamber music even when he is at the point of exhaustion.

In the *New York Times* interview with Stephen Rubin cited above, Stern remarks:

> Whether I'm capable of the same uncaring, unworried pyrotechnics of thirty years ago doesn't make any difference. What has happened is that my music-making has deepened and that cannot be touched. That can only get bigger. So that as long as I can hold a fiddle decently and make a good sound, I will always be able to make music.

Criticisms notwithstanding, when future histories of violin art are written, Stern will certainly be honored as a supremely gifted, impulsive, invigorating, productive, driving, insuppressible, caring, silver-tongued, dauntless, and sometimes ruthless musician-activist, who was also one of the most important violinists of his era.

Leonid Kogan, a dazzling artist who tinctured his rigorous Soviet training with the Heifetz influence, while retaining his own individuality.

CHAPTER SIX

Leonid Kogan

W HEN DAVID OISTRAKH took first prize at the Brussels Ysaÿe Competition in 1937, the Soviet music establishment was already well advanced in the process of unearthing the nation's finest violinists and developing them in that arduous, rigid crucible that came to be called the Soviet School. All of Auer's most famous pupils had long since emigrated, with the exception of Poliakin, who, returning from a nine-year stay abroad, was not destined to attain international stardom. However, lesser-known pupils of Auer, some of them leading professors at the Moscow, Leningrad and other Soviet conservatories, carried on his teaching and traditions.

But Auer's approach was by no means dominant. Oistrakh, a pupil of Piotr Stolyarsky, the singularly gifted pedagogue from Odessa, was to lead and influence violinistic and musical attitudes far removed from those of Auer. The USSR was rich in violin pedagogues such as Konstantin Mostras, Boris Sibor (Livshitz), Abraham Yankelevich, Oistrakh and a host of assistants, many of whom were outstanding teachers. Collectively they have produced a continuous stream of fine instrumentalists who generally have lacked marked musical personality but often have dominated violin competitions, at times overwhelmingly. Oistrakh was always above such criticism, and to his final days remained the Soviet Union's most revered violinist. In the more than four decades since his initial success, only one Soviet-trained violinist ever emerged who could seriously challenge Oistrakh's supremacy, despite the plethora of Russian gold medalists and laureates of major international competitions—and that was Leonid Borisovich Kogan.

Apart from the unchallenged dominance of Oistrakh, Kogan had to triumph over many superb violinists in his own country even before being permitted to compete abroad. For example, from 1922 to 1933, at least a dozen outstanding rivals had been born. There was Boris (Busya) Goldstein (b. 1922), who as a teenager was singled out by Heifetz as being the

USSR's most brilliant violin talent. Others were Julian Sitkovetsky (1925 - 1958) Mikhail Vaiman (1926 - 1978), Nellie Shkolnikova (b. 1927), Rosa Feyn (b. 1930), Igor Bezrodny (b. 1930), Edmund Grach (b. 1931), Igor Oistrakh (b. 1931), Valery Klimov (b. 1931), Boris Gutnikov (b. 1931), Mark Lubotsky (b. 1931), Viktor Pikaizen (b. 1933) and Albert Markov (b. 1933). Later we will discuss many of these individually, as well as the better-known of the younger Soviet luminaries.

Kogan was born in 1924 in Dnepropetrovsk (formerly Ekaterinoslav) in the Ukraine during a period of extreme economic hardship. His parents were both photographers; his father, a nonprofessional violinist. By the age of three he was already fascinated by the sound of the violin, and he states that he began musical study at age six. His first teacher was Philip Yampolsky, a former Auer pupil, with whom he studied through his ninth year. At ten, following a successful public recital in Kharkov, his parents decided to take him to Moscow where he was accepted as a pupil in a special children's group connected with the Moscow Conservatory. His teacher was Abraham Yampolsky (neither related to Philip nor a pupil of Auer), with whom he continued study at the Central Children's Music School, and subsequently at the Moscow Conservatory, from which he graduated in 1948. As a youngster he practiced about three hours a day while carrying a full course of academic subjects for general education. His violin training included mastery of all the standard études: Kreutzer, Fiorillo, Rode, Gaviniès, Dont and Paganini, as well as those by his teacher, A. Yampolsky (unknown in the West). In 1941 he made his orchestral debut as soloist with the Moscow Philharmonic in the Brahms concerto. At twenty-two he played his first foreign concert in Prague.

Following World War II, the Soviet authorites were extremely eager once again to gain top honors in the Brussels Ysaÿe Competition (now called the Queen Elisabeth Competition), suspended since 1937 when the Russians had their historic success. Oistrakh's advice was to send Kogan, as a guarantee of victory. Kogan promptly won the gold medal, with Vaiman garnering second prize. He married Elizabeth Gilels (sister of the celebrated pianist Emil Gilels), one of the country's leading violinists, who had taken third place honors at Brussels in 1937 after Oistrakh and Flesch's pupil Riccardo Odnoposoff.

Like the Oistrakhs, the Kogans became parents of a boy, Pavel, who developed into a concert caliber violinist, and is now forging a major career as a conductor. They also have a daughter, Nina, who toured as piano collaborator with her father in sonata masterworks during the final phase of his career. Though Elizabeth Kogan continued to play and perform, her concertizing career was subordinated to her husband's.

Kogan made his debut in London in 1955, in Vienna in 1956, and in the United States with Monteux and the Boston Symphony in 1958. His

Kogan in concert with his pianist-daughter Nina

A close-up of Kogan's hands and long, powerful fingers

violin, a 1907 Stradivarius, was owned by the state. At the height of his career in 1958 he received 2,000 rubles per performance in the USSR. He eventually became chairman. of the violin department at the Moscow Conservatory. His hobby was collecting and tinkering with automobiles.

In appearance Kogan was a slim, wiry man a bit under medium height, with a high forehead, deep set eyes shaded by thick, prominent eyebrows, and a generous sprinkling of gold teeth. Despite his immense violinistic stamina developed through a herculean practice regime, one could detect a hint of pain in his face which grew more pronounced as the years passed, as if he were suffering from an illness. It is said that his ailment was chronic ulcers, and for all his great instrumental command, he was often prey to nervousness before performances. His stage presence was unusually sober, almost reticent, devoid of body or facial mannerisms, though he was capable of an occasional smile and could be warm and affable to those he favored. He had good-sized hands with long, powerful fingers, and there was no digital challenge or expressive subtlety he could not negotiate with ease. He used a bow grip recalling that of the Auer pupils, with the index finger, highly placed, regulating the pressure and strokes, although his right wrist and elbow were held comparatively low for that school of playing. In sostenuto bowings, and for that matter every type of stroke, his control was immaculate; his staccato, though exceedingly brilliant and fast, was not of the "stiff-arm" variety. Another striking feature of his bowing was its wondrous Heifetz-like articulation.

Toward his mid-forties Kogan's tonal consistency and emotional projection clearly began to decline, although his technical powers were only marginally below his highest standards.

During what was to be his final tour, Kogan had performed the Beethoven concerto on five successive days in Vienna. He then left for the Russian city of Yaroslavl where he was to have given two performances with Pavel conducting the Yaroslavl Symphony, playing Bach's E-major Concerto, Shostakovich's Concerto No. 1, Saint-Saëns' *Havanaise*, Chausson's *Poème*, and the Castelnuovo-Tedesco setting of *Largo al Factotum* from Rossini's *Barber of Seville*. The programs never took place. Following a career second only to Oistrakh among his compatriots, Kogan succumbed quietly to a massive heart attack while enroute by train from Vienna to Yaroslavl. And so died a violinist of exceptional modesty and scarcely rivaled instrumental mastery. Elizabeth had been scheduled to travel with him, but feeling unwell, did not make the trip. Sadly, Leonid Kogan passed away alone, among strangers, at fifty-eight, the same age as Paganini, whose music he played so superlatively.

In evaluating the artistry of Kogan, it is necessary to refer constantly to Heifetz, whose playing during a 1934 tour of the Soviet Union had utterly entranced the ten-year-old boy. In contrast to Oistrakh's manner of play-

Kogan—a study in rapt concentration

Kogan with his conductor-son Pavel

ing, Kogan can be considered the perpetuator of the Auer heritage as influenced by his idol. Whereas Oistrakh was a heartwarming poet of the violin, essentially descended from the line of Ysaÿe, Kogan's glittering blend of crystalline yet impassioned lyricism with hair-raising virtuosity emanates from the Heifetz tradition. He performed Paganini and other bravura works that Oistrakh, for all his vast technical prowess, preferred not to perform in public. Kogan was certainly no crass Heifetz imitator, but eventually his technical equipment, sound and style came to resemble more closely those of Heifetz than of any of the official Heifetz pupils, except perhaps Erick Friedman in his youth. Indeed there are certain compositions in which their violinistic effects are remarkably similar. In any case it can be said that Kogan was the preeminent disciple of Heifetz, in the loftiest sense. He was, however, trained in an atmosphere quite different from that of Heifetz, and traces of this in his vibrato production and general musical ethos could frequently be noted.

Kogan's finger-bow coordination and muscular reflexes came closer to those of Heifetz than did those of any other violinist. He could play with unsurpassed speed, but unlike Heifetz, he never permitted his marvelous facility to dominate an interpretation. His scintillating exactitude of intonation also recalled Heifetz. One of the most stunning of his digital assets was his ability to connect smoothly vibrant lower-position singing notes with those at the topmost reaches of the fingerboard without losing an iota of tonal intensity, comparable to the standard Heifetz had previously introduced. And Kogan well understood and mastered not only the gamut of tasteful expressive slide intricacies, but also the even more subtle art of one-finger horizontal position changes that sustain a sense of legato expressivity without any vestige of overt sliding. This too was a Heifetz speciality which Piatigorsky also employed and taught. He was expert in negotiating the familiar Heifetz expressive slide, but generally reserved its use for passages of extreme intensity.

Boris Schwartz states in *Great Masters of the Violin*, (p. 471) that Kogan's "tone was lean, with a tight and sparse vibrato." This description might be applicable to Kogan's final years, when his playing had deteriorated tonally and emotionally to an infirm state that was little more than a caricature of his glorious playing. But Kogan possessed one of the most effective vibratos in memory, impeccably controlled, with reflex fingertip intensity of the Heifetz type, capable of all speeds, absolutely thrilling in the high stretches of the G and E strings. This can be easily corroborated by his recordings prior to the mid-1960s. Among other superb recordings, his playing in Wieniawski's *Original Theme and Variations*, Op. 15, apart from its dazzling pyrotechnics, is one of the most incredible exhibitions of lush tonal vibrance anyone could ever hope to hear. Like Heifetz's 1918 recording of Paganini's *Moto Perpetuo*, this recording of

Kogan in performance stance; note the length of his fourth finger.

Wieniawski's work represents the ultimate performance in its genre. I recall an incident backstage after one of Kogan's solo appearance with the Los Angeles Philharmonic around 1960. He was demonstrating a few passages to some of the orchestra violinists. At one point he scampered up the G string, ending his runs with an electric vibrance, without the need to "get set" manually, in a way that had the musicians shaking their heads in disbelief and admiration. The strength in his fingers was awesome. Nevertheless, his application of vibrato was wisely eclectic, and he would never think of using a sensuous Tchaikovsky vibrato in music of Bach or Mozart. Kogan's basic tone, while not exceptionally large, had pronounced penetrative power and was uncommonly compact in texture. There is no air in the sound. For all his ability to produce stunning intensity, his tone, like that of Heifetz, could be angelic in its purity.

There was, however, one important difference between Heifetz's use of vibrato and Kogan's. Heifetz had an almost magical ability to sustain a sense of vibrance at all times, even in non-vibrato passing tones. Kogan, probably as a result of his Soviet backgound, was not entirely immune to the employment of "on-and-off" vibrato in a single lyric phrase to no musical purpose (as discussed in the Oistrakh chapter). Yet it must be stressed that unlike many fine violinists who have fallen prey to this misuse and who do it as a sort of technical crutch, Kogan's left hand possessed both the flexibility and sharpness of reflex needed to abstain from it completely, had he thought of it as a negative factor. The best playing of his earlier years contained only intermittent traces of this habit, so slight that only a hard-nosed critic would call it to account. In fact, I have never heard criticism of his playing on this point. Admittedly, it was not a vitiating factor in his finest performances. As he grew older his inner fires began to cool and his physical capacities waned. His playing became more stolid, impersonal and aloof, and the "on-and-off" vibrato syndrome increasingly became an integral element in his interpretations. It was distressing to hear him perform this way, knowing what a magnificent and communicative violinist he had been in his prime.

For technical development, Kogan, like Heifetz, emphasized daily scale practice. He criticized the Flesch scale system for its noninclusion of four-octave scales and arpeggios, being convinced that the three-octave method was insufficient for developing complete fingerboard mastery. In daily practice he advocated devoting at least fifty percent of the time to scales, exercises and études, and the rest to pieces. One of the many rewards of such a regime was a fourth finger of immense strength, and he used it regularly in vibrant lyric passages, as well as in purely technical flights.

Kogan was a musician of utmost integrity and intelligence who sought to play each genre of composition in its proper context without misusing his vast violinistic equipment in the service of interpretative exaggeration or personal whim. In this regard he is considerably less vulnerable than Heifetz is to adverse criticism. In compositions of overt violinistic persuasion (as differentiated from the most profound masterworks), Kogan was among the foremost stylists of the twentieth century. This is not meant to imply that he was incapable of musical introspection, but he was first and foremost a spectacular virtuoso. And while his interpretations of the so-called heavyweight works were thoughtful and well-ordered, they tended to reflect good taste and suavity of execution rather than heightened spirituality or graphic imagination. His comprehensive repertoire ranged from Corelli, Bach and Rameau to Berg, Bartók, Stravinsky, Jolivet and Mannino. I heard him play the Berg concerto with grandly intense romanticism and an insight into the knotty music equal to anyone. Among contemporary Soviet works he performed not only those by Shostakovich, Prokofiev, Khachaturian, and Khrennikov, but also lesser-known major works of Vainberg, Barsukov and Karaev. Numerous compositions were dedicated to him.

Kogan's violinistic personality was well defined, but lacked the striking individuality of Ysaÿe, Kreisler, Elman, Heifetz, Menuhin and Oistrakh. Thus Heifetz does not recall Kogan—rather, it is Kogan who conjures up the Heifetz image. Heifetz, once fully matured, never recalled any pre-Heifetz violinist either in living or recorded memory. It is no reflection on Kogan's stature as an artist to say that in terms of individualized personality, he belongs in the category just below that of "The Great Per-

Taking his bows in the Big Hall of the Moscow Conservatory

The informal Kogan

sonalities of the Violin," while purely as an executant he was perhaps closest to Heifetz.

Kogan's recordings number about 160 compositions, masterworks and miniatures, plus some 40 rerecordings, comparable to the discographies of Stern, Milstein and Francescatti. Only a minority were originally recorded in England, France, and the USA, though many were officially rerecorded or pirated from Soviet discs and tapes. Some of the Soviet performances were reasonably well engineered. Unfortunately, the overall body of Kogan recordings are less known to listeners in the West than those of his most noted colleagues. A partial survey of his more important discs in all categories reveals many that are staggering performances with which dedicated violin fanciers should be acquainted. Only a minority of these are less than extraordinary. Kogan's sound, like that of Heifetz, was wonderfully adapted to the recording process.

There are at least eight or ten exceptional recordings of the Paganini Concerto No. 1 in D-major, but none excels the Kogan rendition, with Charles Bruck and the somewhat tinny sounding Orchestre de la Société des Concerts du Conservatoire, in electric tonal tension and technical perfection. And it compares with that of the boy Menuhin in dramatic force, though perhaps projecting less sheer spontaneity. The brilliance of his scale and arpeggio endings are practically without peer. Had Heifetz recorded the opus, it would certainly have sounded much like this. Each phrase is exquisitely polished.

He recorded the Tchaikovsky Concerto in D-major three times. My favorite, with Vassili Nebolsin and the (Soviet) State Radio Orchestra, contains all of the Auer embellishments, including the two climactic endings in the first movement composed of rapid triplet batteries of thirds and tenths. The variation section just before the cadenza is especially sensitive. It is a warmly expressive, personalized interpretation with emphasis on lyric values. The tempi are quite deliberate, never rushed, an approach which benefits the first two movements, but deprives the finale of the ultimate sense of abandon and excitement. Overall it has a decided Russian flavor, as does the performance of Oistrakh. They differ in style from that of non-Soviet players, and, of course, from each other. A later recording with Constantin Silvestri and the Paris Conservatoire Orchestra, without the Auer first movement climactic endings, is the version best known in the West, and is marginally less fresh and ardent. The third is also with the Paris ensemble.

His Lalo *Symphonie Espagnole*, including the *Intermezzo*, (Bruck, Paris Conservatoire Orchestra) easily ranks among the very finest of this work. The G string sound is invariably opulent and the high E string notes scintillate. All is subtle, crisp and graceful. One can detect some "on-and-off" vibrato in the *Andante*, but generally Kogan's tone sustains intensity of the Heifetz type. The orchestral sound unfortunately does not emulate the quality of the soloist. Overall it is a memorable, stylish violin performance.

A 1961 recording of Mendelssohn's Concerto in E-minor (Silvestri, Paris Conservatoire Orchestra) features both glittering finger intensity and "on-and-off" vibrato in the first movement. The *Andante* is songful, and the finale offers superb bowing articulation that emphasizes phrases often sloughed over even by great violinists, in the interest of speed. Yet Kogan takes care not to rush the final sections of the outer movements, and heightens the effect of the lyric passages with tasteful, cannily selected slides and position changes. The other side of the disc presents Mozart's Concerto No. 3, with the cadenza by Sam Franko. Here Kogan is eminently relaxed, combining sweetness of sound with a sense of virility, clearly in the Heifetz mold, but never projecting a feeling of haste. This recording is somewhat more elegant than a better-engineered one with Otto Ackerman and the Philharmonia Orchestra which features the idiomatic, smartly crafted Oistrakh cadenzas. A noteworthy factor is Kogan's adaptation of his vibrato to the classical Mozart style. These performances, together with a charming, multifaceted rendition of Concerto No. 5 in A-major (Rudolf Barshai, Moscow Chamber Orchestra, Joachim cadenzas) establish Kogan as an elite Mozart interpreter.

Vieuxtemps' Concerto No. 5 (Kondrashin, State Radio Orchestra), like the Paganini, is a miraculous tour de force of finger and bow articulation, and stylistic panache. In my opinion, it is second only to the Heifetz recording, although those of Perlman, Zukerman, Menuhin and Chung provide strong competition. Also in the Heifetz image is his cool, jewel-like recording of Prokofiev's Concerto No. 2 (Basil Cameron, Philharmonia Orchestra). The Khachaturian concerto, with extraordinary collaboration from Monteux and the Boston Symphony (1958), technically immaculate in the outer movements and voluptuously exotic in the *Andante sostenuto*, vies with that of Oistrakh in idiomatic descriptiveness.

In the two greatest musical challenges of the concerto repertoire, those of Beethoven (recorded four times) and Brahms (three times), Kogan falls somewhat short of the topmost echelon. This, of course, has nothing to do with instrumental factors, but rather with such ephemeral elements as spiritual force and inner grace. The Beethoven (Kondrashin, USSR State Symphony, early 1950s, Joachim cadenzas) is a perfectly beautiful performance, exactly as I heard him in concert. All is pure in sound, buoyant, and musically well-ordered. The trills scintillate; the high E string notes resound superbly. Only a couple of minor soloist-conductor loose ends slightly detract from a vigorous, exuberant *Rondo*. It is difficult to find fault with such a performance, yet one cannot say that is as strikingly personal and individual as those of Kreisler, Oistrakh, Szigeti, Heifetz,

Menuhin or Stern. The Brahms (Kondrashin, Philharmonia Orchestra, mid-1950s, Joachim cadenzas) is also an outstanding rendition, though its inspiration is not fully consistent; some climactic phrases soar, others are neatly polished, but almost matter-of-fact.

One of his most masterful concerto performances is of the Shostakovich No. 1, Op. 99 (Eugene Mravinsky, Leningrad Philharmonic), a vehicle ideal in every respect for Kogan's temperament and violinistic attributes. The disc is taken from a live concert. At the opposite end of the stylistic spectrum are Vivaldi's Concerto in G-minor, Op. 12, No. 1, and Rameau's Concerto No. 6 in G-minor, a work much like a *concerto grosso*, replete with quaint ornamental devices. Both are played with chaste spirit and delicacy (Barshai, Moscow Chamber Orchestra). Also with the same ensemble is Bach's Concerto in E-major, with some unwisely selected slides and "on-and-off" vibrato—not actually a poor performance, but decidely earthbound. This is paired with the Bach Double Concerto, an efficient but routine reading. Kogan gallantly relaxes his sound to coincide with the slower vibrato of his partner, wife Elizabeth.

Other Soviet concerto recordings include the Khrennikov No. 1, Op. 14, a readily listenable work standing somewhere between the simplistic Kabelevsky concerto and the popular Khachaturian; quasi-oriental lyricism and brilliant passagework add up to what is essentially superficial, ingenuous fare. (Kondrashin, USSR Radio Symphony). This work and the composer's second violin concerto, written fifteen years later, are both dedicated to Kogan. The 1959 concerto of Moishe Vainberg, dedicated to Kogan, recorded in 1971 (Kondrashin, Moscow Philharmonic Symphony) is strongly influenced by Shostakovich, and colorfully orchestrated. Some of the basic material is rather banal, but the concerto contains much that is festive and exciting. Essentially it is in a category above the Krennikov No. 1, and easily assimilable at first hearing. Kogan's performance is superlative. A much less palatable item is the Barsukov Concerto No. 2, written in 1962, a fragmented hodgepodge of difficult passagework with many trite fortissimo effects that lead nowhere. Barsukov seems to be a better orchestrator than composer, and only the *Lento, quasi Berceuse*, reminiscent of Szymanowski, offers a flicker of talent. Why Kogan chose to expend the time and energy necessary to learn it is anybody's guess (Rozhdestvensky, Great Symphony Orchestra of Moscow Radio, inferior orchestral sound).

An interesting work in the contemporary idiom is the Triple Concerto by Franco Mannino, written in 1966 and recorded by Leonid, Elizabeth and Pavel in 1974. The opus is weakened by excessive repetition, but Mannino weaves the busy, three-violin tapestry with admirable skill, fortified by a variety of powerful percussion devices. A successful, adventurous family project (Mannino, State Academy Symphony of the

USSR).

Kogan ranks among the chosen few in showpieces and short numbers demanding digital viruosity, tonal beauty and stylistic flair. In addition to the previously mentioned, fabulous Wieniawski *Original Variations*, the mercurial Castelnuovo-Tedesco setting of Rossini's *Largo al factotum* easily equals the Heifetz recording, and possibly even communicates a bit more humor. Professional violinists hearing Kogan's record simply marvel at his overwhelming blending of agility and sound. Saint-Saëns' *Introduction and Rondo Capriccioso* (Alexander Gauk, State Radio Orchestra), the *Havanaise* (Monteux, Boston Symphony, 1958) and Ravel's *Tzigane*, all spotlessly clean, vividly recall Heifetz but are not imitative; Kogan's playing is a little less sleek and sophisticated, but masterful in all phases. His Sarasate *Carmen Fantasy* (Nebolsin, State Radio Orchestra) is not quite as spectacular as the truncated, precipitous 1924 Heifetz version, but is musically superior. Among contemporary recordings, Perlman's dulcet-toned performance is perhaps the closest competitor, though Oistrakh, Rabin, Ricci, Spivakovsky and Rosand also have outstanding *Carmen* recordings. The Paganini *Nel cor piu non mi sento* Variations and *I Palpiti* are tossed off brilliantly in pellucid Italianate style.

Wieniawski's *Faust Fantasy*, once considered by many to be the finest of the innumerable nineteenth-century violin operatic transcriptions, is not often played outside of the USSR these days. It is one of the most demanding and delightful medium-length works of its genre, and Kogan's recording is delectable from first note to last. How unfortunate that the recording is not reengineered and circulated in the West! This *Faust* version, while certainly not devoid of occasional superficiality, represents the very heart-beat of late nineteenth century bravura and sentiment, and the orchestral accompaniment is considerably more varied and colorful than any by Paganini or Sarasate (V. Degtiarenko, USSR State Symphony). Another of Kogan's triumphs is Wieniawski's little-known *Adagio Elegiaque*, containing vibrant singing octaves unsurpassed by anyone (A. Kaplan, piano). And although there are several excellent recordings of Polonaise No. 2 in A-major, Kogan's cogent, unhurried interpretation more fully captures the polonaise spirit than any I have heard. (A. Mitnik, piano).

Kogan possessed a high degree of the stylistic subtlety and discipline necessary to play violin-piano sonatas with meaningful musicality in his prime years. Later I heard him perform a charmless "on-and-off" vibrato Handel sonata, and about two years before his death, a Beethoven four-sonata program with his daughter Nina that was dry sounding, almost cerebral and unimaginative. In fact, Nina's playing was the more communicative of the two. But he left several sonata recordings of outstanding merit, including the Strauss Sonata in E-flat major, Op. 18, strongly influenced by Heifetz, and Brahms's Sonata No. 1 in G-major, Op. 78, which after a somewhat overrelaxed first movement, is delivered with admirable thoughtfulness and serenity, building to intense climaxes. Both are with the expert partnering of his principal piano collaborator, Andrei Mitnik. Prokofiev's Sonata in D-major, Op. 94, recorded in the mid-1960s, is one of the few best of the many recordings of the work; highly charged, though varied in tonal texture, technically immaculate and tremendously muscular in articulation. The single vitiating element is the underplayed pianism of Ephraim Koenig, which may or may not be the fault of the Soviet engineering.

Bach's Solo Sonata No. 3 in C-major, violinistically impeccable, exudes a sense of power, and makes no pretense of trying to achieve academic authenticity, although it never stoops to patent romanticism. The disc sounds exactly like Kogan's performance of the work in concert as I heard it. Yet for all its instrumental impressiveness, there are instances where one gets a feeling that he is still in the process of formulating his interpretation.

More than a few of the Soviet-born violinists, both citizens and émigrés, criticize the Soviet School for giving insufficient training in chamber music. But both Oistrakh and Kogan were excellent players in this area. Beethoven's String Trio in E-flat major, Op. 3, with Kogan, Barshai and Rostropovich is performed with meticulous phrasing, purity of tone and elegant classicism. And the polished recording of Tchaikovsky's *Souvenir of Florence*, in which Kogan is joined by Elizabeth, Barshai, Heinrich Talalian, Knushevitsky and Rostropovich, compares with the finest performances on record. His sound is commanding, but not utterly dominating as is Heifetz's in much of his group playing.

It is clear that Kogan made an exhaustive study of Heifetz's manual production and performance style. Nowhere is this more apparent than in his playing of short pieces of all types, and glaringly so in Heifetz transcriptions. One cannot fault Kogan for performing Heifetz vignette settings in the Heifetz style any more than those elite players who try to emulate Kreisler tidbits in the Kreisler manner. Let us remember that if one hundred of the world's finest violinists were to spend years trying to recreate Heifetz's sound, articulation, and expressive subtleties, just about all of them would fail. For example, although Perlman plays many choice pieces of the Heifetz repertoire in the Heifetz style (the Conus concerto, Saint-Saëns' sonata, etc.), the softer-grained texture of his tone clearly differentiates his performance from that of Heifetz. And this is apart from such Heifetz-oriented players as Erick Friedman, Pierre Amoyal, Joseph Silverstein, Eugene Fodor and David Nadien. Frankly, how effective can performances of such pieces as Gershwin's *Tempo di Blues* from *Porgy and Bess* and Prelude No. 1 be in any style other than that of Heifetz?

Suffice it to say that Kogan plays them smashingly, as he does the
Godowsky *Alt Wien*; Dvořák's *Humoresque* (brimming with sophisti-
cated contemporary harmonies); Prokofiev's *March*, Op. 12, No. 1;
Albeniz's *Sevillanas*; Poulenc's *Presto*, another dextrous tour de force; and
Prokofiev's *Masques* from *Romeo and Juliet*. Less consistant are the
Debussy-Heifetz *Beau Soir* and Krein's forgettable Dance No. 4.

Other choice renditions are the Vieuxtemps *Rondino*, which does not
reflect the inimitable swagger or modal variety of the Ysaÿe recording but
is nonetheless glistening and captivating; Bloch's *Nigun*, heartfelt, and
perhaps the most tonally ravishing of all the *Nigun* recordings; the
Shostakovich-Tziganov Four Preludes, played with whimsy, gaiety, and
acute rhythmic pulse; Sarasates's *Zapateado*, with the staccato passage
executed in thirds, after Oistrakh, and the swift harmonic scale passages
all on the A string, a memorable performance; Khachaturian's *Folk Bards*,
an intensely lyric piece strong in Armenian motifs; Achron's *Hebrew
Melody*, at time a bit aggressive, but in the category just below Heifetz,
comparable to the discs of Elman and Josef Hassid in tonal opulence. The
Mendelssohn-Kreisler *Song Without Words*, Op. 62, No. 1 (*May Breezes*), is
played with neatly disciplined lyric splendor; Kreisler's *Caprice Viennois*
begins with surpassing rhapsodic imagery, but the doublestop waltz theme
misses the requisite Kreislerian lilt. And surprisingly, Sarasate's *Caprice
Basque*, powerful and dashing in the doublestop repetition of the opening theme, falls slightly below Kogan's technical standard in the whirl-
wind final variation.

Kogan, a stern taskmaster, had taught as many as seventeen pupils and
postgraduate students from the USSR and abroad in his Moscow Conservatory class. Oddly, neither Viktoria Mullova or Ilya Grubert, his prize-
winning pupils, registers even a modicum of Kogan's tonal beauty or
stylistic acumen and breath, though both are well-trained, technically
formidable instrumentalists. Talents of Leonid Kogan's caliber are indeed
rare, and no amount of drilling and practice can produce playing of his
instinctive artistry.

Apparently Kogan, though Jewish, was not liked by many of the Jewish
émigré violinists, who charge that Kogan's authority over Soviet string
players was similar to that of Khrennikov among Soviet composers.
Practically all of the leading Soviet musicians are either active or nominal
members of the Communist party. Naturally, the competition for concert
bookings, especially those of importance, is just as fierce in the USSR as
in the United States.

The dissatisfaction with Kogan's alleged misuse of power somewhat
coincides with accusations against Stern, except of course that Stern's
authority has no connection whatsoever with government political ma-
neuverings. Few, however, will dispute his stature as the single authentic

Soviet competitor to Oistrakh, and there are those who even preferred Kogan.

With Kogan's untimely death, there remain, at this writing, no Soviet-trained violinists either living in the USSR or aboard who can approximate the splendor of his finest years. Indubitably, he deserves to be ranked high among the elite violinists born in the twentieth century.

CHAPTER SEVEN

Survey of Soviet Violinists

AVID TO PROVE WHAT IT BELIEVES to be the superiority of the Soviet system in promoting mass culture, the Soviet government has given tremendous support to its musicians throughout the years. It can be fairly argued that this support has been cultivated for political ends. But whatever the motivation, a musical establishment capable of continually producing world-class instrumentalists has proven its strength since the 1937 Brussels competition, when Oistrakh led a team of Soviet players that captured five of the first six places.

At a time when other, far more affluent governments callously ignored the economic welfare of their musicians, both before and after World War II, the Soviets organized their efforts in the manner of an army marching to, and determined to win, a war. They saw to it that their representatives were totally prepared musically, amply seasoned in concerts at home, and given every physical comfort available. For many years during the Great Depression and well into the postwar era, gifted, qualified Western musicians who were without hope of a concert career, or even an orchestral job paying enough to earn a decent livelihood, were prone to envy their Soviet colleagues. As late as 1960 the pay scale in many major American symphony orchestras hovered around $3,000 per year. It is no secret that in 1958, just before Van Cliburn won the piano first prize honors at the Moscow Tchaikovsky Competition catapulting him into a golden career, he was floundering about with scant prospects for a success worthy of his talents. And his was by no means an isolated case. With the proliferation of major international competitions and the realization by leading Western musical organizations of the political value of such events, private support for Western hopefuls slowly began to materialize.

The situation today is no longer one-sided, though it must be stressed that even during the most difficult years, individual young artists of the West proved their mettle by challenging, and at times besting their Soviet counterparts. Among them during the lean years before 1965 in the Queen

Elisabeth Competition were Berl Senofsky, U.S.A., first prize, 1955; Jaime Laredo, Bolivia, first prize, and Joseph Silverstein, U.S.A., third prize, 1959; Arnold Steinhardt, U.S.A., and Charles Castleman, U.S.A. third and fifth prize respectively, 1963. Sidney Harth of the U.S.A. took second prize in 1958, and Charles Treger, U.S.A. first prize in 1962 at Poznan's Wieniawski Competition, and Shmuel Ashkenasi of Israel took second prize at the Tchaikovsky Competition in 1962. All have gone on to brilliant major careers in various areas of performance. In later years Miriam Fried, Israel, Eugene Fodor, U.S.A., Elmar Oliveira, U.S.A. and Dylana Jenson, U.S.A., either defeated or tied the Russians in top-level competitions.

It would be naive to suppose that international politics have not played a role at various competitions, just as conflicting opinions of what constitutes "good playing" are held by jurors who stem from diverse musical and cultural backgrounds. Many a behind-the-scenes deal has been made to appease and satisfy the demands of national pride, deals that have unfairly victimized one or another competitor.

One of the advantages the Western contestant enjoys is knowing that if his credentials warrant acceptance, he can enter any competition as long as he can raise sufficient funds to pay his expenses. Not so his Soviet counterpart, who can compete only if he is selected by the Soviet authorities. Oistrakh himself touched upon the frequent injustices of this system. At this writing, the number of international competitions has grown by leaps and bounds. The result has been double-edged. On the one hand, a number of young talents have received sizable cash awards that may well have contributed to their personal well-being. On the other hand, most of these awards do not guarantee more than a limited number of concert appearances, and certainly do not promise a significant international solo career. Oistrakh, Kogan and now Kremer, among Soviet prize-winners, have had extended careers on the international circuits, and to a lesser degree so have Klimov and Igor Oistrakh. But other Soviet laureates of major competition have been forced to settle for less, including many who have made international appearances. The oscillation of Soviet-American cultural exchange programs has had some bearing on their comparative downgrading. But the truth of the matter is that the winning of a gold medal, no matter how sensationally it is publicized, does not necessarily signal the emergence of a truly or even a potentially great artist, as opposed to a superb instrumentalist. Naturally this applies to non-Soviet laureates as well. And it is still possible for an exceptionally gifted young artist to reach the top echelon without ever having won an international competition, if that individual has extraordinary sponsorship such as that of Stern or Karajan. It must be remembered that in the Soviet Union just as in the United States or any other country, there are violinists who have a natural affinity for the "political game" in self-advancement, and there are others who know nothing but practicing the violin.

However, no music educational system, no matter how rigorous and well organized, can hope to produce consistently a flood of outstanding instrumentalists unless it has a vast reservoir of talent upon which to draw. In discussing the reasons for the many Soviet violin successes, it is necessary to examine briefly a phenomenon of Russian violin artistry both before and after the 1917 revolution.

The predominant force of prerevolutionary Russian violin art stemmed from Leopold Auer (of Jewish extraction) and his Jewish pupils Elman, Zimbalist, Heifetz, Seidel, Poliakin, Piastro and others. Multiple factors historically inherent in the lifestyles imposed upon the wandering Jewish people and the heritage of Hasidism that sparked a wider range of self-expression among the poor and persecuted Jewish masses, served to generate a spate of Jewish violinistic talent that was no less overwhelming after the Communist revolution than before.

Emulating nineteenth-century Liège, hub of the old Belgian non-Jewish hegemony that culminated in the mighty Ysaÿe, Odessa and its environs became a veritable wellspring of Jewish violinists, both before and after the revolution. Among those who lived and studied there were Elman, Milstein, David Oistrakh, Boris Goldstein, Mikhail Vaiman, Samuel Furer and a galaxy of noted Jewish musicians, writers and cultural figures. But the Odessa contribution was merely a part of the Soviet heritage. After the departure of Auer and his star pupils, such Jewish professors as Stolyarsky, Yankelevich, Yampolsky, and later, Oistrakh, Bondarenko, Kogan and numerous others played the leading role in training Soviet violinists of all national backgrounds. They have been responsible for the education of such outstanding non-Jewish violinists as Klimov, Tretyakov, Grindenko, Mullova and many more.

In addition to the most noted Jewish violinists, a host of excellent Jewish players of the second and third categories from Moscow, Leningrad, Kiev, Kharkov and other great centers have been trained in the leading conservatories of the USSR. The 1970s saw a steady stream of fine Jewish violinists emigrating to the West, disappointed with what they considered to be a lack of opportunity worthy of their talents and a prevailing undercurrent of anti-Semitism as expressed by the quota system. The promise of fame and fortune in the West under conditions of superior personal freedom beckoned temptingly. But despite the massive emigration, the number of Jewish violinists still residing and performing in the USSR is proportionally higher than their percentage of the population. And more graduate from the conservatories each year.

Yet no matter how vast the reservoir of talent, its organization and quality of training ultimately determine the extent of its success. The Soviet music establishment systematically sought out talented youngsters throughout the country, enrolled them in special schools allied to the leading conservatories which combined musical and secular education in spartan curricula. Only the most hardy and gifted could survive the arduous competition over a period of ten to fifteen years.

Although Auer's influence continued under the Soviet aegis through Poliakin and other Auer pupils, it rapidly diminished after the emergence of Oistrakh. It is important to recognize a certain resurgence of the violinistic precepts of the nineteenth-century Belgian School in Soviet training, precepts that had been introduced into Russia by Vieuxtemps and later, by Wieniawski and Ysaÿe. To this day, Soviet violin students study and perform extremely difficult and ultrastylistic, lesser-known violinistic showpieces by Vieuxtemps, Wieniawski, Paganini and Ernst that have not been stressed in Western training for five or six decades. The Ysaÿe solo sonatas, only now gaining popularity in the West, were widely performed in the USSR thirty or more years ago. Even after the Western successes of Oistrakh and Rostropovich, some observers, while praising their overall artistry, felt it to be somewhat old-fashioned.

Nevertheless, the fierce concentration on sheer instrumental mastery in their training produced a host of formidably equipped young Soviet violinists, against whom only a handful of their Western contemporaries could successfully compete in purely technical feats. More than a few of these Russians, however, have publicly decried the lack of sufficient chamber music playing in the Soviet curriculum, and its single-minded emphasis on virtuoso-type accomplishment. To a great extent this musical imbalance still dominates Soviet training. But with the ever-increasing exposure to Western violinists and musical concepts through cultural exchange programs and recordings, the influence of such artists as Heifetz, Stern, Szigeti and other Westerners has made a deep impression upon many Soviet violinists. Transcriptions by Kreisler and Heifetz are widely performed, and if the Kreislerian style has eluded them, a few have played Heifetz arrangements with reasonably convincing style and, of course, we have already discussed the singular Heifetz-Kogan compatibility. In the decades of the 1930s through the 1960s there was still a wide gulf in both musical approach and instrumental production between the Soviet and the various Western sounds and styles of performance. In listening to Russian recordings, particularly symphonic solo passages played by a Soviet concertmaster, an experienced listener could (and almost invariably still can) immediately recognize the performer to be a Russian as indicated by vibrato usage, overall sound production, phrasing and general musicality. This dichotomy continues, especially in the Soviet players trained before World War II, but the gap is slowly diminishing.

Certain Western observers have a tendency to label all of the leading

Soviet violinists (except possibly Oistrakh and Kogan) as supertechni-
cians and violinistically oriented musicians who possess little, if any,
personal magnetism or individual style. It may be true that except for the
two aforementioned, the Soviet musical personalities are not strikingly
marked, as compared with Ysaÿe, Kreisler, Elman, Heifetz, Menuhin,
Stern or even Perlman. But the same can be said for just about all of the
world's current leading violinists, including a legion of superlative
violinist-musicians. Great personalities of the violin have been rare in
every era, and the extremely personalized violinist of yesteryear is now out
of fashion—let us hope only temporarily. It is far more difficult today for
a violinist to emphasize his or her personality under the existing rules of
stringent musical discipline, although it is certainly not impossible for an
extraordinary artist. While Soviet training is rigid and tends to discourage
any wide divergence from their interpretive norms (though the Russians
would deny this vehemently), Soviet artists, like everyone else, represent a
diversity of sound, style and temperament, if not of basic musical values.
Since we have already discussed Oistrakh and Kogan at length, let us
briefly survey a broad cross section of other leading violinists.

Miron Poliakin

Miron Poliakin (1895 - 1941), nominally a Soviet violinist, does not
strictly represent the so-called Soviet School although he ultimately became a member of its teaching corps and in his maturity, he concertized
throughout eastern Europe.

He was born in Cherkassy near Kiev. At ten he went to study in Kiev
with Vousovskaya, a pupil of Ferdinand Laub. When he was twelve he
was accepted into Auer's class in St. Petersburg and studied with him for
six years. One of Auer's favorite and most gifted pupils, Poliakin was
often afflicted with nervousness. Not possessing the sovereign mastery of
Heifetz, the golden tone of Elman, the exciting vibrance of Seidel or the
musical intelligence and polish of Zimbalist, he nevertheless was an
extraordinary natural talent who, at his best, deserved ranking among the
first four or five Auer pupils. His playing, as bequeathed to posterity
through recordings, reveals a fiery temperament, a facility that if not
actually immaculate, was of virtuoso caliber, a beautiful vibrant tone, and
a colorful style that stamped him as a thoroughgoing romantic of the
prerevolutionary era. It is said that he played far better in private than in
public, and that on his best days his communicative ability in live concert
was electrifying.

Poliakin came to America in 1922, and in 1925 won a contest for
international violinists. But he was essentially, despite some success,
another victim of the Heifetz phenomenon. Not until Milstein's appear-

ance was another Russian-trained violinist to establish a lasting career on the world level. Returning to the USSR in 1927, Poliakin became a stellar figure among Soviet violinists and a principal professor at the Leningrad Conservatory, which was locked in spirited rivalry with the Moscow Conservatory. Admired as a soloist by his colleagues, including David Oistrakh, he was eventually eclipsed by Oistrakh and died comparatively young.

Consistency of performance and musical (or personal) sophistication were not Poliakin's strong points, nor were his teaching methods highly respected. As is often the case with enormously gifted instrumentalists, his intellectual horizons were limited, quite the opposite of Oistrakh's wide range of knowledge and interests. The contemporary music of his time was almost nonexistent in his repertoire. Soroker relates in his book, *Oistrakh* (p. 115):

> Among the sharp-tongued students the following story was popular: M. Poliakin had read a methodological lecture; he got on the rostrum, spread around a pile of books with bookmarks for references. After a long reflection, he exclaimed, 'The main thing is exercises!' and left to the accompaniment of the booing audience.

Poliakin made only about a dozen recordings, which clearly manifest his strengths and shortcomings and corroborate the more reliable reports of those who heard him in person. Chief among the recordings is the Glazunov A-minor Concerto (1941), with A. Orlov and the USSR Academic Symphony. Inconsistent in execution, it nonetheless projects the singular broad sweep of Auer's influence. His sparkling, though not opulent sound, is particularly impressive on the E string, as are his scintillating trills and instinctual expressive phrasing. There is no vestige of the annoying "on-and-off" vibrato of some of the later Soviet violinists. A decidedly personal note is heard in his playing, but it is not as overpowering as that of Heifetz, Elman or Seidel, among the Auer pupils. For all its minor imperfections, the performance is convincing, ranking below those of Heifetz, Oistrakh, Milstein and Rabin, but high in contention among other competing versions.

The first movement of Beethoven's *Kreutzer* Sonata (1938) in collaboration with Heinrich Neihaus, despite poor engineering, is a reading of excellent violin sound, good ensemble, verve and surprisingly well disciplined musicianship. A dramatic cadenza to the Beethoven concerto (1938) by Isaac Dunayevsky, extremely brilliant technically, shows Poliakin in top form, and is stunningly and artistically played. Tchaikovsky's familiar *Melodie* (1936), with pianist Yampolsky is effectively sentimental and intensely vibrant in sound, if rather naive musically, even for its genre. Sarasate's *Habanera*, with pianist A. Dyakov, is stylish, but neither consistent in tonal quality nor one of the best technical performances of the work.

Poliakin did not leave a lasting impression upon Soviet playing, but he must be regarded as an important violinist of ultra-romantic persuasion who, were it not for the dominance of Heifetz, might have enjoyed a far more spectacular career.

Galina Barinova

Galina Barinova (b. 1910) was at one time known as Russia's foremost woman violinist. A pupil of V.A. Zavetnovsky in Leningrad, she won third prize in the first All-Union Musical competition in 1937, and in 1949 was named a Stalin Laureate. Early in the 1950s she was given one of the two Stradivari violins belonging to the State collection which for many years had been played by Oistrakh. On what basis this decision was made must remain conjectural, since there were so many more outstanding violinists in the USSR sorely in need of a fine instrument.

She recorded 54 compositions, all made in the USSR, of which only the concerto by Mieczyslaw Karlowicz, Prokofiev's solo sonata and several Bach sonatas with keyboard collaboration (and one for two violins, cello and clavier) can be considered major works.

The Karlowicz, a traditional Polish favorite composed in 1902 and a typical romantic work of late nineteenth-century spirit and devices, is little played outside of eastern Europe. However, it is an engaging, neatly constructed work that permits the soloist to exhibit the range of her virtuosity. Unfortunately the concerto demands a more heroic violinist than Barinova for optimum performance. Her playing suggests a hard worker of serious purpose, with no more than moderate expressive powers. Her tone, hampered by a slow vibrato, is solid but neither especially sweet nor suave. The total impact of her Karlowicz is somewhat less than that of Wanda Wilkomirska; both are patently inferior to the excellent recording of Konstanty Kulka. Though she is a contemporary of Oistrakh, it was Elizabeth Gilels and Marina Kozelupova who brought honors to the USSR in the 1937 Ysaÿe Competition (third and fifth prizes, respectively), not Barinova. One can only wonder at the reason for Barinova's inflated reputation in the USSR, particularly in view of the superior talent and ability of such younger women players as Nelli Shkolnikova, Rosa Feyn, Nina Beilina (all current émigrés), and the even younger Tatiana Grindenko and Viktoria Mullova, among others of both sexes.

Boris Goldstein

Boris Goldstein (b. 1922), pupil of Stolyarsky in Odessa and Yampolsky in Moscow, was considered a prodigy in his youth. At fourteen he took fourth prize in the 1935 Poznan Wieniawski Competition won by Ginette Neveu (Oistrakh took second prize), ahead of such exceptional talents as Ida Haendel (seventh) and Bronislav Gimpel (ninth). Two years later at the historic Ysaÿe 1937 Competition in Brussels, he again placed fourth in a powerful field. Though highly respected, Goldstein's career did not attain international renown. Doubtless it was Oistrakh's domination of the Soviet sphere, like Heifetz's earlier supremacy in the West, that was responsible for moderating his career. As a recent émigré, he is no longer mentioned in Soviet violinistic annals or journals. Nevertheless he is a brilliant violinist whose natural gifts are close to those of Oistrakh.

His roster of some 40 recordings includes concerti of Mendelssohn, Conus, Arensky, Gliere, Bach and the Soviet concerti of Rzayev and Feltzman, plus major sonatas by Bloch No. 1, Szymanowski No. 1, Poulenc, Honegger and Beethoven's *Spring*. How he would fare in the concerti of Brahms, Beethoven and Mozart, or the intricacies of Bach's solo works and Paganini, is not, of course, possible to judge from his recording roster. His recordings of smaller works do not include any of the repertoire bravura virtuoso items—which is surprising for a top Soviet-trained artist.

Goldstein's recording of the Gliere Concerto in G-minor, Op. 100, orchestrated by Liatoshinsky, with V. Esipov and the Symphony Orchestra of the Moscow Philharmonic Society, reveals an artist of superlative assets. The intensely Russian, seventeen-minute one-movement work, closely akin in spirit to the Glazunov concerto, deserves wider international exposure than it has received, though admittedly it is not sufficiently large in scope to be counted among the major romantic concerti. Its main themes are lyrically compelling and their exposition skillfully developed. The Goldstein interpretation is ravishing, of first-level artistry. His style indicates some Heifetz influence, but his comparatively soft-grained sound, projecting a smartly diversified vibrato, readily recalls that of Oistrakh, albeit without any of the latter's idiosyncracies. The articulation of his bowing is masterful, and his sostenuto is seamless. It is highly polished, acutely sensitive romantic playing with a strong personal note that is perhaps a bit less pronounced than those of the most striking international violinistic personalities, but it ranks with the topmost echelon of Soviet players.

Julian Sitkovetsky

Julian Sitkovetsky (1925 - 1958), a pupil of Yampolsky, died of a brain tumor at only thirty-three, same age as Ossy Renardy, another brilliant gymnastics-oriented violinist who was tragically killed in a car accident.

Sitkovetsky was married to Bella Davidovich, now a Russian émigré pianist who has been forging a major career in the West.

Highly respected in the USSR, Sitkovetsky remained somewhat in the shadow of his countryman and contemporary, Leonid Kogan. In 1955 he took second prize at the Queen Elisabeth Brussels Competition won by the American Berl Senofsky, a particularly bitter defeat for the Russians.

Fortunately he left behind some 35 recorded compositions, which include the Sibelius, Glazunov, Paganini No. 2 and Lyapunov concerti, the Bach Solo Sonata No. 2, Tartini's *Devil's Trill* Sonata and Mozart's Sonata K. 378, three string quartets with A. Sharoyen, R. Barshai and Y. Slobodkin, and numerous bravura virtuoso showpieces. From these it is possible to make a broad assessment of his playing.

Sitkovetsky's performances give the impression of a violinist who did nothing but eat, sleep and practice. Purely as a digital technician he was the equal of anyone. It is in the finer points of artistry that he fails to attain the heights. The Sibelius, recorded from a live concert of the 1950s with Nikolai Anosov and the Czech Philharmonic, is a specific case in point. Among the least impressive of his recordings, it reveals a tone that is taut and one-dimensional, and a fast, pinched-sounding vibrato. His general instrumental command is authoritative, but the intonation is all too often not right on the mark, as it is in his recorded virtuoso pieces. Emotionally the performance is matter-of-fact, and favors muscularity over tenderness and spiritual grace. Perhaps he was having a bad day.

In the showpieces Sitkovetsky displays both temperament and a positive sense of style, although his sound remains rather tough-grained and commonplace, and the totality of his phrasing and expressivity lacks the ultimate in suavity and sophistication. His Ernst *Last Rose of Summer* étude and Paganini-Kreisler *Witches Dance*, (the latter with Davidovich providing accompaniment) are superlative models of daredevil virtuosity rivalling those of the young Ricci. Fingered-octaves, double harmonics and left-hand pizzicatos are tossed off as if they were child's play. Paganini's *Moses Fantasy* with scordatura tuning a minor third higher in pitch, Lipinski's Caprice, Op. 20, No. 3, Bazzini's *La Ronde des lutins*, Wieniawski's caprice, *Cadenza*, Op. 10, No. 7 and *Polonaise in D* are handled in similar fashion. However, Saint-Saëns' *Konzertstück*, with A. Mitnik, alternates between brilliance and stodginess, and the Saint-Saëns-Ysaÿe *Valse-Caprice* contains too many rhythmic liberties. Sarasate's *Malaguena* and *Habanera*, Bartók's piquant Sonatina and Szymanowski's *La Fontaine d'Aréthuse* are all played with extraordinary dexterity. But Sitkovetsky's E string sound is far superior to that of his G string. For all his marvelous fingerboard agility, he was neither a striking musical personality nor an artist to compete with the world's greatest. His son

Dmitri (with Bella Davidovich), a pupil of Yankelevich in the USSR and Galamian in the USA, won the first Kreisler Competition in Vienna in 1979, at age 25. The younger Sitkovetsky is a violinist of excellent instrumental authority and studied musicianship. His tone tends to be cool and lean, and like many trained in his generation he appears to be of the opinion that subtlety consists mainly of deliberately stopping his vibrato. One can respect and even admire such playing in certain compositions that do not appeal directly to the emotions. But it is essentially impersonal.

Mikhail Vaiman

Mikhail Vaiman (1926 - 1978) had an Odessa background as a Stolyarsky pupil in his youth, but was nominally a Leningrader. He first studied with his father, who was later killed in World War II. A graduate of the Leningrad Conservatory, Mikhail ultimately became a leading pedagogue there. He died suddenly at age fifty-two.

I heard Vaiman in a comprehensive recital when he was forty-one and in top form. He was an exceptional violinist of the second category, comparable to the finest concertmaster-soloists in the West. Like nearly all of the Soviet violinists he was essentially a romantic player, though his recordings of the Haydn Concerto in F, Telemann's Concerto in B-major and the Vivaldi Concerto Op. 3, No. 6 avoid any traces of romanticized exaggerations, and his vibrato is meticulously chaste.

Vaiman's recordings number about 40. In addition to the concerti mentioned above, they include those of Sibelius, Mozart No. 5, Bach No. 2, Arapov, Machavariani and the Bach Double Concerto with Boris Gutnikov, a Tchaikovsky Competition gold medalist. Major sonata recordings are of the Bartók No. 1, Prokofiev No. 1, Beethoven Nos. 1, 7 and 10, and Ravel No. 2, all with M. Karandashova.

The Machavariani concerto, with Odyssei Dmitriadi and the USSR State Radio Orchestra is practically a Georgian replica of the Khachaturian; a product of that period in Soviet musical life when anything suggestive of folkishness was extolled, no matter how transient or banal. Actually the concerto is a benignly exotic item cast for immediate mass consumption, about on par with that of Kabalevsky. Vaiman's performance reflects Oistrakh's influence, but is not crassly imitative. His violinistic equipment is commanding and his expressive powers strong, if not overwhelming. The Shostakovich Trio No. 2 with Rostropovich and Pavel Serebryakov, finds the great cellist dominating, but Vaiman plays with vigor and authority.

I found Vaiman's art more exciting in live concert than recordings. In a 1967 concert he displayed an ardent temperament and a sonorous tone abetted by bowing that was generally close to the bridge, utilizing all or most of the hair. His vibrato could project medium intensity as well as the extremes. It was healthy, sincere, expansive, exuberant, mostly intelligent playing. The Bach *Chaconne* was powerful, with virile chordal salvos; an outstanding performance. The Handel Sonata in D-major, broad in concept, live in sound and incisively bowed, was buoyant throughout. In Prokofiev's Sonata No. 1 he lacked Oistrakh's serenity in the muted filigree passagework, but otherwise it was a masterful delivery. Beethoven's *Spring* Sonata, joyous in spirit, was vitiated by occasional overrapid vibrato resulting in steely tones, and in a few instances strayed perilously close to the "Romany" border. Saint-Saëns' *Introduction and Rondo Capriccioso* represented his only serious breach of musicianship, victim of an accelerated tempo that sabotaged the music's inherent rhythmic pulse. Yet it contained many seductive phrases. Bloch's *Nigun* was heartfelt and Tchaikovsky's *Waltz-Scherzo* displayed exceptional verve and virtuosity. Unfortunately his inferior instrument was not worthy of his artistry. Alla Zokhova (Mrs. Vaiman) contributed sensitive, sympathetic piano collaboration. In all it was a most satisfying recital.

Vaiman's playing possessed positive character, though like Sitkovetsky, he was not a striking musical personality, nor a fingerboard gymnast of the latter's stamp. But Vaiman was superior in beauty of sound and artistic detail—one of the most well-rounded musicians among Soviet violinists.

Nelli Shkolnikova

Nelli Shkolnikova (b. 1928), born in Zolotonosha in the Ukraine, moved to Moscow at age two with her family. At age five, her father, a musician, enrolled her at a music school for children that is connected to the Moscow Conservatory. Her first instructor was Lilia Fidelevo-Kossodo, an Auer pupil. Upon her teacher's death when Nelli was ten, she went to study with the noted Professor Yuri Yankelevich at the Secondary School of Music, and continued with him at the Moscow Conservatory. After receiving an Honors degree from the conservatory in 1954 she completed postgraduate studies there in 1957. During that period of studies she won many competitions in the USSR. In 1953 Shkolnikova was sent to Paris by the government to compete in the Long-Thibaud Competition. She won both first prize and the special Ginette Neveu award for the best concerto performance in the final round. This victory launched her international career, and she has since concertized in Europe, Canada, Japan, the United States and Australia. Her second American tour was highlighted by appearances with Eugene Ormandy and The Philadelphia Orchestra in 1967. Among other leading conductors with whom she has performed are Kondrashin, Munch, Cluytens, Rozhdestvensky, Sanderling and Masur. After 1970, the Soviet authorities confined her appearances to

Nelli Shkolnikova

the Eastern bloc countries. From 1975 to 1980 she taught at the Moscow Gnessin Music Institute in the capacity of a Senior Lecturer, and in 1978 was named an "Honored Artist of the Russian Soviet Federated Socialist Republic (RSFSR)." At her first opportunity to revisit the West in 1982, she defected in West Berlin, and is now pursuing her career based in Melbourne, Australia. Recently she has been combining her activities as a soloist with conducting violin master classes at the Victorian College of the Arts.

Shkolnikova's Russian recordings and recent taping of live Australian performances confirm the high esteem in which she is held by her Soviet colleagues, both "loyalists" and émigrés. Of the numerous Soviet-trained women violinists I have heard, her playing projects the most satisfying overall blend of technical mastery, expressive communication, stylistic awareness and artistic finesse. Her tone is warm and appealing; her vibrato, basically of medium speed, is wisely controlled and applied naturally to the spirit of the specific music she is playing. At times her performance reflects Oistrakh's influence, but it is neither openly imitative nor as highly personalized. It is expressive playing in the Russian romantic tradition, although Shkolnikova is capable of disciplined restraint as well as propulsive brilliance. And her technique is nearly impeccable.

Judging by the top aesthetic standards, one might prefer a bit more introspection and subtlety of phrasing in the slow movements of her interpretations of the Beethoven concerto and Sonata No. 8 in G-major, though both contain many passages of suave declamation. Her Tchaikovsky concerto, ardent yet admirably controlled, compares favorably with the best versions of this era. Veracini's Sonata No. 8 in E is imbued with charm and nobility; her Shostakovich Ten Preludes run the expressive gamut with winsome lyricism, glittering virtuosity when demanded, and strong rhythmic impulse. Paganini's *Moses Fantasy* (tuned in scordatura) and Caprice No. 2 are instilled with amiable musical probity rather than gymnastic emphasis. Her recordings include about 50 works of varied lengths. It is to be hoped that Shkolnikova will have the opportunity to win wide exposure in the Western world while her powers are still at their peak.

Igor Bezrodny

Igor Bezrodny (b. 1930) was born in Tbilisi, capital of Georgia, USSR. Both parents were violinists; he began study at age six with his father. In 1937 he entered the school for gifted children affiliated with the Moscow Conservatory, and from 1949 to 1953 was a pupil of Yampolsky. He won gold medals at the Prague Kubelik Competition in 1949 and the Bach Competition in 1950 at Leipzig.

I heard Bezrodny in 1961 playing Khrennikov's Concerto No. 2, a work of vigorous, mass audience appeal, recalling both Khachaturian and Kabelevsky. But it did little for the violinist except to demonstrate that he possessed instrumental powers of a high order, and a mediocre violin. (Since Khrennikov has been the permanent Secretary-General of the Union of Soviet Composers for over thirty-five years and a deputy to the Supreme Soviet, he has had no difficulty getting his works performed either by Soviet musicians or by foreign musicians seeking Soviet connections.)

Bezrodny's recordings number around 60. The single major concerto is the Beethoven along with the minor concerti of Kabelevsky and Foerster. No major violin-piano sonatas are listed, though he has recorded two Handel sonatas, the Locatelli-Ysaÿe *Le Tombeau* Sonata and Bach's *Chaconne*, as well as Ravel's *Tzigane* and Chausson's *Poème*. However, throughout his recordings of many short works, it is apparent that Bezrodny is one of the more Western-oriented among Soviet violinists, and one of their finest stylists, particularly in that genre.

He has an effusive temperament, knows how to use tasteful slides and position changes for expressive purposes, and understands the role of tenderness and poetry in performance. Like most Soviet-trained violinists, he displays a prodigious facility. But his range of tonal color is rather limited. And while the sound quality is engaging, it is not a sound of compelling beauty. The root cause of this is a rapid vibrato that at times becomes too fast, vitiating the solidity of his tone.

Outstanding among his recorded brevities with pianist Abram Makarov are the Gershwin-Heifetz *Three Preludes*, clearly under the Heifetz influence; a heartwarming Bloch *Nigun*; a lilting Kreisler *Gypsy Caprice*; a spicy, rhythmic performance of Lillian Fuch's *Jota* and Harold Trigg's *Danza Braziliana* (the latter dedicated to, and first recorded by the American Louis Kaufman); a jaunty Prokofiev-Grunes *Theme and Processional* from *Peter and the Wolf*; and a gracefully sensitive Mompou-Szigeti *Jeunes Filles au Jardin*. From the origin of the selections it is obvious that Bezrodny's tastes are eclectic, and he was closely in touch with Western repertorial items of the 1940s and 1950s.

In recent years Bezrodny has turned seriously to symphonic conducting and currently is busily occupied with podium chores.

Valeri Klimov

Valeri Klimov, son of Alexander Klimov, a well-known conductor of the Kiev Opera, was born in that city in 1931. Originally a Stolyarsky pupil, he concluded his studies with David Oistrakh at the Moscow Conservatory. In 1955 he only placed sixth at the Paris Long-Thibaud Competition but in 1956 won first prize in the Prague Spring Festival "Ondricek" Competition, and in 1958 was awarded the gold medal in the first Moscow Tchaikovsky Competition. Following this victory he was sent abroad as soloist with the Moscow Philharmonic performing the Tchaikovsky concerto. Klimov has toured the U.S.A. several times, though not all have been top-level bookings. A personable blond man with a winning stage presence, he has appeared successfully throughout the world.

Klimov rightfully belongs in the echelon of Soviet violinists just below Oistrakh and Kogan. Polish, clarity of line and refinement, rather than fiery temperament and bravura virtuosity, characterize his playing. He does, however, possess formidable technical equipment and warmth of sound. His vibrato, basically of medium speed, flows naturally and is smartly controlled, with no "on-and-off" aberrations. And he employs expressive slides and position changes with tasteful selection. Quite free of idiosyncrasies, his playing reflects the utmost in musical integrity, and is in many ways exceptional, but not of striking individuality.

The Klimov recordings number about 35 at this writing. They include the Tchaikovsky, Mendelssohn, Mozart No. 3 and Beethoven concerti; the sonatas of Franck, Prokofiev No. 2, Beethoven No. 3 in E-flat and *Kreutzer*, Schubert's *Fantasy* Op. 159, Bach No. 3 in E, Handel No. 4 in D-major (nearly all are with pianist Yampolsky). Klimov's virtuoso showpiece records are limited to the ubiquitous Tchaikovsky *Waltz-Scherzo*, Sarasate's *Caprice Basque* and *Jota Aragonesa*, and Ysaÿe's Solo Sonata No. 6. Obviously he is not one of the many Russians who make a specialty of fingerboard gymnastics. No chamber ensemble recordings are among his listings.

The Tchaikovsky concerto recording (Kurt Eliasberg, Moscow State Philharmonic, 1958) is much as I heard him in live performance—pure, sensitive, warmly affectionate but not impassioned. The finale (with none of the usual brief cuts in the repetitive rapid spiccato passages) is not truly exciting. But overall it is a sleek, fluent, fastidious interpretation.

Klimov's Mendelssohn concerto disc is one of his finest: sparkling, propulsive and amiably expressive, an outstanding performance in every respect. And Mozart's No. 3, with Oistrakh's superb cadenza, stressing buoyance and nobility of style, is equally impressive. (Both with Maxim Shostakovich, USSR State Symphony, 1967). His Bach Sonata No. 3, for violin and piano, cool and limpid in sound and approach, contains a somewhat joyless second movement *Allegro*. More satisfying is his elegant, stately rendering of Handel's Sonata No. 4.

After the death of David Oistrakh, when it was assumed by most that Igor would succeed to his father's pedagogical chair at the Moscow Conservatory, Valeri Klimov, rather surprisingly, was given the post. Whatever the reasons given by the powers that be, whether justified or not, one cannot deny that Klimov's standing as an artist qualifies him for the position.

Igor Oistrakh

In the post-Paganini era, the Oistrakhs have been the first example of father and son violinists to attain solo careers on the international level. Igor, born in 1931 in Odessa, first took piano lessons, then switched to the violin at age six, studying with Valeria Merenbloom. After two years he was taught briefly by his father, but was, as he put it, "very lazy." It was Stolyarsky who finally motivated the recalcitrant boy to work seriously, and at age twelve he began a ten-year period of study with that master, though he was coached intermittently by his father. In 1949 he played his first major recital in Kiev, and in 1952 won the gold medal at the Poznan Wieniawski Competition. His initial European concerts took place in 1953, and in 1962 he appeared in the first of many American tours.

As the son of the great David Oistrakh, Igor enjoyed many advantages and, of course, was subject to extraordinary pressures. How onerous and frustrating it must be to constantly hear oneself unfavorably compared to a universally beloved and respected father. But this was only part of Igor's burden. In addition, the powerful influence of his father's playing and its

Igor Oistrakh

personalized style impressed upon him daily and at intimate range when David was home, could scarcely fail to engrave itself upon all of his artistic sensibilities. Imagine any young violinist striving to form his own musical personality while living with a Kreisler or a Heifetz—or an Oistrakh!

Igor has always been "the other Oistrakh," and as such he all too often has been underrated as a violinist. Yet in spite of this handicap, the younger Oistrakh has honestly earned his position among the topmost Soviet violinists, against fearsome competition.

Even though it is essentially unfair to insist upon comparing Igor with David, it is scarcely possible not to do so. Igor's concept of tone production, interpretive approach, texture and usage of vibrato, phrasing, and the important expressive horizontal movements involved in position changes and slides, are markedly similar to those of David. In fact, there are passages in which even an experienced ear can have difficulty in telling them apart. Naturally it is a prodigious feat in itself to make music that resembles so formidable an artist as David Oistrakh. However, in the process, Igor obviously sacrificed whatever potential for strong individualism he might have possessed.

As an instrumentalist, Igor is a formidable virtuoso who handles any genre of music with aplomb, though he does not specialize in the most gymnastic of the "variation" showpieces of Paganini and Ernst. His superlative recording of Hindemith's *Kammermusik* No. 4 demonstrates that his technical resources can cope readily with the most severe demands of twentieth-century unviolinistic bravura facility. To his credit, unlike many of his contemporaries and colleagues, he is willing to accept this type of challenge.

At this writing Igor's recordings number about 100, including duets with his father and several collaborations with such colleagues as Pikaisen and Barshai, as well as the outstanding Soviet pianists, Yampolsky, Makarov, N. Zertsalova, A. Ginzburg, B. Davidovich and I. Kollegorskaya. His disc repertoire encompasses most of the basic major concerti, sonatas, medium-length showpieces and a broad sampling of shorter works.

In assessing Igor's art, it is necessary to stress two vital factors. First, in live concert his playing is not fully consistent. Even within a single program his instrumental authority and emotional projection may vary in different works. I have heard him in several performances playing below his highest standard. Secondly, his playing is constantly beset by the "on-and-off" vibrato syndrome, which vitiates his lyric flow. This shortcoming, of course, is less blatant in the music of Bartók, Stravinsky, Hindemith, Shostakovich and most twentieth-century works than it is in nineteenth-century, overtly Romantic staples. Also, unlike David, that steady "Rock of Gibralter," Igor at times will mar a performance by playing rapid passage segments too fast, losing the inherent rhythmic pulse of the music. A vivid case in point occurred at a concert I attended in which Igor, obviously upset by a technically inferior performance of the Sibelius concerto, quickly returned on stage offering as an encore Ysaÿe's Sonata No. 3 (*Ballade*). Played at breakneck speed, it was a technical tour de force, but an incongruous example of music-making.

One of the more impressive of Igor's recordings is the Tchaikovsky concerto with his father conducting the Moscow Philharmonic. It is extremely agile digitally, pure of line and stylistically in the finest tradition of the Soviet musical approach, ranking high among the more than 70 recordings of this work. Although not as emotionally consistent as David's interpretations, it projects warmth of spirit, and contains less "on-and-off" lyric vibrato than most of Igor's performances of ultra-romantic works.

Other outstanding discs are Prokofiev's Concerto No. 1 (Rozhdestvensky, Moscow Radio Orchestra) and Bartók's Concerto No. 2 (Rozhdestvensky, Moscow State Philharmonic). Lalo's *Symphonie Espagnole* is brilliantly idiomatic, though more sweet than sensuous. His Beethoven concerto is sensitive and thoughtful in a musical approach similar to David's (D. Oistrakh, Vienna Symphony), but again his uneven vibrato usage is sometimes irksome. His Rakov concerto and Szymanowski's *La Fontaine d'Aréthuse* are strong in David's influence; Ravel's *Tzigane*, while medium-weight in tonal texture, is highly polished and ardent in sound and phrasing. Chausson's *Poème*, otherwise elegant, is impaired by "on-and-off" vibrato, as are to an even greater extent, Saint-Saëns' *Havanaise*, Vitali's *Chaconne* and Paganini's *Moses Fantasy* (no scorditura).

Ysaÿe's *Lointaine Passé* Mazurka No. 3, absolutely exquisite, and Vieux-temp's *Tarantelle*, a breathtaking exercise in facility, dominate a superb collection of recorded brevities from the mid-1950s. Eight of Paganini's caprices, 1973 (with wife Natalia Zertsalova playing the simplistic Schumann accompaniments), are straightforward, scrupulously clean, propulsive renditions, and the Kreisler version of *La Campanella* is scintillating. Turning to the viola, Igor, also conducting the Solo Ensemble of the Moscow State Philharmonic, with Viktor Pikaisen on violin, offers a performance of Mozart's *Duo Concertante* that is neatly limned, resonant in sound and musically alert.

In retrospect, one might say that David Oistrakh's legacy to his son has been both bountiful and deleterious. Irrespective of any shortcomings, Igor Oistrakh is an artist to be admired.

Viktor Pikaisen

Viktor Pikaisen, born in 1933 in Kiev, is the son of Alexander, concert-master of the Kiev Opera Orchestra. His mother, a pupil of Simon Barere, was a pianist-accompanist at the same theatre. Viktor began violin study with Joseph Gutman, a well-known teacher of children in Kiev. The family was relocated in Alma-Ata, Khazhakstan, after the war broke out, and at age nine the boy made his debut in Wieniawski's Concerto No. 2 with the Alma-Ata State Symphony. Meanwhile he continued lessons with his father. In 1946 David Oistrakh accepted him as his pupil and taught him in Moscow for fourteen years, longer than any other pupil. Among his many awards were second prizes in 1957 at the Thibaud Competition and in 1958 at Moscow's Tchaikovsky Competition, and first prize in 1965 at Genoa's Paganini Competition. He has concertized extensively on an international scale but has never been sent to the United States.

I met Pikaisen at the Moscow Conservatory where he has been a leading professor since 1966. A man of gentle mien, he bears a striking physical resemblance to David Oistrakh, and is a close friend of the Oistrakh family. His repertoire is broad. He has performed all 24 of Paganini's caprices in a single concert more than fifty times, and the full cycle of Bach Solo Sonatas and Partitas on numerous occasions. He favors recitals for solo violin, and often programs the solo sonatas of Bartók and Geminiani. Both Aram Khachaturian and Boris Tchaikovsky have dedicated major works to him. In recent years he has given many concerts with his

Viktor Pikaisen

pianist daughter Tatiana.

Piakaisen's recordings number about 40, and in addition to the solo vehicles and various violinistic showpieces, they include the concerti of Beethoven, Mendelssohn, Dvořák and Wieniawski No. 1 in F-sharp minor.

When Pikaisen took second place to Klimov in the 1958 Tchaikovsky Competition, more than a few observers preferred his fiery, intensely vibrant performance to the polished, patrician playing of Klimov. Surprisingly, despite his long years with Oistrakh, Pikaisen is not an imitator of his master, and while one can pinpoint instances of "on-and-off" vibrato usage, it does not occur to an annoying extent.

Pikaisen's interpretations represent two distinctly different approaches. Basically he is a full-blooded romantic, an impassioned performer with exceptional virtuosity. His recording of the Wieniawski No. 1 (Rozhdestvensky, Moscow Radio Symphony) vies with those of Rabin and Perlman, as a stunning tour de force of opulent sound and immaculate authority. And his Dvořák concerto (David Oistrakh, Moscow Philharmonic), with its lush tone and fervent temperament, ranks with the better recordings of this work. The Beethoven concerto, with a lengthy unorthodox cadenza by Wolfgang Schneiderhan, and including a certain amount of material unrelated to the themes, punctuated by drum beats (Igor Oistrakh, Central Television and Radio Orchestra), is vitiated by a loggy, uninspired opening orchestral tutti. Pikaisen's performance is admirable technically and his high E string sound is excellent. But there are moments of prosaic playing, and in general it is not memorable as a celestial interpretation.

The dichotomy in Pikaisen's playing is most evident in his Paganini caprices and Bach solo sonatas. Here his inherent fire is deliberately curbed by his intellectual devices. The caprices are scrupulously delivered, clean and neat in detail, and one can scarcely be unimpressed with many of his attempts at originality of interpretation. Yet in the process, the bravura character of the music is often sacrificed. And in the Bach, his square-cut approach inhibits the natural flow of the lighter dance segments (i.e. *Gavottes, Menuettos, Bourrées,* etc.). If Pikaisen were an artist of academic pursuits and cool temperament, this would be understandable. But in his obviously sincere efforts to perform Bach without any vestige of romanticism, he has adopted a quasi-cerebral musicality that is essentially studied and alien to his instincts.

The above observations notwithstanding, Pikaisen is of international stature, and one of the finest of Soviet violinists.

Vladimir Spivakov

Vladimir Spivakov was born in 1944 in Ufa in the Soviet Ural area, after his family had been evacuated from Leningrad during World War II. He first received piano lessons from his mother, but at age seven began study of the violin with Mme. Lubovitch Siegel, also a teacher of Boris Gutnikov. Next he studied with Veniamin Sher at the Leningrad Conservatory, and at seventeen he was enrolled in the Moscow Conservatory where he was a pupil of Yankelevich. In 1965 he took fourth prize at the Paris Thibaud-Long Competition; in 1967, second prize at the Genoa Paganini Competition; in 1969, first prize at the Montreal International Competition; and in 1970, second prize in the Moscow Tchaikovsky Competition. Spivakov has toured extensively both at home and abroad, and during the Soviet-American political freeze has been one of the very few Soviet artists permitted to play in the United States. His prestige in the Soviet Union is extremely high and his loyalty unquestioned. I met and spent some time with Spivakov during one of his Los Angeles visits, and found him to be a modest, reserved man of striking sincerity, looking younger than his years, and a strongly patriotic Soviet citizen despite his Jewish heritage.

Spivakov was not well received in his various Southern California appearances, and I concurred with this opinion. Of course he is a brilliant instrumentalist, as are so many of his countrymen, but his playing is marked by a major flaw—a vibrato that is consistently too fast, at times almost approximating a whinny. And for all his finger intensity, the "on-and-off" vibrato habit is one of his hallmarks. Thus his sound is

Vladimir Spivakov

either excitedly vibrant or "white," with no intermediate tempering degrees. How this has escaped major adverse commentary from the Soviet violin establishment and certain foreign critics must remain a mystery. He uses practically the same vibrato for a Mozart concerto as for the Sibelius concerto (both of which I have heard live), just as in a recording his sound in a Haydn concerto is scarcely less vibrant than in the Tchaikovsky concerto. There are times, naturally, when this tense vibrato is acceptable, but his tonal palette has little variety and tends to be monochromatic. Spivakov does evince a measure of individuality in his interpretations, but his tonal aberrations prevent him from ranking artistically with such violinists as Perlman or Zukerman.

In a survey of his recordings to date, the most impressive are the Paganini-Spivakov *Witches Dance*, a dazzling performance, and his highly personalized, interesting, if unorthodox renditions of the Brahms-Joachim *Hungarian Dances* 16, 2, 9 and 6. Spivakov has recently formed and presides as leader and soloist with a 27-member group called the Moscow Virtuosi. At this writing he is devoting much of his time and energies to conducting.

Now in his forties, it is too late for any appreciable change in Spivakov's tonal production and projection even if he wished to effect it. This is all the more unfortunate since his natural expressive powers and galvanic, yet controlled temperament, are far superior to those of Mullova, Grubert, or just about any of the younger Soviet-trained violinists of their generation.

Viktor Tretyakov

Viktor Tretyakov (b. 1946), born in Krasnoyarsk, Siberia, is the son of a tuba player in an army band. At age six he began violin study at the Irkutsk Conservatory, and later entered the noted Central Music School of Moscow, the preparatory subsidiary of the Moscow Conservatory. In 1963 he became a pupil of Yankelevich, who taught him until his death in 1973. In 1965 he was named the laureate of young Soviet violinists, and in 1966 won first prize in the third Tchaikovsky Competition in Moscow. He has had many international tours and first appeared in the United States in 1969.

A handsome, engaging stage figure, with a bearing almost military in its decorum, Tretyakov is a model "Russian" violinist, one of the more successful Soviet artists to follow Oistrakh and Kogan.

As an executant his equipment is superb, and his repertoire is broad. A dominating feature of his playing is its obvious sincerity of purpose, disciplined intelligence, and the absence of carelessness or superficiality. In live concert Tretyakov's tone is not very large-scaled, but his vibrato is strong and evenly applied. It is not the type of sound that can thrill an audience by its beauty alone, but can at times project a sense of opulence. There is an aura of formality in his interpretations of masterworks, yet he does possess a warm temperament that infuses a positive glow into these works for which he is best suited. Thus, in one of his recitals that I attended, he generated a dynamic drive to Prokofiev's *March* that attained an overwhelming climax. But Kreisler's *Caprice Viennois*, after a promising beginning, fell victim to a plodding tempo and almost flaccid doublestops that completely lacked the vital intensity and charm demanded by the music.

The best-known of Tretyakov's recordings in the West is the Paganini Concerto No. 1 (Neimye Varvy, Moscow Philharmonic). It is a glittering performance, virile, immaculate in technique and bold in spirit. The first movement Sauret cadenza registers as a tour de force; the operatic *Adagio expressivo* may not project the ultimate drama, but does contain a good measure of intense ariosity. The finale is unusually rapid in tempo, and all, including the double harmonics, is crisply articulated. This is Tretyakov at his zenith, and the disc ranks among the finest half-dozen of this work.

Conversely, in his recording of Brahms's Sonata No. 3, Op. 108, while he obviously strives for introspection in a rendition that is quite individualized, his tempi are decidely elastic and his tone inconsistent. His pace too often tends to plod, and passages of genuine excitement are few and far between. In Ravel's *Tzigane* Tretyakov is essentially miscast, and though the performance is efficiently wrought, it does not have the tonal richness and instinctual fire of an exceptional reading. Again, the Vitali-Charlier *Chaconne* is chaste and conscientious, but lacking propulsion and diversity of pacing, and generally uninteresting.

Tretyakov's recording of Bach's G-minor Solo Sonata is outstanding, highlighted by beautifully delineated fugal patterns and eloquent chordal salvos. Also extraordinary are Paganini's Caprice No. 17, which smartly avoids dull dynamic repetition in the scale filigree passages, and Caprice No. 24, spotless in bowing inflections and purity of intonation, plus a novel loud-and-soft exposition of the left-hand pizzicatos. Even more exciting is the Paganini-Kreisler *I Palpiti*, hair-raising in its technical integrity and clarity in the awesome gymnastic challenges.

A recording of the Sibelius concerto, taken from a live performance (Alexander Dmitriev, USSR Academy Symphony) is estimable overall; the third movement is a bit labored but the *Adagio* contains some sensuous G string tones.

In all, Tretyakov is one of the finest Soviet violinist-musicians though not quite a talent of the highest magnitude.

Gidon Kremer

Gidon Kremer was born in Riga in 1947 of musical parents. His first teachers, at age four, were his father and grandfather. At seven he entered the Riga School of Music where he studied with V.A. Sturestep, and at sixteen won first prize in the Latvian Republic Competition. During the following eight years he was a pupil of David Oistrakh. In 1967 he received third prize in the Brussels Queen Elisabeth Competition; in 1969 won first prize in Genoa's Paganini Competition and second place at the Montreal Competition; and in 1970 was gold medalist in Moscow's Tchaikovsky Competition. Kremer has concertized widely on an international scale, and at this writing enjoys the most prolific and successful career of all contemporary Soviet-trained violinists. This can be attributed to several factors. He was acclaimed as "the greatest violinist in the world" by the eminent conductor Herbert von Karajan. Also, as a de facto citizen of the world he has moved to the West and is, to all intents and purposes, a Soviet émigré. This has enabled him to build his career without the interference and frustration caused by East-West political antagonisms and boycotts. And in addition to the impact of his performances, he has a gift for garnering attention and publicity for himself by means of highly unorthodox musical activities. Kremer was first married to the violinist Tatiana Grindenko, 1972 gold medalist at the Poznan Wieniawski Competition, with whom he has made several duo recordings. His present pianist-wife Elena, daughter of pianist Dmitri Bashkirov, collaborates with her husband in recitals.

Gidon Kremer

Kremer is probably the most idiosyncratic, controversial violinist of his generation. Except for a few glints in his early recordings, his playing reflects no direct influence of Oistrakh's sound or style. As a digital virtuoso he is easily the equal of any of the gymnastics-oriented Soviet violinists; his recordings of Ernst's *Last Rose of Summer* (Étude No. 6) and *Erl King*, Geminiani's Solo Sonata, Bach's Solo Partitia in B-minor and Paganini's Caprice No. 4 are note-perfect gems of technical facility. However, even in these spectacular performances one can discern Kremer's shortcomings as well as his strengths, and understand why he has cleverly elected to make novelty and experimentation the cardinal components of his career.

The crux of the matter is that for all his individuality, vigor and fervor, Kremer possesses a thin, commonplace, impersonal sound, a sound essentially indistinguishable from that of any number of second- and third-rate colleagues. His comparatively thin fingers and slowish vibrato simply cannot produce a tone of sensuous beauty. Inasmuch as sensuality is not an integral element of his performance, he cannot compete directly with tone-oriented artists of the first rank. Since there are so few of them among contemporary international soloists, Kremer's lack of tonal opulence has not proved an insuperable handicap.

Some observers tend to associate Kremer's artistry with that of Joseph Szigeti, who forged a major career despite the competition of such great tonalists as Heifetz, Kreisler, Elman and Menuhin, among others. I be-

lieve this to be fallacious. Any Kremer-Szigeti similarity is merely superficial. Both have sought repertorial novelty and have been champions of
works originally shunned by others. But at this point resemblances cease.
Szigeti, in his prime, could elevate masterworks such as the Beethoven,
Brahms and Mozart concerti with a spiritual grace and inner nobility
quite beyond any of the routinely efficient interpretations of these works
by Kremer, although Kremer is the superior technician. I cannot help but
compare a recent international telecast of Kremer's playing of Vivaldi's
The Four Seasons with the English Chamber Orchestra, an overpropul-
sive, lean-toned, graceless romp, with the lofty elegance Szigeti could
impart to a simple Handel sonata. Apart from comparisons with Szigeti,
Kremer is unable to achieve the tonal intensity and lustre necessary for
impassioned performances of the great romantic concerti of Tchaikovsky,
Sibelius, Bruch, Lalo and others. Even in his recordings of such works as
the Bartók Sonata Nos. 1 and 2, and the Shostakovich Sonata Op. 134,
which he plays with sensitivity and elan, the slenderness of his tone is
always apparent to a professional ear. And because of his unsightly body
contortions and deep knee bends, it is more satisfying to hear Kremer in
recordings than to watch him on the concert platform.

Kremer's fierce independence is well-suited to the talents he possesses.
Thus far, avant-garde compositions for the violin have gained little favor
with audiences, but there has always been a potential audience for contemporary works that do not assault the ear or insult the intelligence. In
his search for material, Kremer has unearthed such curiosities as Milhaud's *Ox on the Roof* arrangement, a saucy, nose-thumbing confection
recalling the jazzy 1920s; several wry, forgettable pieces by Satie; Beethoven's undistinguished *Twelve Variations on a Mozart Theme*; the
early (1897), immature sonata by Ravel (not the familiar sonata with the
Blues movement); and a slight morsel purportedly written by Charles
Chaplin for *Modern Times*. And in his zeal for novelty he has taken up
such rarely performed romantic gambols as Vieuxtemps' *Fantasia Appas-
sionata*, which he has recorded. A recent ploy that won Kremer an enormous amount of attention was his inclusion of cadenzas by the Soviet
avant-gardist Alfred Schnittke, in his performance of the Beethoven concerto. Apparently operating on the proven theory that any publicity, good
or bad, is desirable, Kremer stoutly defended his action against a barrage
of criticism. Actually the cadenzas, aside from being alien to the style and
spirit of the concerto, contain little to cause indignation among the
musically more permissive auditors. They employ a scarcely cohesive
collection of insignificant pizzicato pluckings, rambling doublestops,
chordal salvos and dextrous digital flights that bear scant relationship to
the concerto's basic themes. In some of the climactic bars the violinist is
assisted by drum beats and surging billows of sound from the orchestra's

string players. Kremer is currently presenting a concerto by Schnittke, and no doubt will continue to build his career along these lines while retaining as much of the basic repertoire as he requires to balance his programs.

Kremer can be an extremely interesting artist in "off-beat" and little-known works. Yet even at best, while his playing may be exhilarating, it is hardly exalted, and not calculated to touch the heart.

Other Soviet Violinists

Many a Soviet virtuoso has lived and died, either unknown in the West or known only to a few Western colleagues. One of these was that elegant stylist of the "old school," **Shmuel (Samuel) Furer**, born in 1909, who was more or less a casualty of the Oistrakh hegemony. Today, the number who still live in the USSR or have emigrated to the West is large; as is the case everywhere in the world, more than a few never receive the recognition they deserve.

One who has recorded at least 80 widely diverse works, including Soviet exotica, Western brevities and chamber music, is **Eduard Grach** (b. 1930), an Oistrakh pupil who is little known abroad. **Boris Gutnikov** (1931 - 1986), a winner of the 1962 Tchaikovsky Competition, has performed in the West with rather indifferent success. As I heard him in the Tchaikovsky concerto, he is a brilliant instrumentalist with strong tonal attributes, but projects no particular personal aura. **Mark Lubotsky** (b. 1931), an Oistrakh pupil, now a professor at the Amsterdam Conservatory, boasts a formidable, top-level recording of the Britten concerto.

Albert Markov (b. 1933), now living in the United States, is a fiery player of rhapsodic bent, who took second honors to Jaime Laredo in the 1959 Queen Elisabeth Competition. A smooth, lyric performer, his music-making is not profound, and "on-and-off" vibrato usage mars his delivery, particularly in his recording of the Kvernadze concerto, a sort of Georgian reflection of the Khachaturian concerto. He is nevertheless a sensitive, entertaining stylist, and his recording of Paganini's *Moses Fantasy*, with one of the final variations played pizzicato, is quite dazzling. His transcription, *Second Rhapsody on Gershwin Themes* is a blazing tour de force, cleverly conceived and stunningly executed. Markov's son, **Alexander Markov**, whom I have heard, is an outstanding violinistic talent, and at eighteen was winner of the 1982 Paganini Competition.

Vladimir Lantsman (b. 1942), now in the West, dispatched the Tchaikovsky concerto with sure-fingered agility, but with no more than routine interpretive powers and no particular individuality in a concert I attended. **Oleg Kagan** (b. 1946), an Oistrakh pupil, winner of the 1965

Vladimir Lantsman

Sibelius Competition and second prize winner in the 1966 Tchaikovsky Competition, is a violinist-musician of respectable stature. His recording of Beethoven's Sonatas No. 4 and No. 5 (*Spring*) with pianist Sviatislav Richter, offers playing of sound, alert musicality, a straightforward approach and clean-cut delivery, but lacks any exceptional subtlety. A fast, occasionally fluttery vibrato is a key element in his tonal production.

Boris Belkin (b. 1948), a Yankelevich pupil now in the West, appears to have more powerful contacts than some of the other artist émigrés. Onstage as I saw him, he sported shoulder-length hair and affected a cocky, quasi-Paganini stance. Belkin's recording of Paganini's Concerto No. 1 is far better than the live performance I heard. His tone is small though warmed by a fast vibrato, and he has a sense of drama and verve that so many of his generation lack. Technically his playing is sometimes labored. A violinist of romantic persuasion, he plays the Tchaikovsky concerto in both live and recorded performances with flashes of brilliance. But his performances overall do not project either top-level or significant artistry.

Vadim Brodsky (b. 1950), winner of the 1977 Wieniawski Competition, is another Soviet supertechnician and has recorded the cycle of Ysaÿe sonatas in the United States. Brodsky exhibits top-level instrumental command, and a tone that is strong but commonplace in character and not oriented toward beauty. It is said that he can play Paganini's *Perpetuum Mobile* in fingered octaves in the manner of César Thomson.

Vadim Brodsky

Pavel Kogan

André Korsakov (b. 1950), second to Miriam Fried in the 1971 Queen Elisabeth Competition, plays a recorded Wieniawski collection, including the extremely difficult *Original Variations*, Op. 15, with admirable verve and panache. His digital equipment is superb and his pure tone can be impassioned, though its texture is light. Yet his performance does not denote big-scaled authority or scope.

Philip Hirshhorn, a Vaiman pupil now living in Brussels, was winner of the 1967 Queen Elisabeth Competition. A recording of the Saint-Saëns-Ysaÿe *Valse-Caprice* made at that time displays him as a brilliant virtuoso whose playing is vitiated by an inordinately fast vibrato. **Pavel Kogan** (b. 1952), son of Leonid and Elizabeth Gilels, a Yankelevich pupil, is a violinist of superior attainments. I heard him play in a live performance of the Brahms concerto with excellent command and a disciplined, thoughtful manner. However, his interpretation did not reflect a strong personal note. In a recording of the dark, tension-packed concerto by Franco Mannino, a challenging, difficult contemporary work, young Kogan displays a decided flair for the modern idiom; his technique sparkles and his tone is intense and penetrating. He is presently forging a career as a symphonic conductor, a profession for which he has had considerable training and background.

Tapes of the 1978 Tchaikovsky Competition indicate that cowinner **Ilya Grubert** (b. 1954), a Yankelevich pupil, is a well-trained violinist of undistinguished sound and moderate talent. **Viktoria Mullova** (b. 1959), a Kogan pupil, winner of the 1982 Tchaikovsky Competition and a previous winner of the Wieniawski and Sibelius Competitions, emigrated to the West in order to aggrandize her career. In two comprehensive recitals which I attended, she displayed outstanding technical equipment plus clarity of intonation and musical line that recalls her eminent master. But her tone, while bright and fairly vibrant, tends to be one-dimensional and limited in color, and emotively, her playing is cool. Her performances of Paganini's *Nel cor piu non mi sento* Variations and the entire *La Campanella* movement from Concerto No. 2 was a scintillating tour de force, though quite wanting in subtlety. Bach's Solo Partita No. 1 in B-minor, cleanly wrought, was musically immature, and in the Brahms Sonatas No. 1, Op. 78 and No. 3, Op. 108, the meagerness of her expressive powers would indicate that Mullova's chief virtues are purely violinistic, and that she is not an instinctual talent of elite caliber. At this writing there is still much of the artist-student in her playing.

I have not heard **Dora Schwarzberg**, a Yankelevich pupil, 1976 winner of the Flesch Competition now living in Israel. But **Isaak Shuldman**, a second prize winner of the Flesch Competition, presently a professor at the Oslo Conservatory, sent me taped performances of several major works that show him to be a powerful violinist in the best Soviet tradition. And the immensely gifted **Daniel Shindaryov** (b. 1924), now of Los

Angeles, richly deserves an extensive solo career. A performer of extraordinary spontaneity, he has sought to infuse his playing with the best precepts of Western musicianship while sharpening the stunning virtuosity inherited from his Soviet training. A former concertmaster of the Bolshoi Ballet and Opera orchestra, Shindaryov has blossomed into a soloist of multifaceted tonal color, superb instrumental command and warmhearted lyric expressiveness. He possesses a rare penchant for exciting his audiences.

Nina Beilina and Tatiana Grindenko were cited in my previous book, *Master Violinists in Performance.*

Notable among the current young generation is **Vadim Repin**, born in 1971 in Novosibirsk. His teacher is Zakhar Bron, who studied with Igor Oistrakh at the Moscow Conservatory. Repin started violin at age five, had lessons at a children's music school, and in 1977 began study at the "specialized" secondary music school at the Novosibirsk Conservatory. At nine he played Wieniawski's Concerto No. 2 and Paganini's Caprice No. 16 in concert.

In 1982 he won first prize at the Wieniawski Competition, and at thirteen his repertoire included concerti of Mozart, Bach, Tchaikovsky, Mendelssohn, Khachaturian, Wieniawski, Khrennikov and the Beethoven *Romances*, together with many virtuoso showpieces. At fifteen, he performed the Paganini Concerto No. 1 with the Sauret cadenza.

At this writing Repin has not performed in the West, but a recording made when he was only thirteen stamps him as a genuine child prodigy with the powerful tone of a mature artist and incredible digital facility. His general style recalls David Oistrakh, though his vibrato is faster. Rapin tosses off Ysaÿe's Solo Sonata No. 6 with stunning virtuosity, instills the Tchaikovsky-Bezekirsky *Meditation*, Op. 42, No. 1 with impressive warmth, and plays the quixotic Schumann-Kreisler *Fantasia* in C-major, Op. 131, with considerable charm. His vibrato usage is afflicted with the "off-and-on" habit in lyric passages. It is impossible to determine whether or not his playing has an individual profile or is steeped in emulation. But Repin's career merits close scrutiny. It is hoped that he will develop into a great artist rather than merely just another superb instrumentalist.

Daniel Shindaryov

CHAPTER EIGHT

Survey of American Violinists

W HO, PRECISELY, CAN BE BE DESIGNATED AN American violinist? Certainly one who was born in the United States and received all or most of his or her training in that country from teachers who were themselves taught in the United States. What then of such yesteryear players as Maude Powell, Leonora Jackson, Nettie Carpenter, Albert Spalding and others born in the United States, but whose principal training was in Europe? Would anyone deny them the right to be called American violinists? What of a long list of artists including Zimbalist, Seidel and Piastro, born and trained in Russia, who arrived in America as young men, became American citizens and had many decades of career activity in the United States? And what of Isaac Stern, born in Russia, taught in the United States by the foreign-born, foreign-trained pedagogues Naoum Blinder and Robert Pollak; or Josef Gingold, born in Russia, trained by Ysaÿe in Belgium, yet who, like Stern, is as American as apple pie? Are not any naturalized citizens in any field considered American, even though their training was obtained in the land of their birth? One could conjure up several more variations on this theme to no constructive purpose or definitive answer.

Rather than become mired in chauvinistic contradictions, I prefer to touch all the bases and to discuss American citizens who have made significant contributions to American violin art, irrespective of their national origin or training.

All eighteenth- and nineteenth-century American classical music has European roots. Data concerning the violin in the colonial era is sketchy. We are told that Thomas Jefferson had regular lessons with an Italian violin teacher (in America), practiced three hours a day for at least twelve years, and played music by Purcell, Handel, Corelli, Boccherini and Haydn. In his bachelor days he performed duets with Martha Wayles, his future wife, who had some skill on the harpsichord. And in his latter days he played for his grandchildren despite being impaired by a wrist that had been broken. Patrick Henry fiddled by ear at parties. In the early nineteenth century we read of Mark Beaubien, who fiddled for an audience of six hundred on a river bank.

One of the first European virtuosi of some significance to tour America was the Hungarian-Jewish Miska Hauser (1822 - 1887), an adventurous world traveler and freewheeling personality whose name was linked with the notorious Lola Montez. Hauser trekked as far as the California mining camps in the early 1850s, and was equally at home whether playing on the concert stage or in a mercantile store display window. The Norwegian, Ole Bull (1810 - 1880), whose brash American projects and peregrinations have been comprehensively documented in two biographies (one by his widow, the other by Mortimer Smith), made a striking impact upon the American scene in the middle decades of the nineteenth century. Naive early American audiences were quite enchanted by his superficial vaudevillean tricks and handsome blond image. Bull's rivalry with the Belgian Henri Vieuxtemps (1820 - 1881) in New York created quite a stir. However, for all his great success with the unknowledgeable American audiences of the time, playing mostly light-minded music, Bull's London appearance with Franz Liszt in Beethoven's *Kreutzer* Sonata was a fiasco for the violinist. Bull, like Heinrich Ernst (1815 - 1865), represented the afterglow of the spectacular Paganini tradition (though he was not nearly as schooled a musician as Ernst), and left no influence whatsoever on the gradually developing native American participation in European-oriented classical violin music.

Other noted nineteenth-century continental visitors to American were the Italian Camillo Sivori (1815 - 1894), Hungarian-Jewish Edouard Remenyi (1830 - 1898), Polish-Jewish Wieniawski (1835 - 1880), Wilma Norman-Neruda (Lady Hallé) (1839 - 1911), the French Camilla Urso (1842 - 1902), the Spanish Pablo de Sarasate (1844 - 1908), the German August Wilhelmj (1845 - 1908), the Belgian César Thomson (1857 - 1931) and Eugène Ysaÿe (1858 - 1931).

German émigré musicians played a leading role in the salad days of American symphonic and instrumental performance. Only a minority of conductors have musical backgrounds as violinists, but oddly, the two men most responsible for early American symphonic development, Theodore Thomas (1835 - 1905), who arrived in America in 1845, and his archrival Leopold Damrosch (1832 - 1885), were transplanted German violinists. An 1862 *New York Times* review of Thomas playing the Mendelssohn concerto states... "Mr. Thomas produced a firm tone and stops absolutely in time, and plays without any affection of sentiment. He was completely successful." Another, in 1868, says: "His performance of Beethoven's *Kreutzer* Sonata, Op. 47 did not compare unfavorably with that of Joachim in the same sonata." In his book *Memoirs of a Musical Life*,

William Mason points out that "he had a large tone, the tone of a player of the highest rank. He lacked the perfect finish of a great violinist, but he played in a large, quiet, reposeful manner." Thomas's violin repertoire in his active playing years ranged from Ernst's *Otello Fantasy* and Lipinski's *Concerto Militaire* to Bach's *Chaconne* and the Beethoven concerto. He performed the latter in 1868, well into his conducting years, and Beethoven's Quartet Op. 59 as early as 1855. In 1855, Thomas, Mason and a cellist gave the world premiere of Brahms's Trio, Op. 8, possibly the first publicizing of Brahms's name in America. Ultimately, of course, his fame as a maestro far overshadowed his reputation as a violinist.

Damrosch, of Jewish parentage, came to America in 1871 and shortly thereafter performed the Beethoven concerto with the New York Philharmonic, featuring his own cadenza. He is described as having a tone that was not large, though pure and consistent. Damrosch practiced the violin dutifully two hours a day for many years despite his ever-mounting responsibilites as conductor, teacher and entrepreneur. He also wrote and performed a violin concerto.

It was common practice for American-born violinists of the nineteenth century to go abroad to receive the finishing touches of their training from world-renowned teachers. Thus they could boast that they were pupils of Joachim, Vieuxtemps, Wieniawski, Dancla and other notables. Later generations were to travel to Europe for study with Auer, Flesch, Ševčik, Ysaÿe, Thomson, Rèmy, Schradieck and other famous teachers. In some instances, it was done as much for the sake of status as for knowledge. By the time Auer, Flesch and Ševčik came to reside and teach in America, there were already many highly qualified teachers in this country.

Sam Franko (1857 - 1937), born in New Orleans, a pupil of Joachim and Vieuxtemps, was among the first noteworthy American-born violinists. He edited and performed many compositions that he unearthed in European libraries, and founded and conducted the 65-member American Symphony Orchestra in 1894. Franko's cadenzas to Mozart's Concerto in G-major, No. 3, are still widely played. His brother **Nahan Franko** (1861 - 1930) was also a violinist of prominence, whose teachers included Wilhelmj and Joachim. As a boy of eight, he toured with Adelina Patti. In 1883, Nahan Franko became concertmaster of the Metropolitan Opera Orchestra, and in 1889, organized the Franko Symphony Orchestra, of which he was the conductor.

Leopold Lichtenberg (1861 - 1935), a native of San Francisco, studied with Wieniawski for three years after touring with him in the United States at the age of twelve. At fourteen he won first prize in Brussels, playing Vieuxtemps' Concerto No. 5, with Vieuxtemps a member of the jury. He edited many major violin works and was soloist with Theodore

David Mannes

Thomas and the New York Philharmonic. Detroit-born **Max Bendix** (1866 - ?) was concertmaster of the Germania and Thomas orchestras with which he often appeared as soloist. He also founded his well-known string quartet, in 1900.

David Mannes (1866 - 1959), born in New York, included Karl Halir (1859 - 1909) and Ysaÿe among his teachers. He was concertmaster of the New York Symphony under his brother-in-law Walter Damrosch, organized the "Music Settlement for Colored People," played many major sonata recitals with Clara, his pianist-wife, and in 1916 founded the prominent Mannes School of Music in New York. As a music educator, Mannes occupied a distinguished position in the development of American music.

St. Louis-born **Theodore Spiering** (1871 - 1925) studied with Joachim and Schradieck (1846 - 1918), making his debut in 1893 with the Thomas orchestra. He was also a member of the Chicago Symphony. For twelve years he toured widely as leader of the Spiering String Quartet, then, in 1905, he relocated in Berlin. In 1909 he accepted Gustave Mahler's invitation to become concertmaster of the New York Philharmonic. He gained renown as an editor of violin works for the Carl Fischer publishing firm.

During the dawning of native American violin art, women began to play an important role. **Armah Senkrah** (née Harkness 1864 - 1900), born in New York, pupil of Wieniawski, Vieuxtemps, Massart and Arno Hilf

(1858 - 1909), won first prize at the Paris Conservatoire and toured Europe and England. New York-born **Nettie Carpenter** (1865 - ?) also studied at the Paris Conservatoire and toured Europe and the United States after winning first prize. **Geraldine Morgan** (1868 - 1918), born in New York, worked with Leopold Damrosch, Schradieck and Joachim, and was the first American to win the coveted Mendelssohn prize in Germany. Her American debut in 1892 featured the premiere of the Bruch Concerto No. 3 with Walter Damrosch and the New York Symphony. Morgan also toured Europe and England and once performed the Bach Double Concerto with Joachim. **Olive Meade** (1874 - ?), born in Cambridge, Massachusetts, studied with Franz Kneisel (1865 - 1926). She appeared as soloist with the Boston Symphony in 1898, toured the United States, and formed her own concertizing string quartet. A Joachim pupil, Boston-born **Leonora Jackson** (1879 - ?) won the Mendelssohn prize in Germany, toured with Paderewski and Adelina Patti, was soloist with the Boston Symphony and appeared in more than 150 concerts in 1901. Jackson's reputation was second only to that of Maude Powell. She gave up concertizing after marrying a man named McKim, and ultimately left a fortune to the Library of Congress to establish the McKim Fund.

Except for three negligible vignettes by Lichtenberg, none of these American pioneer violinists left behind any commercially made recordings. Though all were respectable artists of their time, one cannot assert that any one of them was of topmost international caliber. American violin art was still in its infancy.

We now enter the era when it is no longer necessary to rely upon antiquated performance evaluations. The best of these may be reasonably accurate by the standards of their time but they lack that vast knowledge of violinistic and musical advances made during the twentieth century to which we have access today—thanks to the marvel of recordings.

Maude Powell (1868 - 1920) represented a sizable step forward. At the turn of the century she was the leading American violinist and the first violinist to record for the Victor Company. Powell's playing is an excellent example of a first-class violinist whose basic training was completed before 1890. Her teachers included William Lewis of Chicago, Schradieck and Joachim, but while having high praise for Lewis, she considered Charles Dancla (1818 - 1907) to be her most inspiring teacher. Her repertoire was large, and she introduced many works, both major and minor, to American audiences, including the Sibelius and Dvořák concerti. Her 71 recordings, apart from de Bériot's Concerto No. 7 with piano and single movements from sonatas by Bach and Leclair, are all of short numbers, since she died before the era of complete masterwork recordings. These recordings were made in the 1905 - 1919 period, but a rather dull-sounding Vieuxtemps *Ballade and Polonaise* possibly dates even earlier.

Maude Powell

Her playing, of course, sounds quite old-fashioned to modern ears. On the purely technical level, her discs reveal that she could handle the Sarasate pieces with assurance and considerable facility. Her intonation was clean and her bowing fluent. Her innate temperament and expressive phrasing would seem to indicate that had she been trained with modern expertise, she would have been a first-class player even today. She plays with drive, boldness and a keen sense for pacing.

In assessing a cross-section of these discs, we can note that Powell's tone is not voluminous. In the manner of her time, her vibrato (of slow to medium speed) is only partially developed and inconsistently applied. She used it more as a reflex emotional adjunct than as a consciously controlled element of a tonal range that, in her case, was rather limited. Yet her native talent often renders her playing surprisingly communicative. Her slides and position changes are frequently gauche, but her playing is quite well disciplined, if one allows for the romanticized standards of her age.

Powell also played many concerts as leader of her own string quartet (with three male colleagues), and her musical horizons were by no means narrow. She was constantly alert to those special difficulties confronting women artists, and could be outspoken on the subject without sacrificing awareness and pride in her own femininity.

The Grieg-Kreisler *To Spring* has purity of line, and is cannily paced and clean in intonation. Her vibrato fluctuates in intensity and the slides are "dated." Cadman's *Little Firefly* is bland in sound. Bruch's *Kol Nidrei*, however, has warm G string tone and much inner feeling. If some questionable slides and position changes were to be removed, it could be a viable modern performance.

Boisdeffre's *Serenata Champêtre*, an inconsequential genre piece with harp support, helps to display her nicely controlled trill. Ogarew's *Caprice* in A, in part a deft spiccato showpiece, reveals her impressive one-finger glissando, dryness of tone, and agile but not immaculate facility, while it builds to an exciting finish.

Elgar's ubiquitous *Salut d'amour* is delivered with charming sentiment. Moszkowski's *Serenata* shows neat attention to interpretive detail and warmth of sound, except for some rather lifeless doublestops, and is played with sober purpose. The Thomas-Sarasate *Gavotte* from *Mignon*, a weak transcription, exhibits dexterous bowing in the variations and is brightly styled. The de Bériot concerto is a dashing performance, one of her best, with biting articulation and ardent temperament.

The Massenet-Hubay *Crepuscule*, arranged for violin and harp by Powell and retitled *Twilight*, is a brief, forgettable bagatelle, as is the Sibelius-Powell *Musette*, in which the piano support is too loud for the violin. Franz Xavier Neruda's *Berceuse slave d'après un chant polonais* projects some vibrant sounds, but the piece is naive in conception and fails to live up to the promise of its florid title.

Sauret's *Will-O-The-Wisp*, a showpiece of medium difficulty with an uninspired melodic middle, is dry in tone and has many tasteless slides, but is admirably aggressive in style. The Schubert-Kreisler *Entracte III* from *Rosamunde* is nicely lyric, but strongly invites comparison between the yesteryear playing of Powell and the far more modern performance of Kreisler—to her considerable disadvantage.

Sarasate's *Spanish Dance* No. 8 recalls the dry tonal world of Kubelik, but Powell projects much more Iberian flair and shows adroit digital command. Raff's *Cavatina* has good G string tone and clean doublestops, and avoids oversentimentality, but is not consistent in vibrance. Leybach's *Nocturne*, an inferior piece with orchestral support, has unusually bad surface noise. Hubay's *Hejre Kati* is clean, conscientiously phrased and fervent in motivation.

Maude Powell's disc legacy offers a rare insight into the early era of recorded violin playing, and is invaluable to the connoisseur of violinistic lore and highly entertaining, too. At one time she toured as soloist with the famed Sousa band, playing Saint-Saëns' *Introduction and Rondo Capriccioso* twice a day for thirty weeks.

Her husband was H. Godfrey Turner, son of a famous English journalist. He became her manager and chauffeur, driving their Franklin car from town to town, concert to concert, in Gypsy fashion. Inevitably, this rigorous life ruined her health. Her doctor advised her to drink two quarts of milk a day, and when told this disagreed with her, he ordered an increase to three quarts. She complied, but collapsed during a recital and died before her fifty-third birthday.

During the first two decades of the twentieth century, the influx of émigrés from all parts of Europe, representing the many varied schools, immensely raised the stature of American violin art. It became less and less necessary for American-born players to travel abroad for top-level training. Eastern European violinists, most of them Jewish, fleeing czarist oppression and the rigors of the Russian revolution, played a leading role in the American leap forward. Foremost among them were the pupils of Leopold Auer (1845 - 1930), who, as the ranking professor at the St. Petersburg Conservatory in the capitol city, was in a position to procure as pupils all the stupendous Jewish talents from the Russian Pale of Settlement where the Jewish people were incarcerated. It is interesting to note that Auer had taught for many years, but it was not until he gained access to these pupils around the turn of the century that his reputation and production as a teacher became in any way exceptional. (See the Elman chapter of *Master Violinists in Performance*). And Heifetz, originally taught by his father and Ilya Malkin; Elman by Alexander Fidelman; Seidel by Max Fidelman; Zimbalist by his father; and Eddy Brown by Jeno Hubay, were all extraordinary violinists before coming to Auer for "finishing."

Meanwhile the title of greatest American-born violinist had passed from Powell to **Albert Spalding**, born in Chicago, who probably deserved that distinction until the rise of Menuhin. Spalding (1888 - 1953), a scion of the famous sporting goods family, enjoyed personal affluence. Most renowned violinists have come from families of moderate or impoverished economic circumstances. But Spalding's struggles to attain violinistic eminence and his unswerving artistic integrity were in no way less pronounced than those of his colleagues.

According to his written account, the Spalding family spent their winters abroad, and young Albert's first teacher was Ulpiano Chiti, in Florence. In fact, rumors persisted that Spalding was actually an Italian child adopted by the Spalding family, a claim the violinist never took the trouble to deny. Later, Spalding studied with Jean Buitrago in New Jersey and Narcisse-Augustin Lefort as a private pupil in Paris. Spalding did not study at the National Conservatoire in Paris. In 1903 he passed a rigorous examination at the Bologna Conservatory, accompanied at the piano by the then-unknown Ottorino Respighi, with a mark of 48 out of 50, a feat equalled only by Mozart at a similar age.

Albert Spalding in 1906   **Albert Spalding in 1927**

Spalding's Paris debut at sixteen included the Bach *Chaconne* and Saint-Saëns' Concerto No. 3 in B-minor. This was followed by concerts throughout Europe. In 1908 he made his New York debut with the New York Symphony under Walter Damrosch playing the Saint-Saëns concerto, a Spalding favorite. An older-generation violinist who was present told me of Spalding's extreme nervousness in a performance that was a near-disaster. Inexplicably, Spalding was free from that affliction after his service in the American army in World War I, during which he served as adjutant to Fiorello La Guardia who was to become mayor of New York. Greatly inspired and influenced by the art of Ysaÿe, Kreisler, Elman and Heifetz, Spalding continued to forge ahead, gradually building his own audience. Ultimately he recorded about 155 different works, large and small; his best date from the 1920s and 1930s, though a few, like Spohr's Concerto No. 8 (*Gesangsszene*) with Ormandy and the Philadelphia Orchestra, were recorded later. André Benoist was his piano collaborator in most of the shorter works. His compositions include two violin concerti, a violin-piano sonata, a solo violin sonata, a suite for violin and piano, the delightful *Etchings*, Op. 5 (first performed by Elman), and a number of short violin pieces, transcriptions, piano pieces, songs and an orchestral suite.

I heard Spalding on numerous occasions in his mature years and was invariably attracted by his person and impressed by the sincerity of purpose vested in his musicality. It was unfortunate that certain people misused Spalding's deserved reputation as the greatest "American" violinist to insinuate, snidely, that he was not Jewish. This continued long after Spalding had been surpassed by more than a few American-born players. A man of highest ethical principles, he numbered many Jewish artists among his close friends.

Spalding was the proverbial "gentleman and scholar." Onstage he possessed the appearance, poise and presence of a distinguished diplomat. He spoke in an educated, cultivated manner, and as a writer of considerable literary style, he wrote, in addition to his autobiography, an interesting, meticulously researched novel based on the life of Tartini, *A Fiddle, A Sword And A Lady*.

Spalding must be considered part of the "new wave" of violinists, even though his birth year predates that of quite a few widely known players whose antiquated training and musical horizons relegated them to an anachronistic category. Surprisingly, he did not study with any of the eminent "name" teachers, and represented no particular school, but he obviously had the intelligence to shape his playing along progressive lines. His vibrato was highly developed and extremely rapid, contributing to a tone of striking beauty. In music of linear construction and mood, such as the Beethoven and Mozart concerti and the old classical sonatas (*Devil's Trill*, etc.), the extraordinary clarity of his articulation combined with his compelling tone, produced playing of distinction. His trill was of "electric" speed. In general, Spalding's musical inclinations were an extension of his refined personality, and his interpretations were respectful of whatever musical idiom he performed.

Yet for all its tonal vitality, his playing had a decided element of reserve. In overtly romantic music his style could be stiff, inflexible and too tense. His aesthetic muse lacked innate sensuality, and his crystalline phrasing somehow precluded subtlety of nuance and diversity of color, thus imparting a somewhat one-dimensional cast to his art. His technique was not of spectacular virtuosity, but was entirely adequate to handle the exigencies of the masterworks.

Spalding's artistic generosity was uncommon. He wrote of the New York Symphony of 1920: "The orchestra itself was composed of virtuosi; many of the men in the string section, I reflected, could and should take over my (soloist) role." Here was a man to respect!

Spohr's *Gesangsszene* is easily his most impressive recording. The opus, uniquely conceived, is constructed to showcase the finest elements in Spalding's playing, and he responds with an honest, clean-cut performance that is both elegant and pellucid.

In a brief cross section of his discs of shorter works, we find Lily Boulanger's *Cortege* cleanly wrought but occasionally too tense. Suk's

Burleska is nimble, though not impeccable in intonation. Chopin's Waltz No. 10, a Spalding transcription, lacks both pliancy and poetic subtlety, and is strangely alien to his temperament. Spalding's own *Dragonfly*, a cleverly contrived unaccompanied technical study of arpeggios, is deft, neat and conscientious in delivery.

Cassado's *Danse du diable vert* is clean and agile, but has only moderate resilience. The Moszkowski-Sarasate *Guitarre* is much more modern in style and sound than the Vecsey disc version, and reveals some sparkling trills. Clarence Cameron White's setting of the spiritual *Nobody Knows the Trouble I've Seen*, exudes honest, deeply felt sentiment. The Mendelssohn-Achron *On Wings of Song* has fervent G string tone, tenseness on the E string, some galvanic trill-tremolos, and glints of imperfection in the doublestops.

The Schubert-Wilhelmj *Ave Maria* has rich G string sound and admirably vibrant octaves and doublestops, though occasionally one gets the feeling that Spalding is concerned more with execution than with the essence of the music. Sarasate's *Introduction and Tarantelle* (with a brief cut in the intro) is a dextrous, brilliant performance, among the very best of Spalding's recorded virtuoso-type stints.

Wagner's *Prize Song* suffers from too rapid vibrato, and a "stiffish" Chopin-Sarasate *Nocturne* in E-flat is about one-quarter of a tone flat in the basic engineered pitch. The Schumann-Wilhelmj *Abenlied*, sparse in tenderness, has some exciting trills. Schumann's *Traumerei* is one of Spalding's most satisfying vignettes, better balanced in sound production than most.

Albert Spalding may not have been a dangerous competitor to the likes of his colleagues Kreisler, Elman, Heifetz, Szigeti, and Francescatti and the young Menuhin, but he was an exceptional, multitalented man who, on his own terms, could always be relied upon to charm an audience with his violin and personality.

American-born violinists continued to make their mark. **Francis Macmillen,** born in 1885 in Marietta, Ohio, included Joachim, Thomson, Flesch and Auer among his teachers. Auer cites him as one of the best American pupils to study with him in Russia. Macmillen toured in Europe and the United States with a degree of success, and at one time was known for his short violin pieces and transcriptions. An assessment of his vignette recordings reveals him as a neat, conscienctious, small-scaled player, stylistically aware, but no more than a moderate talent.

Frederic Fradkin (1892 - 1963) born in Troy, New York, was taught by Schradieck, Rèmy and Ysaÿe, among others. He won first prize at the Paris Conservatoire in 1909, winning a splendid Caressa violin which he later willed to Joseph Gingold. Fradkin was concertmaster of many orchestras, both symphonic and commercial, among them Diaghilev's Russian Ballet in 1915 and the Boston Symphony (1918 - 1919). In 1911 he performed the Mendelssohn concerto with Mahler. He commanded much respect from professionals, and deservedly so. Some 75 vignette recordings exist, a few in consort with such noted singers as Elisabeth Rethberg and Mario Chamlee. In them his playing reflects the influence of the French and Belgian schools; his sound is smallish, sweet, and of medium vibrance; his delivery, quite polished.

Eddy Brown (1895 - 1974), born in Chicago, studied in Europe from an early age, was a prodigy who studied with Hubay (1858 - 1937), and performed the Beethoven concerto at the Budapest Royal Conservatory at age thirteen. Upon meeting Auer in London, he decided to return to Russia with him for further study. Brown ultimately was regarded as one of Auer's finest pupils and ranked among the first six or eight of these stellar violinists. Following successful recital tours in Europe, he made his American debut in 1915 with Walter Damrosch and the New York Symphony, playing the Beethoven concerto and later that same year performed the Tchaikovsky concerto with Josef Stransky and the New York Philharmonic.

It was Brown's misfortune to be one of that group of major players who were inundated by the Heifetz phenomenon. An outstanding technician in his prime, Brown was engaged for lucrative vaudeville appearances, performing such showpieces as Bazzini's *La ronde des lutins*. In 1933 he became musical director of radio station *WOR*, and with pianist Clarence Adler, was probably the first to perform the cycle of Beethoven sonatas on radio. He recorded some 65 pieces including the Mendelssohn and Tchaikovsky concerti, and in later years, when his powers had waned, the concerto by the American woman composer, Mana-Zucca (originally Zuckerman).

Brown's most impressive recording was undoubtedly the Tchaikovsky concerto with the Berlin Philharmonic, made in the mid-1920s, now a collector's item, which I have heard. It is a brilliant technical performance by any standards, somewhat small-scaled but warm in temperament. At its best, his tone is pleasantly vibrant, though not thoroughly consistent; at times one can sense Elman's influence in the projection of his lyric playing, but of course, without Elman's sumptuous timbre. His trill is extraordinary. Brown's musical personality and expressive powers are considerably less definitive than those of his fellow Auer pupils: Elman, Seidel, Heifetz and Poliakin, but he was undoubtedly one of the premier American-born violinists of the pre-1925 period.

Frank Gittelson (1896 - 197?), born in Philadelphia, was Flesch's student for three years. In *The Memoirs of Carl Flesch* (p. 275), Flesch states:

> Few Americans realize that (Gittelson) is the most talented violinist (not excepting Spalding) that America has so far produced, and that

Francis Macmillen   **Eddy Brown**

he was only prevented by a combination of adverse circumstances, by extreme bad luck, from taking the place he deserves in the musical life of America...Not only I but many others, among them Nikisch and Godowsky, regarded him as a possible successor to Ysaÿe. Forced by Walter Damrosch to play the Bach E-major Concerto, which was quite unsuitable for an American debut and which, to make matters worse, he did not know too well, he suffered a sensational failure which caused a grave depression, paralyzed his willpower, and for years gave him a distaste for the concert platform.

Later he became the head violin teacher at the Peabody Institute in Baltimore, and ultimately concertmaster of the American Ballet Theatre orchestra. In the late 1940s I had occasion to play in that orchestra during one of its Los Angeles sojourns. Gittelson, an enormously stout, bald unprepossessing figure, played the Tchaikovsky ballet solos with a voluminous, vibrant sound, a striking sense of style, and granite solidity. I cannot recall having heard them performed so beautifully. Gittelson left only about ten recordings, all vignettes. But even in these it is obvious that his gifts were bountiful.

John Corigliano (1901-1975), born in New York, was one of Auer's pupils in America. Succeeding Mischel Piastro in 1935, he served as concertmaster of the New York Philharmonic for thirty-one years and performed both staple and contemporary works as soloist with that organization. Corigliano's concerto stints, often broadcast nationally on radio, were always engaging and of admirable stature. His tone was extremely vibrant and penetrating, though at time slightly taut—not sensual in character, but coolly beautiful, somewhat reminiscent of Spalding's clean-cut sound. One can note Heifetz's influence in his subtle position changes. His listed recordings both as soloist and concertmaster number about 15 works, including Beethoven's *Triple Concerto* with Leonard Rose and Walter Hendel, Bruno Walter conducting; the *Scheherazade* solos and Vivaldi's *The Four Seasons* with Leonard Bernstein; and several more Vivaldi concerti with Guido Cantelli, all with his New York colleagues. Perhaps the most impressive of his records is the colorful sonata (1963) by his son John Jr., one of America's significant composers, with pianist Ralph Votapek. The work itself deserves much more exposure than it has received. The elder Corigliano performs it with brilliant articulation and bravura flair. He ranks among the more important twentieth-century American concertmasters.

Benno Rabinof (originally Rabinowitz, 1908 - 1975), was the archetypal poor Jewish boy in New York's Lower East Side in an era when Elman's magical tone inspired Russian-born parents to make every economic sacrifice to rear their sons in his image. His early teachers included Kneisel and Victor Kuzdo, and it is said that in later life he studied briefly with Thibaud and Enesco. It was Auer, however, already seventy-three, newly emigrated from Russia, who became his teacher around 1919, and taught him for a period of nine years. In his playing, Rabinof represented the continuation in America of Auer's most brilliant pupils from Russia, perhaps more so than any of the numerous violin hopefuls who flocked to the Auer banner after his American arrival. Auer conducted the nineteen-year-old Rabinof's 1927 Carnegie Hall debut in the Tchaikovsky and Elgar concerti, with a sixty-member orchestra chosen from the New York Philharmonic. But like so many others in the Heifetz shadow, Rabinof was unable to generate a top-level career, despite encouraging reviews. In the early 1930s he played a 28-week concert cycle of nationwide radio broadcasts with Alfred Wallenstein conducting. I recall being thoroughly impressed by these broadcasts.

Rabinof was a fervent admirer of Heifetz, though his own sound and temperament more resembled that of Seidel. His tone, dominated by a rapid fingertip reflex vibrato rather than by the slower wrist and arm vibratos currently in vogue, was sumptuous and intensely virile in the tradition of Kreisler, Elman, Heifetz and Seidel. And he thoroughly understood and employed the expressive devices in position changes of both Heifetz and Kreisler with good taste. Technically he could handle any genre of music in the staple repertoire with ease. In the hierarchy of ear-titillating violinists, Rabinof ranks among the elite. However, it was essentially instinctual, spontaneous, visceral playing. His violinistic personality was strong but not as overpowering as those of the already entrenched superstars. His bad luck was to have reached his prime around

John Corigliano

Benno Rabinof
and his pianist-wife, Sylvia

the onset of the Great Depression, with its deflated box office returns, plus the established competition. And as was the case with Seidel, there was no more room at the top for another violinist of his genre. Rabinof concertized successfully with his pianist-wife, the former Sylvia Smith, in sonata recitals, often performing the complete Beethoven sonata cycle. In 1955 they commissioned a Double Concerto from Boleslav Martinu, that they played with Ormandy and the Philadelphia Orchestra.

He continued to develop his musicianship through the years, but it was the violin-oriented works of ardent lyricism and virtuosity that best suited his gifts, rather than works demanding intellectual profundity. Only a dozen compositions on phonograph recordings represent his available legacy most of which are on the Decca release, *Gypsy Violin Classics*. The best of his volcanic, supremely romanticized art is illuminated in Sarasate's *Introduction and Tarantelle* and *Zigeunerweisen*, Kreisler's *La Gitana* and *Gypsy Caprice*, Brahms's *Hungarian Dance*, No. 20, the Kreisler arrangements of Dvořák's *Slavonic Dance*, No. 1, Albeniz' *Tango*, Granados' *Spanish Dance*, No. 5 and the de Falla-Kochanski *Jota*. The listener who can come into possession of this disc is in for a treat of beguiling aural splendor and colorful stylizing.

Rabinof died unexpectedly of a heart attack shortly before he was to have played a concert in North Carolina.

KNEISEL AND HIS PUPILS

Franz Kneisel (1865 - 1926), born in Bucharest of German parents, was destined to play an important role in the coming-of-age of American violin art. A pupil of Grün and Hellmesberger at the Vienna Conservatory, he possessed a violinistic aura typical of the vibrato-poor, dry-sounding nineteenth-century playing of middle Europe, as exemplified by Joachim. But while his tone would probably sound dull and dry to modern ears, Kneisel was a master musician who possessed a comprehensive knowledge of musical architecture, aesthetics and stylistic probity. After his arrival in America in 1885, it was no longer necessary for American-born pupils to travel abroad for instruction in high-minded, intelligent musicianship.

At seventeen Kneisel performed the arduous Joachim *Hungarian Concerto*, and at nineteen became concertmaster of the Bilse Orchestra (later the Berlin Philharmonic), a chair once occupied by Ysaÿe. Upon emigrating to America, he was appointed concertmaster of the Boston Symphony and made his debut in the Beethoven concerto. He held this position until 1903. However, it was as a chamber music player and teacher that Kneisel was most successful. The Kneisel Quartet helped to popularize and win acceptance for chamber music throughout the United States. They played the American premieres of quartets by Brahms and Dvořák, and on their programs gave special emphasis to the late Beethoven quartets. As a forward-looking musician, Kneisel championed such "modern" works as the Debussy quartet when many colleagues still considered it hopelessly avant-garde.

As was to be expected, the group adhered to the late nineteenth-century, cool, often "whiteish" tone of the old German school, and as far as he could, Kneisel influenced his quartet colleagues to play in this vein. Yet their musical standards were unusually high for their time. The quartet performed until 1917. Such Kneisel pupils as Sascha Jacobsen, Jacques Gordon and William Kroll eventually became leaders of prestigious string quartets.

As a teacher, Kneisel was a typically Prussian, tyrannical disciplinarian. On the one hand he molded a number of exceptionally talented pupils, who were originally raw and uncultivated, into fine musicians at the Institute of Musical Art in New York. But he also broke the spirits and crippled the playing of certain gifted pupils who were too sensitive to resist those of his demands that produced negative results. More than a few left Kneisel and went abroad to study with Auer, Flesch or Ševčik. His own son and daughter, Frank and Marianne, were never more than mediocre violinists. The best of Kneisel's students were Jewish, and their hot-blooded musicality and vibrant tonal production (which they had

Franz Kneisel String Quartet: Franz Kneisel, first violinist, Hans Letz, second violinist, Louis Svecenski, viola, Willem Willeke, cello.

acquired before they came to Kneisel) were an anathema to his unaffectionate methodology and latent anti-Semitism. Yet somehow this teacher-pupil dichotomy was productive, and Kneisel merits recognition as a significant pedagogue of his era.

At least eight of Kneisel's pupils made their mark upon the American Scene and deserve mention. **Samuel Gardner** (1892 - 1982), born in Russia, came to America as a child and, before becoming Kneisel's pupil, studied with the violinist-composer Charles Martin Loeffler and Felix Winternitz. His teacher in composition was Percy Goetchius at the Institute of Musical Art. In 1918 his String Quartet in D-minor won a Pulitzer Prize, and his Symphonic Poem for Orchestra was awarded the Loeb Prize. However, as a composer Gardner is best known for a catchy syncopated trifle, *From the Canebrake*, a fillip of Americana which has continued to delight young violinists for more than six decades. During the 1924 - 1925 season he was soloist in the Mendelssohn concerto with the New York Philharmonic under Mengelberg, and shortly after in a concerto of his own. Gardner's recording output lists about a dozen vignettes which reveal his playing as well ordered, sensitive and free of exaggerated expressive devices. His tone and musical ethos register a bit cool but are quite congenial. He devoted many decades to teaching, and was a venerable figure in the New York violin world.

Elias Breeskin (1895 - 1969), born in Russia, possessed a discriminating musicianship and controlled temperament that made him a Kneisel favorite. Unfortunately, as one of the most freewheeling personalities among American violinists he became well-known to his colleagues for his practice of borrowing instruments and money that were seldom returned. Married to a wealthy woman and much sought-after for lucrative jobs as concertmaster, he nevertheless found himself constantly in embarrassing predicaments owing to his compulsive gambling. As a result he moved from city to city, ultimately landing in Hollywood in the 1940s. His introductory recital in Los Angeles, crowned by a scintillating technical display in the Saint-Saëns-Ysaÿe *Caprice in the Form of a Waltz*, ensured a huge success, even in this ferociously competitive jungle. But again his peccadillos destroyed the goodwill that his playing had created. He retreated to Mexico, where he succeeded in escaping the Mexican version of Devil's Island by the skin of his teeth. In 1950 I found him playing salon music as a strolling musician in a Mexico City restaurant. His performance had begun to deteriorate, but the remnants of his formidable equipment and disciplined musicianship were still impressive. His recordings, numbering 13 vignettes, are marked by a purity of tone and style somewhat recalling Zimbalist; the sound is only moderately vibrant, although the scope of his playing is large-scaled. In his final years he returned to the United States, but by this time his performance was no more than a hollow shell of his prime. Had Breeskin been more stable, he might have enjoyed a sustained career as a top concertmaster and soloist, and as a conductor of respectable ability.

Sascha Jacobsen, born in 1895 of Russian-Jewish parents in what is now called Helsinki, arrived in America at age eleven. Considered a star pupil of Kneisel (though Flesch refers to him as "a former pupil"), he won the 1915 Loeb prize at the Institute of Musical Art in New York, and made a successful debut later that year. But Jacobsen, for all his superior ability, became yet another casualty of the 1917 Heifetz phenomenon. As a soloist he was not quite equal to the best of the Auer pupils, who were tremendously in vogue at the time. At Kneisel's death in 1926, he suceeded him as a teacher at the Institute and then formed the Musical Art Quartet with violinist Paul Bernard, violist Louis Kaufman (later renowned as a violinist) and cellist Marie Roemat-Rosanoff. The quartet performed for nearly twenty years, though there were a few changes in the second violin and viola positions. Around 1945 the group disbanded and Jacobsen resigned his teaching post at Juilliard, moved west, and became concertmaster of the Los Angeles Philharmonic in 1946. Jacobsen's exceedingly warm, meticulously controlled if smallish sound was superbly suited for quartet playing, and in the areas of subtlety and stylistic grace, he merits ranking with the finest quartet violinists. He received wide publicity when, as a result of a driving mishap in which he nearly drowned, his "Red Diamond" Strad was lost in the Pacific Ocean. As luck would have it, someone found the badly soaked, practically ruined instument and returned it to the violinist. Thanks to an incredible job of restoration by violin maker Hans Weisshaar, the violin was saved. Jacobsen left recordings of over 50 works, the most important of which is Saint-Saëns' *Introduction and Rondo Capriccioso*. They indicate basic talent of a high order; his tone is consistently vibrant, and he employs expressive devices with invariably good taste.

Michael Gusikoff (1895 - 1978), born in New York City, was among the most intrinsically talented of the Kneisel pupils. Like Gardner, he studied composition with Percy Goetchius, but the acme of his works is the *The American Concerto* (cowritten with Benjamin Machan), an entertaining potpourri of quasi-jazz lyricism and lightly syncopated rhythms in the popular mood of the 1920s and 1930s. Gusikoff made his debut in 1920, subsequently becoming the concertmaster of the St. Louis Symphony, The old New York Symphony, and concertmaster of the Philadelphia Orchestra under Stokowski. He also held the same position with the NBC Orchestra and was for a time associate conductor of the Pittsburgh Symphony. Gusikoff's recording legacy consists of about seven bits of trivia, such as *I'll See You Home Again Kathleen*, the type of piece demanded of important violinists for mass consumption in the days of ten- and twelve-inch acoustical discs. Nevertheless, these performances reveal Gusikoff as possessing a beautiful, intensely vibrant sound of first-class timbre in the tradition of the Auer tonalists. He had the courage to dress up the simple themes with doublestops of more than average difficulty, in sharp contrast to the way many of his competitors treated vignettes of this type. However, one cannot say that he exhibits exalted aesthetic motivation in his playing.

Jacques Gordon (1899 - 1948), born in Odessa, studied there with Franz Stupka at the Imperial Conservatory, and at age thirteen was already a prize-winning pupil. Emigrating to America, he continued his studies with Kneisel at the Institute of Musical Art. He became a member of the Berkshire Quartet in 1917, a post he held for three years. In 1921 Gordon was selected by conductor Frederick Stock to be concertmaster of the Chicago Symphony, where he remained for nine years. As a soloist it is said that he was the first to perform Respighi's *Concerto Gregoriano* in America. Also in 1921 he formed the noted Gordon String Quartet whose members at one time included violinist Henry Sellinger, violist Clarence Evans and cellist Naum Benditsky.

Once as a publicity stunt Gordon, dressed as an itinerant fiddler, performed on a street corner with his 1732 Stradivarius (claimed to have been played by Paganini, Spohr and Joachim) to prove that passersby

Jacques Gordon

Joseph Fuchs

would toss money into a hat for good violin playing as readily as for any other kind of fiddling. He substantiated his point and received newspaper publicity throughout the country.

Gordon was conductor of the Hartford, Connecticut Works Progress Administration (WPA) Symphony from 1936 to 1939, and in 1942 became head of the violin department at the Eastman School in Rochester, in conjunction with his quartet duties. Following a stroke in 1947, he resigned from the quartet, and he died in 1948 of a cerebral hemorrhage after a musical soirée at the home of Albert Spalding, at which Kreisler had been present. Gordon's recordings were few, but a disc of his quartet in several light music arrangements show him as a player of extraordinary polish and sophistication, with a suave, pure, somewhat small tone ideally suited to quartet playing.

Joseph Fuchs (b. 1901), born in New York, was the eldest of five children. His sister Lillian became a noted violist, and brother Harry was at one time first cellist of the Cleveland Orchestra. Fuchs began study at an early age with Kneisel at the Institute of Musical Art, made his debut in 1920, toured for a time in Europe and became concertmaster of the Cleveland Orchestra in 1929. In 1941 he resigned this post to pursue a solo career. He became director of the New York Musicians Guild, a group dedicated to chamber music, often joining musical forces with his sister Lillian, and he toured abroad extensively. In 1960 he commissioned the Walter Piston concerto (through the Ford Foundation), and gave first performances of concerti by Nikolai Lopatnikoff and Ben Weber. Boleslav Martinu dedicated his *Madrigals* to the Fuchs brother-sister duo. Obviously an outspoken person of strong convictions, Fuchs once appeared on a nationwide television special in the role of pedagogue. Evincing neither prudence nor artistic humility, he unrealistically predicted that his pupil, Christine Edinger, who played a portion of the Brahms concerto not very impressively, would defeat Pinchas Zukerman and Kyung-Wa Chung in a forthcoming competition. She did not, of course (but has since achieved a measure of success as a soloist in contemporary and avant-garde compositions). Fuchs is a formidable virtuoso with considerable temperament. His instrument is the 1722 "Cadiz" Stradivarius.

The Fuchs recordings number about 65 compositions, including the Beethoven sonata cycle, sonatas by Debussy, Fauré, Copland, Piston, Franck, Grieg, Schubert and Strauss, the Stravinsky *Duo Concertante* and the Hindemith and Mozart (No. 3 in G) concerti. These disc performances match closely his live playing that I have heard. Fuch's musical approach is one of consistent drive and tremendous energy, and his articulation is invariably powerful. His tone, brilliant if somewhat hard-edged and muscular, is dominated by a very fast vibrato that often reflects tenseness rather than intensity, and is limited in variety. In general his playing projects visceral force and fervor, while lacking a sense of poetry, particularly in the sonatas of Franck, Fauré and Debussy. His playing seldom smiles. Nor does tenderness, elegance or affection play a prominent role in his music-making. All of the above-mentioned qualities and faults can be readily noted in his performances of the Hindemith concerto, live and recorded. Yet, rather surprisingly, he produces more than a few stylistic subtleties in Grieg's Sonata No. 3 with the splendid piano collaboration of Frank Sheridan. Though Fuch's prowess as an instrumentalist exceeds his impact as an artistic personality, he merits ranking with the finest concertmaster-soloist America has produced. Now in his mid-eighties, he still plays with admirable command.

William Kroll (1901 - 1980) was born in New York and studied at the Berlin Hochschule as a youngster with Henri Marteau, from 1911 to 1914. After returning to New York in 1915 he became Kneisel's pupil at the Institute of Musical Art where he also studied composition with Goetschius. Kroll's playing was ideally scaled for chamber music. He served as leader of the Elshuco Trio, 1922 - 1929, Coolidge Quartet, 1936 - 1944 and the Kroll Quartet, 1944 - 1969. In 1942 he received the Coolidge medal at the Library of Congress. He held teaching posts at the Institute of Musical Art (1922 - 1938) and the Mannes College of Music as well as at the Berkshire Tanglewood Festival, the Peabody Conservatory, the Cleveland Institute and Queen's College. Kroll played a Guadagnini violin until 1950, then came into possession of the 1709 Strad once owned by Ernst.

Like Gardner, his fellow Kneisel pupil, Kroll as composer is best known for a violinistic trifle, the showpiece *Banjo and Fiddle*, popularized by Heifetz and at one time widely played. As a violinist Kroll was greatly influenced by Kreisler. His playing, meticulous though at times a bit overrefined, was not without glints of temperament. His sweet clear, comparatively small tone, never dominated his colleagues, and the chamber music performances he led were always marked by the suppleness, fluency and polish of his playing.

In terms of violinistic posterity, **Louis Kaufman** (b. 1905), born in Portland, Oregon, may well turn out to be foremost among Kneisel's pupil by virtue of some 125 recorded works, most of them major, plus featured solos in hundreds of film scores. Among the latter are such immortals as *Gone With the Wind, Modern Times* and *The Diary of Anne Frank*. He studied in Portland with Albert Kreitz, Frank Eichenlaub and Henry Bettmann, and at thirteen he went to New York to study with Kneisel. After six months of preparation with Hugo Kortshak, he entered the Kneisel class, where he had two half-hour lessons a week plus the privilege of hearing the lessons of other students, an opportunity he seized eagerly. Kaufman recalled, "Kneisel never told me what works to play. I selected my own music and brought it to him for instruction" (*Strad* magazine, June 1983). Tired of playing second violin to the older pupils in quartet playing, he took up the viola, "though," he states, "at the conclusion of

William Kroll

Louis Kaufman

the quartet session I immediately stashed my viola case under the bed and spent all my time with the violin.''.

Word soon circulated that Kaufman was a fine quartet violist, and eventually he was called upon to play privately on numerous occasions with such stars as Kreisler, Elman, Casals and Zimbalist. "The musical understanding and discipline I received from Kneisel were vital to my education, but my opportunity to learn from the great masters with whom I played quartets significantly influenced my artistic development."

In 1927 Kaufman won the Loeb prize at the Institute of Musical Art and, in 1928, the prestigious Naumberg Award, both on violin. He accepted the post of violist in the Musical Art Quartet, a position he held until 1933. Meanwhile, he acquired Zimbalist's Guadagnini. In 1932 he married pianist Annette Leibole, a pupil of David Saperton, and they collaborated in sonatas. Deciding to seek a major career as a violinist, Kaufman resigned from the quartet. They traveled west, ultimately settling in Los Angeles, where they were soon playing three recitals a week on radio. Heard by film director Ernst Lubitsch, he was engaged to record the violin solos for *The Merry Widow*. Before long he was sought after by all the Hollywood studios.

Kaufman had a rare gift in the commercial realm for endowing a prosaic four-bar phrase with compelling beauty and in lyric solo segments he had few serious rivals. But he never forgot his principal goal, and after fourteen lucrative years made the fateful decision to desert the Hollywood "fleshpots" and to seek recognition in the jungle of the international concert world. Even while fully committed to film work, he had produced successful recordings of the Saint-Saëns No. 3 and Khachaturian concerti, the Smetana trio with pianist Rudolf Firkusny and the Ernst Toch Quintet with the composer at the piano.

Kaufman's first post-Hollywood recording, Vivaldi's *Four Seasons* with conductor Henry Svoboda and members of the New York Philharmonic, was awarded the French Grand Prix du Disque. He has given premiere performances of concerti by Boleslav Martinu (Concerto de Camera), Anthony Collins, Lars-Eric Larsson, Henri Sauguet, Dag Wirén and Leighton Lucas, plus performances of major works by Milhaud, Poulenc, Copland and Robert Russell Bennett. Many of the above grace his list of recordings, together with concerti of Chausson, Vaughan Williams and Giuseppe Torelli. More than a few violin authorities place Kaufman's discs of the Barber, Saint-Saëns, Mendelssohn, Khachaturian and Chausson concerti among the finest recorded versions of these works.

After eight years of touring and recording (with Paris as their base), the Kaufmans returned to their home in Los Angeles. In his mid-seventies, following a detached retina operation, he decide to retire. "I didn't want to decay in public," he remarked wisely.

While Kaufman is a thoroughly well-rounded, disciplined musician, the dominant characteristic of his playing is a bewitching vibrant tone. His impulse-type vibrato is exceedingly fast, and is applied in all compositions from "portal-to portal." Thus, as a hyperromantic artist, the character of his sound is naturally more suited to romanticism than to classic or baroque music, although he has gained much critical acclaim for his classic and baroque interpretations. His style incorporates many of the artful slides and position changes introduced by Kreisler (particularly those involving string crossings), as well as emotive position changes recalling those of Heifetz.

Among those outstanding violinists who have endeavored to recreate Kreisler's sound and style, Kaufman, with his entrancing fast vibrato and versatile emulation of many Kreisler's expressive finger devices, can be counted among the few most convincing. In support of this contention, a comparison of Kaufman's recordings of *Londonderry Air* and *Hymn to the Sun* with those of any other violinist save Kreisler himself, is recommended. And in short confections of popular and jazz-tinted Americana widely performed in the 1930s and 1940s, and even later, Kaufman's stunning sound, sophisticated style and rhythmic verve are of the highest order.

With his comparatively small hands, Kaufman did not specialize in the more gymnastic areas of the repertoire, but had a solid, secure technique which readily conquered the many difficulties and hazards posed by the contemporary compositions of his era. His playing, unusually consistent in quality, can scarcely fail to captivate the ear, and he deserves ranking among the top American-born violinists.

THE COMMERCIAL PHENOMENON

The role of the violin purely as a vehicle of entertainment in dance halls, salons, theatres, restaurants and even bordellos, is one of long standing. In their youth, such luminaries as Ysaÿe, Kreisler, Casals, Thibaud and, of course, the Strausses in Vienna, to mention but a few, played in one or another of these institutions to earn a living. The quality of so-called commercial playing has ranged from the sleaziest pseudo-gypsy shmeerings to stylish vignette performances, in many instances reflecting polished artistry even in music of admitted banality. As the twentieth century progressed, the historic development of the American musical theatre and light opera, and the tremendous proliferation of various types of Tin Pan Alley popular music and jazz, drove many exceptional violinists to the comparatively lucrative theatre pits and movie house orchestras. As phonograph recordings, radio and talking pictures attracted vast audiences, commercial playing escalated to a new, more sophisticated level, demanding violinists capable of playing into an all-revealing microphone with genuine éclat. Film moguls, who invested huge sums to produce movies of quality, insisted on the finest orchestras money could buy. Excellent musicians from the Eastern theatre pits, as well as graduates of the leading American conservatories, flocked to Hollywood to reap the potential bonanza. Others quit comparatively low-paying jobs in symphony orchestras and rushed to the new Klondike. This influx has continued for over sixty years and now includes violinists born in Israel, Japan, the USSR, England, Hungary and other countries. New York, and to a lesser degree, Chicago, are also among the major centers of American commercial recording.

Before Vitaphone, (the first sound track used for the first talking pictures), until 1927, any musician of reasonable skill had his choice of jobs, and the better players might combine a noontime restaurant stint with the theatre pit and a radio show in a single day and night. But talking pictures obliterated movie house orchestras, and the Great Depression found violinists, more than a few of soloist caliber, competing desperately for theatre pit work. (Eugene Ormandy, fresh from study with Hubay at the Budapest Conservatory, was unable to attain a solo career and started as assistant concertmaster to Fradkin at the Capitol Theatre in New York). It is no exaggeration to state that the overwhelming majority of American-born and naturalized violinists, including many with international reputations as soloists, pedagogues, chamber music players and symphony concertmasters, have worked (paid by the hour) at one time or other in the commercial field. Many gifted violinists have found themselves stranded in the commercial field for life, well paid but all too often artistically impoverished.

The key element in lucrative commercial playing of solo caliber is unabashed ear titillation. Vibrant beauty of sound, stylish and emotive phrasing and, of course, an exceptional ability to read any and all types of music with accuracy and rapidity are vital requisites. The vibrato-poor alumni of middle-European academicism that descended from the Joachim precepts and Ševčik-schooled technicians, were soon vanquished by the lush-toned players of the Russian and, to a lesser extent, Belgian schools. This coincided with the situation that (particularly since the advent of recordings after the turn of the century) existed in the concert hall at that time.

The supreme commercial violinists in terms of direct mass appeal were Kreisler and Heifetz, and the ravishing charm and elegance of their vignette playing became the model for commercial violinists. A drab-toned "gymnast" who spent eight hours a day mastering Paganini's finger-twisters was almost certain to be surpassed by the violinist with a beautiful vibrant sound. In earlier years it was possible for dry-toned players to "hide" in the violin section that had a concertmaster with a golden tone, but as the decades passed this became less prevalent unless a

Lou Raderman

colorless player had political job connections having nothing to do with the quality of his performance. Often violinists of comprehensive musical background and intelligence lost out to players of limited training who possessed instinctive expressive gifts and a songful tone. Thus, through the years, and still today, many a violinist who has earned his livelihood in the commercial field is not a commercial violinist in the truest sense of the term, but a well-schooled player displaced from the classical field. Some of the finest commercial violinists belong to the latter category.

Like gifted college athletes from poor families who leave school before graduation in order to enter lucrative professional sports, many violinists in similar circumstances, particularly those of the 1920s and 1930s, curtailed their music studies to earn big money in the commercial field. One could easily compile a lengthy roster of such players who achieved exceptional earnings by virtue of their naturally beautiful sound and expressive talents.

Selections are always debatable, but having worked for more than four decades with the best in the field, if I were to pick the archetypal commercial violinist who was *not* an economic refugee from the classical ranks, it would be **Lou Raderman** (1902 - 1979).

Born in New York, Lou Raderman began playing the violin at the relatively late age of nine. At twelve he was already earning money playing for dance schools. His formal training was meager, but he did mention having had some lessons with Theodore Spiering and Maximilian Pilzer. At fifteen he was a member of the Russian Symphony in New York, and soon after began recording for RCA-Victor with such stars as Caruso, McCormack, Galli-Curci and others. When Nathaniel Shilkret was engaged as conductor for that company, Raderman became his concertmaster. Meanwhile, he held the same position for many nationally broadcast radio shows. In 1938 Shilkret left for Hollywood, and upon becoming music director at MGM studios, monarch of the film scene, he brought Raderman to the West Coast as his concertmaster, a position the violinist held for thirty-five years. Raderman, a guileless, winsome personality, was one of the most natural violinists I have ever heard, equally at home in the frothy strains of *Over the Rainbow* or the tensely dramatic solos in *The Four Horsemen of the Apocalypse*. His vibrato was not much over medium speed, but he employed it with rare sensitivity, and his rhythmic instincts, which permitted him to "bend" a phrase to delectable effect without distorting its essence, recalled those of Kreisler's. Violinists with infinitely more impressive academic credentials held Raderman in enormous respect. The overwhelming majority of them, recognizing his unusual gifts, did not resent sitting behind him in the section. His solos can be heard in most of the vintage MGM films, and record collectors fortunate to possess one of the four or five vignette confections he left, will quickly note the Kreislerian lilt of his artistry.

Specialty groups in the commercial field include jazz's "hot fiddlers," gypsy-type violinists, and bluegrass and country-western fiddlers. The obstreperous Joe Venuti (1903 - 1978) was the undisputed king of hot fiddlers for decades, a position later vied for by the Frenchman Stephane Grappelli (b. 1908) and the Swede Sven Asmussen. The black violinist Eddie South (1904 - 1962), who concocted provocative jazz versions of such pieces as Kreisler's *Praeludium and Allegro*, and the more elemental Stuff Smith (1909 - 1965), together with Ray Nance, Benny Gill and the Curtis Institute graduates Paul Nero and Florian Zabach, deserve mention. Among the more well-known gypsy players in America were the remarkable classically trained Nicolas Matthey and Bela Bobai. Prominent in the country hierarchy are Chubby Wise, an originator of bluegrass fiddling in the 1940s; Scott Stoneman, who imbued bluegrass playing with classical intensity;Richard Greene,a current contributor to bluegrass with western swing; Dale Potter, inventor of doublestop devices in western swing; Tommy Jackson, a slick country commercial fiddler; Johnny Gimble, a top player of western swing style, and Benny Martin, creator of sundry novel effects and intervals in bluegrass on an eight-string fiddle.

At present many of the most talented pupils from around the world come to the United States for advanced training and coaching, thus

To the Schuberts —
San Francisco's fine fiddle doctors —
from a grateful patient!
Louis Persinger —
1947.

Louis Persinger

reversing the former trend of Americans flocking to European pedagogues for instruction and status. **Louis Persinger** (1887 - 1966) born in Rochester, Illinois, was certainly not the first American-born teacher of quality, but he was the first to garner international renown through his leading pupils, Menuhin and Ricci. Other outstanding violinists such as Guila Bustabo, Joseph Knitzer, Miriam Solovieff, Camilla Wicks, Berl Senofsky, Fredell Lack and Zvi Zeitlin numbered him among their teachers. At twelve he was taken to Leipzig and there was graduated with honors from the old Royal Conservatory at age sixteen, winning praise from the famed conductor Arthur Nikisch. But it was his consequent study with Ysaÿe for several years in Brussels, and the summers of coaching with Thibaud, that indelibly stamped Persinger as an exponent of the Belgian and French schools. He made his American debut in 1912 with Stokowski and the Philadelphia Orchestra. In 1914 Nikisch invited him to be concertmaster of the Berlin Philharmonic, but the war exigencies convinced him to return home, and in 1915 he became concertmaster of the San Francisco Symphony. After several years, he decided he had had enough of symphony life and formed a string quartet, which quickly gained recognition and respect. From 1916 to 1928 he was director of the Chamber Music Society of San Francisco and began private teaching. In the wake of the Menuhin phenomenon, Persinger was appointed to the Juilliard faculty in 1930, replacing the deceased Leopold Auer, and remained there for thirty-six years as a violin pedagogue and chamber music coach. He was also an excellent pianist, and collaborated with his star pupils in concerts and recordings.

As a teacher, Persinger emphasized the musical and spiritual elements in performance. He was not one to prescribe backbreaking academic toil as a way of life for his students, holding that an hour and a half of practice at one time was sufficient for maximal results. His was a rare gift for inspiring his students. But in the case of Menuhin, his failure to demand uncompromising technical discipline, in favor of accomplishments on the purely musical and communicative levels, undoubtedly was a significant factor in the serious technical problems later incurred by Menuhin.

However, Persinger possessed unusual musical sensitivity and imagination. His violinistic philosophy, as exemplified in his fascinating 64-page booklet, *Why the Violin?*, in which he briefly touches upon an amazing number of technical and musical points, indicates a searching, inquisitive mind and a willingness to challenge rigid orthodoxy. The material in the treatise ranges from a discussion of the "singing" nature of the violin to the frequency of rosining the bow. The ideas and presentation of his booklet also suggest that profound, hair-splitting analysis was not his forte. But he could be a wonderful, liberating influence upon tense, inhibited students who had been "manhandled" by professional martinets. He encouraged individuality in his pupils; thus, there is no palpable Persinger stamp in their performance.

In my youth I once heard Persinger's quartet and was impressed by the sweetness of his tone and by his affectionate lyrical musicality. All he left behind were a few duet recordings and a lecture illustration of the Mendelssohn concerto that reveal similar propensities. As a performer, Persinger ranked among the best American concertmaster-level violinists of his era. Who, among those present at the time, can ever forget the obvious love and solicitation with which he tuned their violins and presided as a bastion of support at the piano for the young Menuhin and Ricci?

SOME NOTEWORTHY NATURALIZED AMERICANS

Paul Kochanski (1887 - 1934) died prematurely at only forty-seven. It is sad that an artist of his exceptional gifts, who concertized as late as 1934, has left so small a heritage of recordings. This scion of an orthodox Jewish family (his surname at birth was Kaganoff) was born in Orel, Russia, but he is generally included in the hierarchy of great Polish violinists (Lipinski, Wieniawski, Huberman, Szeryng, et al.) inasmuch as his residence, early training and first important successes were in Warsaw. Following his initial training with his father, Kochanski studied with Emil Mlynarski, himself a pupil of Auer. Considered a prodigy, Kochanski was the first soloist with the newly founded Warsaw Philharmonic at age

Paul Kochanski

thirteen. Two years later he went to Brussels, where he continued his studies with César Thomson, ultimately winning first prize at the Conservatoire with the highest distinction. Indeed, Kochanski's playing, as evinced in his recordings, is a marvelous blend of the Russian school (emerging into international prominence), sparked by Auer, and the older, grandly romantic Belgian school, as epitomized by Ysaÿe. In 1915, he succeeded Auer as professor at the St. Petersburg Conservatory, and in the mid-1920s became a professor of violin at Juilliard.

In his maturity, Kochanski was greatly respected as a brilliant conversationalist and a musician of sophisticated, cosmopolitan tastes and interests—all of which is mirrored in his playing. He had an active interest in music contemporary to his time, and was an ardent champion and performer of the violin music of his friend Karol Szymanowski, as well as works of Stravinsky and others.

Kochanski left only eleven commercially circulated recordings, one a major work, the others vignettes, They reveal him as an artist who would equate (except, perhaps, for an occasional dated slide) with standards of today. Though he was older than Heifetz or Elman, his playing, among other fine attributes, reflects the new revolutionary singing propensities of the violin that ultimately rendered the old dry, vibrato-poor playing anachronistic. Whereas the playing of Vecsey, born in 1893, and Přihoda, born in 1900, for all their digital feats, could in no way compete in quality of tone and sophistication of style with first-class (not to mention elite) modern artists, the playing of Kochanski, born earlier, would be highly respected. One need only take the time to compare Vecsey's Beethoven Sonata No. 3 disc and the non-bravura pieces played by Přihoda with Kochanski's Brahms Sonata No. 3 in order to substantiate the above statement.

Unfortunately, the few Kochanski discs cannot prove conclusively whether or not he was a large-scaled player capable of giving "heavy-weight" top-level performances of such masterworks as the Beethoven, Brahms and Tchaikovsky concerti. We must therefore be satisfied with the evidence of his recordings unless we wish to rely on the contradictory reports of indivduals who heard the violinist in his prime.

No matter what he plays, Kochanski enchants the ear at all times. In addition, he combines an exceptional, intuitive talent for expressive phrasing with a suave, musical intelligence that rarely transcends the bounds of admirable discipline. It is the discipline of romanticism rather than academicism. Needless to say, his vibrato is highly developed, capable of varied speeds and colors, and his bow arm is ever fluent, as is his entire musicality. His intonation is pure and his technique facile, though it is almost always used in the service of musical cognition, rather than virtuoso display. On occasion, the very propulsion of his melodic outpourings will result in a sort of breathless transition from one phrase to the next, but this idiosyncrasy is not of serious consequence. His art radiates sensitivity, and he is always a provocative stylist. One can note an affinity between Kochanski and Elman in certain position changes, but the Kochanski tone is less opulent and his musical personality not as strikingly personalized as is Elman's.

Kochanski's Brahms Sonata No. 3 disc enjoys the piano collaboration of Artur Rubinstein, who plays with uninhibited, romantic gusto. The opening *Allegro* is sensually lyric, the pace brisk, the violin-piano rapport superbly integrated as befits two artists who have performed together countless times and know each other's heartbeat. On a few occasions the piano overpowers a bit, but the cause could be in the original engineering. One can note a few slides that hearken back to the Belgian manner of the turn of the century. The G string sound of the *Adagio* is exquisitely sweet, the trills fast, the doublestops vibrant—an exceptionally fluid reading. The *Poco presto e con sentimento* is carefully honed to chamber music disposition, relaxed and finely etched. The *Presto agitato* finale is alternately songful and incisive, indicating Kochanski's knowledge of the art of musical diversity. In all, the interpretation is passionate, eloquent and poetic.

The Wagner-Wilhelmj *Prize Song* is ardently vibrant, the high E string passages extraordinarily so. One can note vividly Kochanski's relationship to both the Russian and Belgian schools. The Rachmaninoff-Gutheil *Vocalise*, containing a few more slides than most of Kochanski's short pieces, muses dreamily and beautifully. Kreisler's *La Gitana* bears the composer's influence in the playing, but is in no way imitative, and is delightfully piquant. Sarasate's *Malaguena* is almost lascivious in sound and languorous in mood; a few brief cuts are made; the G string themes are equally impassioned. The disc's only technical tour de force is Wieniawski's *La Carnaval Russe*, a tricky theme and variation work. Kochanski makes much of what is essentially musical trivia, instilling it with a flavor that is unmistakably Russian; the left-hand finger pizzicatos are swift and clean; the harmonics pure, the trill-tremolos exceedingly rapid. It is not a Heifetz technique, but is still admirable. Frank Tresselt is the conscientious piano collaborator.

Kochanski's brother Joseph, an excellent pianist, collaborates in Tchaikovsky's *Melodie* and the salon style *Chant sans paroles*. Both recall Elman. The tempi move along brightly; all is sweet but never mawkish. Pierne's *Serenade* is elevated far above its intrinsic value and invested with a silvery sheen. The Raff *Cavatina* cannot rival Elman's G string sound, yet is exceptional, with superbly clean and vibrant doublestops. The Brahms-Joachim *Hungarian Dance* No. 1 is dashing in style; the trill-tremolos, electric. Several of the phrases are strung together without adequate "breath." The approach is quite individual.

There can be no doubt that with the death of Paul Kochanski, the world lost a violinist of redoubtable qualities. His discs are an invaluable testament to an artist every violin fancier should know and esteem.

Efrem Zimbalist (1889 - 1985) was born in Rostov-on-Don, Russia. His father, a violinist and conductor at the Rostov Opera, was his first teacher. Around 1904 he was taken to St. Petersburg by his mother. Like other budding violinists of Jewish lineage, he required special permission from the czarist authorites for his parent to remain in the city—in this instance, for a single week. This was obtained through the efforts of Leopold Auer. Following preparatory work with Auer's assistant, Nalbandyan, at the St. Petersburg Conservatory, the boy was admitted to Auer's class in 1907. Biographers generally point out that Zimbalist was a "red-shirt" leader of the conservatory student strike during the abortive 1905 revolution. However, his intimate association with extremely wealthy society figures dating from shortly after his arrival in America, would indicate that Zimbalist was a realist in terms of advancing his career. Upon graduation, he won the conservatory's Gold Medal and the 1,200 ruble Rubinstein Prize. On November, 1907, he made a successful Berlin debut with the Philharmonic in the Brahms concerto and a month later, his London debut. He also studied for a short period with Ševčik.

Arriving in the United States in 1911, Zimbalist made his American

Efrem Zimbalist

debut with Max Fiedler and the Boston Symphony in the relatively new Glazunov concerto. His introduction to the American music scene is related by Samuel Chotzinoff, his early piano collaborator (later brother-in-law of Heifetz, and a New York music critic), in his nostalgic auto-biography *Days at the Morn*. Surprisingly Chotzinoff's evaluation of Zimbalist's playing is neither unbiased nor knowledgeable. In 1914 the violinist married the noted soprano Alma Gluck, a divorcee and mother of the writer Marcia Davenport. Zimbalist, an accomplished pianist, often served as accompanist for his wife. The couple had two children, Maria and Efrem Jr., the well-known actor. Gluck died in 1938. In 1943 Zimbalist married Mrs. Mary Louise Curtis Bok, a benefactor of the Curtis Institute of Music, daughter of the Philadelphia publisher, Cyrus Curtis .

Zimbalist performed on and off until 1955, when he played the Bee-thoven concerto with the Philadelphia Orchestra. While his solo career was of longer duration than that of many other victims of the Heifetz phenomenon, it ultimately slackened. He continued to play many concerts throughout the 1920s and 1930s, after which the frequency of his public performances abated. In 1928 he became a faculty member at the Curtis Institute and from 1941 to 1968 held the post of director. Many American violinists of stature count Zimbalist among their teachers, including Oscar Shumsky, Shmuel Ashkenasi, Joseph Silverstein and Norman Carol.

There can be no doubt that Zimbalist was one of the most sophisticated and intelligent violinists of his era. His overall career as a musician was long and honorable. He moved in the highest social circles and was the intimate of the music world's greatest figures. His ability to perform successfully such masterworks as the Beethoven and Brahms concerti placed him in a more exalted category than many highly gifted, tonally oriented violinists whose musicianship and essential artistry were comparatively limited. As late as 1954, Zimbalist gave the premiere performance of Gian Carlo Menotti's violin concerto. During his later years he retired to the Reno, Nevada area.

In his autobiography, *Memoirs of Carl Flesch* (p. 225) Flesch states:

> I must confess that (Zimbalist) interested me the least of the best Auer pupils...His playing offered no evidence of a significant personality...I regard it as an injustice of fate that (Toscha Seidel) is not considered the third in a triumvirate with Heifetz and Elman.

This was a direct slur against Zimbalist, who was invariably cited as the third. Flesch also complains about the slowness of Zimbalist's vibrato, a problem he well understood since he was plagued with a similar shortcoming. One might consider Flesch's appraisal to be prejudiced, since his relations with the Curtis Institute were strained during the period before his resignation from the faculty. He makes a point of writing that "the eighty-four-year-old Auer and Efrem Zimbalist, *who had never before taught the instrument,* (author's italics) became my successors." Flesch also rather uncharitably states of the elderly Auer's private lesson in America, "The chief condition of admission for a prospective pupil consisted in his ability to pay 360 dollars for six lessons." Alas, it was all too true. (At the time Kneisel, the premier teacher in America, was receiving 20 dollars for a private lesson, one-third of the outlandish Auer fee. But Kneisel was not the reputed teacher of Elman and Heifetz.) However, regardless of Flesch's disposition, the many occasions on which I heard Zimbalist in person and on recordings generally support Flesch's evaluation.

I particularly recall a Zimbalist recital during the early 1930s. About three hundred people were in attendance on a Sunday afternoon in the 3,500-seat Philharmonic Auditorium, a hall invariably filled by Kreisler, Heifetz and the boy Menuhin. Zimbalist, a thoroughly poised, imperturbable figure, never one to be afflicted by nervousness, began with Bach's E-major concerto, which he delivered with bland accuracy. He then proceeded to play Bruch's *Scottish Fantasy*, all with piano support. It was then that I understood why Zimbalist, for all his polished artistry, could not sustain a solo career in competition with the top artists of the day. His playing was practically devoid of emotional projection, though he was well skilled in expressive finger devices. He would, for example, make a long Heifetz slide on the G string, and one could almost count the oscillations of his vibrato on the pallid landing note. Everything seemed on the surface of the instrument, and his vibrato was not only inherently slow and undistinguished, but ineffective in terms of producing warm-hearted sentiment, temperamental fire, sensuality of sound or dramatic tension. Yet there were elements of his playing that one could admire greatly, such as his ability to sustain the "long bow" in lyrical phrases. The recital continued with several Zimbalist favorites: amazingly fleet, cogently phrased, crystalline renditions of the Popper-Auer *Spinning Song* (originally for cello), Hubay's *Le Zephyr*, the Glinka-Auer *The Lark*, the Chopin-Spalding *Waltz in G-flat*, No. 11 and Sarasate's *Carmen Fantasy*, in which the technical passages were of stellar brilliance and almost birdlike clarity. Interspersed were cool, glassy-toned performances of Glinka's *Persian Song* and a little Japanese trifle titled, I believe, *Kukura-Kukura*, both Zimbalist settings.

Zimbalist recorded about 89 different compositions, the most significant of which are Brahms's Sonata No. 3, Op. 108, Ysaÿe's Solo Sonata No. 1 and two movements of Hubay's Concerto No. 3. All closely mirror the impression of his live playing. He also tried his hand at composition, the most significant of his output being his Sonata in G-minor, which can be heard in a highly capable recorded performance by his one-time pupil Philip Frank, and pianist Bernard Frank. It is a congenial work containing many glints of Zimbalist's Russian past, liberally sprinkled with clever violinistic effects. Unfortunately, it also has an unrelieved meandering quality that may be one of the reasons it has never become a repertorial staple of his celebrated colleague-friends. Irrespective of how one assesses Zimbalist as a soloist, his influence on American violin art was considerable, and his overall contribution was of major stature.

In the same age group was **Naoum Blinder** (1889 - 1965), born in Eupatoria, Russia, a pupil of Alexander Fidelman in Odessa and of Adolf Brodsky in Manchester. His early years included a post on the Moscow Conservatory faculty (1923 - 1925), and numerous solo appearances throughout the USSR and Japan. Coming to America in the late 1920s, he became concertmaster of the San Francisco Symphony in 1932. Grossly underpublicized nationally, he was Stern's teacher from 1932 to 1937. The single time I heard Blinder, he impressed me as a major talent with outstanding technical equipment, broad expressive powers, a richly intense sound and tasteful musicality. Had he been with one of the major East Coast organizations, undoubtedly his career would have attained greater scope. He left only ten recordings of short pieces.

Among the leading pupils of Auer who were unable to sustain top-level

Naoum Blinder

Mischel Piastro

solo careers were several who became concertmasters of major symphony orchestras. In the vanguard of these was **Mischel Piastro** (1891 - 1970), born in Kerch, Russia. He was generally included as one of the best six or seven of the pupils Auer taught in St. Petersburg. His violinist father, who had once been an Auer pupil, was his first teacher. His older brother, Josef Piastro-Borissoff, also a pupil of Auer, was prominent as a splendid technician and teacher, though his tone was less vibrantly beautiful than that of the younger violinist. Mischel studied with Auer for about four years, starting in 1906, and in 1911 won the 1,000 ruble Auer prize. Together with Elman and Zimbalist, he was one of three military-age Jewish violinists exempted from military service by the czar.

In 1914 he began a tour eastward to the Orient, and ultimately arrived in San Francisco in 1920, where he became concertmaster of the San Francisco Symphony from 1925 - 1931. Engaged by Toscanini to become concertmaster of the New York Philharmonic, he enjoyed a brilliant career, winning nationwide renown through his annual broadcasts as soloist with the orchestra, performing most of the major concerti from Brahms to Miaskovsky. Piastro's broadcasts were eagerly awaited by young violinists of the era, including myself. During John Barbirolli's leadership of the orchestra (1941 - 1943), he became assistant conductor, but was later victim of a purge of first-chair players by the new leader, Artur Rodzinski. Piastro, while still concertmaster, had already been serving since 1941 as conductor and violin soloist of the highly respected Longine Symphonette which performed for many years on radio and recordings.

Flesch says of Piastro: "Instrumentally, he is of Heifetz's class, while his personal aura is, of course, far weaker." The latter part of the statement is true, but Piastro, although a brilliant violinist of exceptional polish with a sweetly vibrant tone of medium intensity and disciplined musicianship, was certainly no competitor of Heifetz, instrumentally. His playing was smaller-scaled, but be had the true instinct of a soloist, as opposed to quite a few solid, highly regarded concertmasters who do not. His left hand expressive devices bore Elman's influence. This can be heard in the more demanding works among the 19 recorded pieces he left, such as Wieniawski's *Faust Fantasy*, *Le Carnaval Russe* and *Souvenir de Moscou*, all made early in his career. Piastro's style possessed the heroic thrust and breadth of the best Auer pupils. Undoubtedly had he been able to concentrate purely on solo playing, his artistry would have been considerably enhanced. (The same holds true for so many brilliant concertmasters of the 1920s, 1930s and 1940s, and for that matter, today.)

I once had the opportunity to spend about three hours privately with Piastro, reminiscing about his early days with Auer. Since he could be counted among the best tonal pupils of Auer, I asked about Auer's

Richard Burgin

teaching of vibrato and tone production. Why, I wondered, in view of Auer's eminence as a teacher, did the vibratos of his pupils range from the one extreme of Elman, Seidel and Heifetz to the other of Zimbalist, Achron and Borissoff? He replied that Auer would discuss *usage* of the vibrato, but not its development and manner of production. Either the pupil already had a viable vibrato before coming to Auer, or he did not. Auer's lessons, he stressed, offered no clinical instruction about vibrato. And like Milstein, he stated that the most fruitful moments of his association with Auer were during the twice-weekly master classes in which he was inspired by watching and listening to the other extraordinary talents.

Other Auer pupils of note were **Richard Burgin** (1892 - 1981), born in Warsaw, who was concertmaster of the Boston Symphony from 1920 to 1967, and **Alexander Hilsberg** (1897 - 1961), born in Russia, who was concertmaster of the Philadelphia Orchestra for some two decades. Burgin had also studied with Lotto and Joachim, and after four years with Auer he won the Gold prize at the St. Petersburg Conservatory in 1912. After concertmaster stints in Helsinki and Oslo, he came to the United States in 1923, and in 1927 combined his concertmaster duties with those of assistant conductor under Koussevitzky. He married violinist Ruth Posselt in 1940. Hilsberg, who studied with Auer for only about a year, also became addicted to the baton, and ended his musical career successfully as

Mischa Mischakoff String Quartet

a conductor of the New Orleans Symphony, a position he accepted in 1952. Both Burgin and Hilsberg were superb section leaders, but not in Piastro's category as soloists.

A powerful member of this company was **Mischa Mischakoff** (Fischberg), (1895 - 1981), born in Proskouroff, Russia, son of a flutist. He studied with Korguyeff, himself an Auer pupil, at the Imperial Conservatory in St. Petersburg, receiving the Rubinstein prize of 1,200 rubles in 1913. Arriving in America in 1921, he was successively concertmaster of the New York Symphony (not the Philharmonic), the Philadelphia Orchestra and the Chicago Symphony. His stature can be judged by the fact that Toscanini selected him from a large number of the finest available candidates to be concertmaster of his "all-star" NBC Symphony in 1937. Mischakoff also appeared often as soloist; his 14 recordings, capped by the Brahms Double Concerto with cellist Frank Miller (Toscanini, NBC Symphony), are mostly single movements from concerto staples. I heard him many times on radio as soloist and in orchestral solo excerpts. His performance was impeccable, his tone warm and solid, his rhythmic stability unshakeable. It was neither highly personalized nor particularly imaginative playing, but he was certainly one of the finest concertmasters of his era. He continued his concertmaster assignments well into his seventies with the Detroit Symphony.

The career of **Samuel Dushkin** (1895? - 1967) is proof positive that a violinist need not be a heaven-storming virtuoso, a member of an elite quartet or trio, or a brilliant concertmaster-soloist to make a valuable contribution to his art. Essentially a pupil of Rèmy in Paris, he also had some lessons with Auer in New York. Dushkin commissioned the Stravinsky Violin Concerto in 1931, in which he collaborated with the composer in matters of violinistic detail. From that time on the two were intimately associated, and Dushkin played an important role in the creation of the *Divertimento, Duo Concertante,* and *Suite Italienne.* He also fashioned arrangements of short pieces from selected Stravinsky works. The two performed together in Europe and America, popularizing Stravinsky's music at a time when much of it was considered avant-garde and sensationalist. In music other than the novel Stravinsky compositions, Dushkin's playing might be described as no more than capable and efficient. This is borne out by his recordings. Wisely, he opted for contemporary works that did not place him in direct competition with the elite among his colleagues. In addition to Stravinsky, he performed works by Martinu, Victor Rieti, Virgil Thomson, William Schuman and Gershwin, and he is said to have been the first to introduce Ravel's *Tzigane* to America. His 13 recordings are mostly pieces by Stravinsky, with the latter at the piano, and his recording of the concerto (with Stravinsky, Lamoureaux Orchestra) was the first of many since recorded. Dushkin was a pioneer whose efforts merit respect and emulation by enterprising violinists, who may or may not be fortunate enough to find new violin works by composers who understand the instrument and are able to exploit its lyric propensities with some degree of talent and inspiration.

Had Heifetz not come along, **Toscha Seidel** might well have joined Kreisler and Elman in the topmost echelon in terms of mass public acceptance during the late teens and 1920s. Born in Odessa (1900 - 1962), Seidel was yet another prodigy from that incubator of violinists. He started lessons with Max Fidelmann, an Auer pupil, and at age twelve began study with Auer himself in St. Petersburg. At fourteen he shared programs with Heifetz (one year his junior), both of them winning resounding success. Seidel was dubbed "the devil of the violin"; Heifetz, "the angel." His major debut in 1915 was in Olso playing the Tchaikovsky concerto, followed by his St. Petersburg debut a year later. After numerous European concerts, he made his Carnegie Hall debut in 1918, a year after Heifetz, again with great critical acclaim.

One of the most instinctive and exciting violin talents ever to draw a bow, Seidel possessed a thrilling tone that was sumptuous and voluptuous, motivated by one of those "meaty," impulse-type vibratos, and abetted by a sonorous Russian-style bow arm. It can be safely asserted that

Toscha Seidel

Left to right: Max Rosen, Jascha Heifetz, Leopold Auer, Toscha Seidel

among presently concertizing violinists there is no violin tone to compare with Seidel's in sheer impassioned sensuality. His fiery, extravagant romanticism, dominated by a rare, completely personalized, readily recognizable tonal timbre, was vastly different from the pellucid clarity of the far more disciplined, seraphic Heifetz muse. Professionals who were familiar with his live performances still rhapsodize about the "Seidel sound." Like his sound, his musical approach and interpretations were tinged with an ingenuous gypsy spirit and rhythmic liberties recalling Elman, but even more exorbitant in overt emotive thrust. Although his playing was of massive scale, he could also charm the listener in short pieces. Seidel's emotive slides and position changes were occasionally overused, but generally in good taste and devastating in effect. He did not specialize in Paganinian gymnastics, although his technical equipment was comprehensive and fluent. However, pure intonaton, marvelous singing doublestops, a brilliant trill and a fine staccato were cardinal elements of his playing.

Why, then, after his triumphant early years did Seidel's career fail to sustain itself on the highest level. True, he might be considered yet another victim of the Heifetz phenomenon. But others such as Menuhin, Szigeti, Milstein, Francescatti, and later Stern, built careers while Heifetz was still in his prime. Seidel had the advantage of a start as early as 1918, an advantage not enjoyed by many important talents who reached maturity during the Great Depression. The downturn in Seidel's career can be attributed to two main factors. First, for all the aural beauty of his playing, Seidel could not be considered a profound, perceptive, all-encompassing musician in an era in which these qualities were becoming increasingly in demand by critics and the concert-going public. As an incorrigible romantic, musical introspection was alien to his nature, intellect and temperament. His tone and musicality were too singular for the impersonal glories of the Bach sonatas, or even to an extent for the music of Beethoven, though his brawny Brahms concerto was impressive, as were his Tchaikovsky, Bruch, Lalo and Mendelssohn concerti. Historically, by the mid-1930s, freewheeling violinists like Elman were gradually becoming anachronistic at the topmost level. Second, unlike the worldly wise Zimbalist who was utterly at ease in any cosmopolitan company, Seidel was a somewhat naive, unsophisticated personality, who was most at home with the violin under his chin. I knew him very well after he had been relegated to the Hollywood milieu in the late 1930s, in which he was totally miscast and not really comfortable. During this period he played considerable chamber music, which broadened his musicianship, but his playing was far too individualistic for a concertmaster "section-leader" in commercial orchestral work. However, many of his film score solo excerpts are memorable. His mental powers retrogressing through illness, this one-time prodigy of the violin ended his career playing in a Las Vegas show orchestra.

Around 1930, while still in his prime, Seidel performed a weekly series of CBS nationwide radio broadcasts featuring a different concerto each week. Unfortunately, the transcriptions have not been preserved. Thus we cannot hear his finest large-scale work, though he did record the Brahms Sonatas No. 1, Op. 78 and No. 2, Op. 100, and Grieg's Sonata No. 3 with pianist Arthur Loesser. These were recorded during the 1930s, when he no longer performed regularly on the concert stage. In them his playing is artistically inconsistent. Thanks to James Creighton's Discopaedia Records, 17 of the short pieces among the 57 Seidel recordings have been restored. The early Columbia discs have much more surface noise than their Victor counterparts, but the dedicated listener can scarely fail to be delighted by such extraordinary playing. Among them the Rimsky-Korsakoff *Chanson Arabe* is saturated with lush tone. *Eili-Eili*, a Seidel setting, is heartfelt and freely intoned. Hubay's *Hejre Kati* is a Romany delight. Burleigh's *Indian Snake Dance*, a piece tritely imitative of Kreisler, is forgettable. Kreisler's *Caprice Viennois* is ultrarhapsodic, but perhaps the most tonally impressive performance, along with Elman's, after that of Kreisler. The Paderewski-Kreisler *Minuet*, once ubiquitous, is gleamingly beautiful and demonstrates Seidel's excellent digital and bowing flexibility.

Some later noiseless Victors are Saint-Saëns' *Prelude to the Deluge* and the Wagner-Wilhelmj *Albumblatt*, both broadly conceived, overtly extroverted and voluminous in sound. *Brahmsiana*, a banal vaudevillean paraphrase of *Hungarian Dances* No. 4 and No. 5 by V. Bakaleinikoff, and the Brahms-Joachim Hungarian Dance No. 1 have gut-shattering G string sound, though the latter contains some notes almost too intense for the violin to project tastefully. The Mozart-Burmester *Minuet* from *Divertimento* No. 17 is rather muscular, ornate in sound and resonantly buoyant in the flying staccato bowings.

And, of course, there is his lengendary, gorgeous performance of Provost's *Intermezzo* from a film recording which, for an extended period, popularized the violin with millions of listeners.

Little-known to modern audiences and the younger generations of players, Seidel was one of the elite violin talents of the twentieth century, an artist who, irrespective of certain musical shortcomings, has much to offer violin fanciers who revel in playing of spontaneity and inner warmth, exquisitely virile sound and grand-manner perspective. At his best, Seidel deserves inclusion, after Heifetz and Elman, in the leading triumvirate of Auer's Russian pupils.

Raoul Vidas

Raoul Vidas (1901 - 1978) was born in Rumania (of Jewish parentage, according to the noted American critic James Huneker), but was considered a French violinist since he came to Paris at age eight. After initial lessons with his father, he studied privately with the blind Henri Berthelier, who was a professor at the Paris Conservatoire. Vidas enjoyed a brilliant career as a child prodigy and was tremendously acclaimed in France. He made a successful New York debut in 1918, and once when Heifetz fell ill Vidas was recruited as his substitute. As an artist and representative of the French School, Vidas stood somewhere between Thibaud and Francescatti. His playing was influenced by Ysaÿe, Kreisler and Thibaud. The few recordings he made reveal him as a stylist of decided elegance. Like so many fine violinists who had the misfortune to be born in the Heifetz generation, Vidas, a person of gentle spirit, hampered by a serious injury to his right thumb, retired after a comparatively short adult career. When his injury healed, he tried to make a comeback in New York around 1938, including in his program (of all things!) a violin transcription of the Grieg piano concerto. He soon retired permanently, living alone with his mother in Los Angeles and devoting all his waking hours to composition. However, when he played privately on occasion, he performed with the sweep, sound and authority of an important Romantic violinist. Among his compositions were his tribute to Americana, violin-piano transcriptions of numerous Stephen Foster songs, and many complex contemporary works that were rarely performed. An affable man who loved to "talk violin," he seemed quite content to exchange the rigors of the concert and commercial worlds for his self-imposed isolation. Vidas willed his beautiful Guadagnini violin and exquisite Tourte bow to the Paris Conservatoire.

Moving ahead chronologically among foreign-born Americans, we veer to the opposite extreme of the violinistic and musical spectrum with **Louis Krasner** (b. 1903), born in Cherkassy, Russia. Brought to America by his parents at age five, he began lessons in Providence, Rhode Island, and graduated from Boston's New England Conservatory in 1922. Subsequently, he studied in Europe with Flesch, Capet and Ševčik. Like Dushkin, Krasner gained renown through his association with leading contemporary composers, and in 1934 he commissioned Alban Berg to write his violin concerto, which he premiered April 19, 1936 in Barcelona, shortly after Berg's death. Krasner continued to introduce the hyperromantic work elsewhere, and succeeded in winning converts to its cause in New York and Boston.

At that time, the concerto was considered by some to be hopelessly avant-garde, but today, like Prokofiev's Concerto No. 1 and the Stravinsky concerto, it is in the repertoire of nearly every concertizing artist, including several from the USSR where twelve-toned music was once an anathema. He also premiered in 1928 Joseph Achron's concerto in Vienna and Alfredo Casella's concerto in Siena and Rome, neither of which has won acceptance into the standard repertoire. The Achron (which I heard played by the composer), is an interesting worthwhile work, unfortunately neglected. Krasner then accepted the supreme challenge of being the first to perform Schoenberg's violin concerto in 1940 with Stokowski and the Philadelphia Orchestra. Several violinists have since performed and recorded the work which at once reveals the limitations of the violin by consistently abusing its intrinsic nature as the instrument closest to the human voice. One can understand the thrill of accomplishment experienced by those violinists who have scaled the heights of cacophony and applaud their Herculean labors. But after nearly half a century, a performance of the Schoenberg concerto, no matter how brilliant, remains a sensationalist feat, appealing only to a limited audience. Krasner, concertmaster of the Minneapolis Symphony in the 1940s, plays with a dry tone production that hearkens back to the Ševčik pupils, but his playing style is aggressive, and he surmounts the massive Schoenberg obstacles with courage, accuracy and poise. His handful of recordings include the Berg (Rodzinski, Cleveland Orchestra) and the Schoenberg (Mitropoulos, New York Philharmonic). And whether one does or does not like these concerti, violin art like any other needs its pioneers, and in this area, Krasner has made an important contribution.

Born in 1906 in Greenock Scotland, where his father served as cantor for the local Jewish congregation, **Henri Temianka** has enjoyed an exceptionally diverse musical career. Both parents had come from Poland, but Henri spent most of his childhood in Holland. He studied with Carel Blitz for eight years in Rotterdam and later with Willy Hess in Berlin, Jules Boucherit in Paris (whom he credits with "doing wonders for my bow arm") and ultimately with Carl Flesch at the Curtis Institute and at Baden-Baden. In 1935, while residing in London, he became a last-minute entry in Poland's politicized Wieniawski contest, and was awarded third prize after Ginette Neveu and David Oistrakh. Subsequently he served as concertmaster of the Scottish Orchestra under George Szell and from 1941 to 1942, with Fritz Reiner and the Pittsburgh Symphony. After World War II he became first violinist of the Paganini String Quartet, whose members performed on Stradivarius instruments once belonging to Paganini. After two decades and many personnel changes, the quartet disbanded in 1966. The immensely enterprising Temianka founded the California Symphony in 1960, a group that, despite an amazing number of personnel changes through the years, prospered and won deserved respect in the Los Angeles area under his leadership, which was honed in the strict Szell-Reiner image. A number of the world's greatest artists: Oistrakh, Menuhin, Stern and Szeryng, among others, performed with the ensemble. Temianka premiered works of such contemporary composers as Shostakovich, Ginestera, Milhaud, Menotti, Copland, Chavez, Arnold, Krenek, William Schuman and Castelnuovo-Tedesco. His pupil, Nina Bodner, won first prize in the 1982 Thibaud Competition, and Camilla Wicks and Leo Berlin number among his former students.

Temianka is an extremely articulate man, and his many writings include the witty, semi-autobiographical *Facing the Music*. As a remarkably knowledgeable public speaker on musical subjects he has few peers. And he is a tough-minded musician who has publicly stood up to newspaper critics and survived their often scurrilous attacks.

Temianka is an unusually consistent violinist and a stylist of uncommon stature. In the many times I have heard him in concert, whether in Mozart, Mendelssohn or Chausson concerti, or Beethoven sonatas, his tone is invariably sweet, his technique facile and his delivery polished.

His recordings number about 40, fifteen of which are Handel sonatas with harpsichord. Among the best of his 1935 - 1937 recordings are Pugnani's Sonata in E-major, Op. 1, No. 6 and Schubert's Rondo in A-major (the latter with chamber orchestra). One might pinpoint some anachronistic expressive slides (which are not to be heard in his postwar playing), but these works, so difficult to perform convincingly, are rendered with exceptional purity of line and sound. Other pieces are a ridiculously fast performance of Wieniawski's *Scherzo Tarantelle*, in which the inherent pulse of the music is mostly lost, and a neatly phrased version of the Polonaise Brillante in A-major with much verve and crackling staccatos. The post-1960 Handel sonatas, with Malcolm Hamilton, display chaste classical grace, and the post-1970 three Grieg sonatas with the late pianist, James Field, though evincing a noticeable slackening of his vibrato, are sensitive and admirably romantic. Temianka's career has been kaleidoscopic; he must be counted as one of Flesch's important pupils, and his contribution to the American music scene has been considerable.

Without doubt, the most unorthodox, individualistic, independent violinist among the significant soloists of this era has been **Tossy Spivakovsky**, born in Odessa in 1907. At a very early age, he was taken to Berlin, where he studied with Arrigo Serato and later with the domineering Willy Hess. However, Spivakovsky was exclusively "his own man" as an artist, uninfluenced by any specific school or colleague. At ten he made his debut, and at eighteen became one of the concertmasters of the Berlin Philharmonic for several seasons, then resigned to concentrate on solo playing. When the Nazis came to power he left Germany for Australia, and eventually identified himself with the musical life of that area. From 1933 to 1940 he taught at the University Conservatorium of Melbourne. In 1941 he moved to America, and from 1942 - 1945 was concertmaster of the Cleveland Orchestra.

Spivakovsky appeared often as soloist with the orchestra, and in 1943 scored a sensational triumph in Bartók's Concerto No. 2 with Rodzinski and the New York Philharmonic, which was nationally broadcast. I vividly recall the occasion. The Bartók ideally showcased the best elements of Spivakovsky's playing. For the moment it seemed as if he belonged to the elite few among international stars. This success was the catalyst that enabled him, within two years, to retire from orchestral playing and pursue a solo career.

Shortly after, in the Tchaikovsky concerto, it was obvious that while he was a brilliant virtuoso, his playing was not quite of superstar stature. I heard him in many live concerts, both in concerti with orchestra and in recitals. The results in the standard repertoire were generally uneven. In a single work he was capable of interpretive logic, discipline, superficiality, stunning virtuosity and ill-conceived musicality, particularly in such works as the Beethoven and Mozart concerti. Yet it must be said that his performances of the Beethoven sonatas were well ordered and respectful of the composer.

Spivakovsky might well be thought of as the alchemist of the violin—an indefatigable experimenter. His choice of bowings, and to a lesser extent, of fingerings, were different from those of any other violinist. It was a disturbing experience for professional violinists to view him in action because his bowings were so utterly divergent from the various traditional modes. However, these seeming aberrations worked beautifully for him. His bow grip was unusual, held a bit above the frog. This rendered his bowing exceptionally smooth, supple and powerful, but limited in variety of textures. In the Bach solo sonatas he used a curved bow in the slow movements. It was both impressive and disquieting to hear sonorous three-note chords played unbrokenly in the baroque manner, and in the same work, vibrato employment that at times was patently romantic. His facility was tremendous in both hands. His playing of Sarasate's *Carmen Fantasy* and *Introduction and Tarantelle* compared favorably with anyone's, except Heifetz's in dazzling speed and clarity. But when not at his best, intonation problems would creep in. Spivakovsky's vibrato was exceedingly fast, and coupled with certain somewhat peculiar, sensuous slides that he used, it gave to his sound a glittery gypsy cast that recalled salon playing, but, of course, on an infinitely higher level. In contemporary music such as the concerti of Roger Sessions, Leroy Robertson, Gian Carlo Menotti, Leon Kirchner, Bartók and Stravinsky, these idiosyncrasies did not vitiate his interpretations seriously. Indeed, his performances in these works were of extraordinary caliber. In the romantic repertoire and technical pieces his playing, though ever intensely expressive, was more convincing in shorter episodes that did not require a full range of color, nuance and modal scale. And apart from his Bach, which was always interesting whether or not one agreed with his approach, classical compositions were not really in consonance with his sound and fervent temperament. All this can be verified by his 53 recorded works.

Spivakovsky was a violinist whose playing was never less than provocative, interesting and entertaining, and in top form he was a superlative instrumentalist.

Prominent among the hierarchy of post-Huberman Polish-Jewish violinists, among them, Paul Kochanski, Stefan Frenkel, Henri Temianka, Bronislav Gimpel, Roman Totenberg, Ida Haendel, the tragic Joseph Hassid, and the formidable Henryk Szeryng, is **Szymon Goldberg**, born in Wloclawek, Poland in 1909. He began study in Warsaw at age seven with Czaplinski, and later with Mihalowicz; at ten he became Flesch's pupil in Berlin. Following a Warsaw debut at age twelve, he made a Berlin debut with Flesch's blessing at only fifteen in a program of three concerti, Bach's E-major, Paganini's No. 1 and Joachim's arduous *Hungarian*

Concerto. Gaining experience as concertmaster of the Dresden Philharmonic at the tender age of sixteen, he was chosen by Furtwängler four years later to be one of the Berlin Philharmonic's concertmasters, a position he held from 1929 to 1934. Replacing Josef Wolfsthal, who had died unexpectedly at age thirty-one from the after effects of influenza, Goldberg joined Hindemith and Feuermann in a string trio. Purged from the orchestra by the Nazis, along with all the other Jewish members, he left Germany. During the next six years he toured mostly throughout Europe and the Far East, appearing both as a soloist and in sonata concerts with pianist Lily Kraus. Theirs became one of the notable collaborations of the era. In the course of his travels he made a New York debut in 1938, then, unfortunately, left to tour the Orient. While playing in the Dutch East Indies, he was interned by the Japanese for three years, as was Kraus. In 1946 he resumed his international concert career.

From 1951 - 1966 he was a faculty member of the Aspen Festival and a member of the Festival Piano Quartet with violist William Primrose, pianist Victor Babin and cellist Nikolai Graudan. Goldberg became conductor-soloist of the Netherlands Chamber Orchestra in 1955, after which he played and taught in London, and since returning to America in 1978, he has taught at the Curtis Institute, the Juilliard School and Yale University.

Goldberg is not a violinist of the largest scale, but in such matters as refinement and impeccability of taste, his best playing can be superb. He is certainly one of the most patrician musicians among the Flesch pupils (or any others). I vividly recall his performance of the Beethoven concerto in its unfamiliar original form with the New York Philharmonic. It was a noble effort, pristinely played, but one that set him apart from the mainstream virtuosi by virtue of its novelty.

While Goldberg's intensely vibrant yet pure sound bespeaks romanticism, his musical and repertorial inclinations tend to stamp him as a classicist. He has, however, successfully recorded such contemporary works as the Berg concerto and the chamber music of Hindemith and Milhaud. Disdaining the use of expressive slides, his playing is warmhearted, intelligent, clean-cut and beautifully polished. And his overall facility is formidable, if not honed in the image of the romantically-oriented, heaven-storming virtuosi.

In the Goldberg performances that I have heard, admittedly, some of his interpretations were more stylistically impressive than others. But in works well suited to his aristocratic musical instincts, his playing was impressive.

The Goldberg recordings number 47 different compositions, a large portion of which are chamber music. Among his finest efforts are recordings of the Mozart Concerto Nos. 3, 4 and 5, a glowing account of

Josef Gingold

Brahms Sonata No. 3 with Balsam, cultivated readings of Beethoven Sonata Nos. 2, 5, 6, 9 and 10 with Kraus, and numerous Mozart sonatas both with Kraus on old 78's and with Radu Lupu on LP's. These belong in the record collection of every violin fancier.

Goldberg has been one of those musicians whose artistry has considerably exceeded his publicity, and in its genre, his playing is greatly respected by professionals.

There can be no higher goal to which a young violinist can aspire than to pattern his or her life and career in the image of **Josef Gingold**. Born in Brest-Litovsk, Russia, in 1909, he has come to exemplify a rare amalgamation of superb instrumentalism, legendary pedagogy, and human being extraordinaire. He began study of the violin at age three. At the end of World War I his family resettled in New York, where from 1922 to 1927 he studied with Vladimir Graffman, an Auer pupil. In 1927, Gingold went to Brussels to work under the great Ysaÿe for three years, with whom he studied all the masterworks of the violin repertoire, as well as Ysaÿe's own compositions. His Brussels debut included the first public performance of Ysaÿe's Solo Sonata (*Ballade*) No. 3, now a staple of the repertoire. Gingold ranks among the few top Ysaÿe pupils, and following in the footsteps of Persinger, he ultimately became the leading advocate of Ysaÿe's method and style in America.

Upon his return to the United States he was faced with the stern rigors of the Great Depression. Like many other outstanding violinists, he was forced to "tread water," doing commercial work while toiling assiduously to develop his art. From 1937 to 1943 he was a first violinist in the elite NBC Orchestra under Toscanini, and a member of William Primrose's String Quartet. Gingold was also first violinist of the NBC Concert Orchestra, an offshoot of the NBC Symphony, with whom he appeared as soloist each week for more than a year. Subsequently he became concertmaster of the Detroit Symphony, but after only three seasons was lured away by George Szell to become concertmaster of the vaunted Cleveland Orchestra, an "act of piracy" in view of Karl Kruger, then the Detroit conductor.

During Gingold's thirteen-year tenure in Cleveland, he was soloist with the orchestra eighteen times. In a letter to Gingold written on Christmas Eve, 1956, Szell wrote to Gingold:

> In this tenth of my years with the Cleveland Orchestra when we can look back on a very considerable progress, I am convinced that this type of unfolding of a variety of virtues of an orchestra would have been unthinkable without you. This broad statement is meant to cover both your superb artistry and your moral influence on the consciences of us all.

In 1960 Gingold retired from orchestral playing to join the Indiana University School of Music, where his present title is Distinguished Professor Emeritus of Music. For thirty summers he headed the Chamber Music Department at New York's Meadowmount School of Music.

Gingold combines encyclopedic knowledge of the violin and its repertoire with the ability to analyze instantly any technical problem and to demonstrate personally the correct procedure. His temperament enables him to handle pupils with both firmness and compassion, and his cosmopolitan musicianship, garnered by association with such giants as Ysaÿe, Toscanini and Szell, stamps him as a rare mentor. Above all, in a world in which horrendous competition so often warps the character of many a fine (and not so fine) instrumentalist, Josef Gingold has maintained his profound sense of humanity along with the virtues of patience and generosity. He not only gives instruction—he gives of himself! These qualities, of course, have long been apparent to his students and colleagues the world over, and must account for their virtual adulation of Gingold, not unlike that special reverence reserved for giants like Kreisler and David Oistrakh.

Among those who have studied with him are Miriam Fried, Jaime Laredo, Joseph Silverstein, Yuval Yaron, Nai-Yuan Hu, Eugene Fodor, Ulf Hoeschler, Joshua Bell and other pupils holding major concertmaster posts from San Francisco to Hamburg. These include Raymond Kobler, Isador Zaslav, Yuval Waldman, Otto Armin, Jacques Israelevitch, Andres

Cardenes, Richard Roberts, Carol Sindell, Herbert Greenberg, William Preucil and Roland Greutter.

To complement his teaching, Gingold has edited many solo works and studies for the violin, and his compilation of orchestral excerpts is a standard text used throughout the world. He was the moving spirit in the creation of the Quadrennial International Violin Competition of Indianapolis for which, in 1982, he served as Honorary Chairman and President of the Jury, and has represented the United States at the Queen Elisabeth, Tchaikovsky, Wieniawski, Sibelius, Paganini and Kreisler international competitions, plus the Leventritt and Naumberg contests in New York. His seventy-fifth birthday celebration was a spectacular event widely publicized by the national press, radio and television.

Gingold's laurels as a pedagogue and international ambassador of the violin in recent years, have tended to obscure his stature as a soloist. Fortunately his recording output of some 25 works, incorporating several major sonatas together with a broad sampling of vignettes, reveal him to be, in his prime, one of America's elite violinists, a talent of extraordinary impact. His is romantic playing marked by a blazing temperament, virtuoso technique, rich vibrant sound and sophisticated musicianship. More than that, he is a master stylist in the most exalted tradition, whose interpretations communicate a definite personal note. He employs ingeniously those subtle expressive devices utilized by Ysaÿe, Kreisler and Heifetz to fulfill his own aesthetic needs. While the experienced listener can detect Ysaÿe's influence, Gingold is distinctly "his own man." Lest the reader feel these statements are exaggerated, I invite him to listen to Gingold's elegant, suave Fauré Sonata, Op. 13 (1966); the brilliant Walton Sonata (1964) with pianist Walter Robert, taken from radio broadcast tapes; a variety of vignettes recorded from 1942 to 1976 in the two-record album released in honor of his seventy-fifth birthday; or the searing G string sound and contemporary swagger of Roy Harris's Sonata with pianist Johanna Harris. And in a 1976 album of Kreisler pieces, Gingold evinces an ultrasensitive penchant for Kreisler's lilting imagery, which is approximated by less than a handful of living violinists. Upon hearing this record, even the most critical auditor is impelled to shout "Bravissimo, Joe!" Historically, Josef Gingold ranks in the topmost echelon of America's brilliant concertmaster-soloists.

Bronislav Gimpel was born in Lwów, Poland, in 1911, of a family immersed in cultural activities. His grandfather created the Jewish Theatre in that city, and his older brother, Jakob, is an internationally prominent pianist. Gimpel's father, originally a clarinetist, also played violin and conducted the small theatre orchestra in which Bronislav played at about age eight. After first taking lessons from his father and then from a cousin of the noted violinist Josef Wolfsthal, he studied at the Vienna Conser-

Bronislav Gimpel

vatory of Music from 1922 to 1926 with Robert Pollak, who shortly after became Stern's early teacher in San Francisco. A child prodigy, he played in Italy and was invited to perform on the Paganini Guarnerius del Gesù, which rests in Genoa's City Hall, and he played for both Pope Pius XI and the Italian king. He joined the Flesch class in 1928 but remained with him at the Berlin Hochschule for only about a year, though he is commonly regarded as a Flesch pupil. Advised by Flesch to get some orchestral experience in order to improve his musical discipline, Gimpel served in 1928 as leader of the second violins under Herman Scherchen in Konigsberg. In 1930 he became concertmaster of the Göteborg, Sweden orchestra where he remained for seven years until Otto Klemperer recruited him as concertmaster for the Los Angeles Philharmonic in 1937. In 1935 Gimpel had competed in the Wieniawski Competition won by Neveu, and was cited at the time by David Oistrakh as "a wonderful violinist with wide international experience." He was unaccountably given only ninth place, behind several violinists who were never of his caliber; so much for politics-riddled competitions!

I heard Gimpel play a broad range of concerti, including those of Brahms, Mozart, Glazunov, Mendelssohn, Wieniawski and Tchaikovsky. He was not like Neveu as a stylist, but was rather a large-scaled virtuoso of the Heifetz, Milstein, Menuhin, Stern, Perlman order. He had a fiery temperament, and his tone was among the most vibrant of the Flesch disciples; his vibrato, cannily controlled. Not quite of maximal opulence, his sound nevertheless was rich and multifaceted. Although the central European discipline of Flesch and Pollak was evident in his playing, Gimpel was essentially an eastern European artist whose temperament was emphatically romantic. A performer of unflappable poise, his single concession to stress was a disposition to turn beet-red while playing. If one compares him to the very greatest artists, perhaps his imagination was a bit less vivid and his musical personality not as striking. But these things were marginal. After serving three years in the United States Army during World War II, Gimpel returned to Europe where he scored many a triumph. However, he could not reach the summit in America. For all his talents, they were not calculated to displace any of the six or eight reigning violinists. Nor did he enjoy a sponsor of Artur Rubinstein's importance, as did Szeryng.

Gimpel's recordings include the Beethoven, Brahms, Dvořák, Glazunov, Goldmark, Sibelius, Tchaikovsky, Wieniawski No. 2, Mendelssohn and Paganini-Wilhelmj No. 1 (first movement with a slightly abbreviated Sauret cadenza) concerti, and the cycle of Bach Solo Sonatas and Partitas. The Goldmark compares favorably with that of Milstein and of Perlman, and the others are all stunning performances in every respect. The Bach cycle may not be the most profound, but neither is it overprecious and fussy. His interpretations tend to be straightforward and conscientious, inclined more toward contemporary stylization than an amorphous striving for baroque authenticity with modern violin and bow.

Concurrent with his postwar years of international concertizing, he taught in Karlsruhe, at the University of Connecticut from 1967 to 1973, and at the Royal Academy of Music in Manchester until 1978. According to Jakob, Bronislav was the first to perform the Britten concerto in London. On occasion he conducted, and played concerti with orchestra while conducting. He also performed chamber music with the New Friends of Music Quartet, the Mannes Piano Trio and the Warsaw Quintet, and gave sonata recitals with his brother. By nature he was somewhat of a "rolling stone."

Like that other brilliant Flesch pupil, Ricardo Odnopossof, Gimpel failed to achieve the career he deserved. In 1979 he met with success during a three-month sojourn in Venezuela and was reportedly in fine spirits. A short time later, only few days before a scheduled sonata recital with Jakob in Los Angeles, he died of what was described in the press as a medical overdose.

Roman Totenberg, born in 1913 in Lodz, Poland, started violin lessons at age seven. Like Szymon Goldberg, he had lessons with Mihalowicz in Warsaw, and in the late 1920s, with Flesch. Though generally considered a Flesch pupil, he also studied with Enesco. After winning the Mendelssohn prize in 1932, he toured in South America with pianist Artur Rubinstein, and concertized with the composer Szymanowski in the mid-1930s. After emigrating to the United States in the late 1930s he combined his solo appearances with teaching assignments which included posts at the Music Academy at Santa Barbara, the Aspen Institute in Colorado, and Boston University as head of the string department. In recent years he has been director of the Longy Music School in Boston.

Totenberg's career has been perhaps less spectacular than those of some of Flesch's other leading pupils, but he is an admirable violinist. I have heard him play the Mendelssohn concerto with felicity and sparkle. His performance repertoire ranges from Bach to such contemporaries as Berg, Bartók, Milhaud, Prokofiev, Stravinsky and William Schuman. Numbering around 50 works, his recordings display his playing as medium-scaled, sweet-toned, clean-cut, warmly expressive and tempered with sincere, intelligent musicianship. In particular, his disc of the Bloch concerto with Golschmann and the Vienna State Opera Orchestra is deeply felt, sensitively wrought and technically brilliant.

Ossy Renardy, born Oskar Reiss in Vienna in 1920, belongs to that lamented company of exceptionally gifted string player whose careers were cut short by death or debilitating illness, either before full artistic maturity or in mid-flight. This group includes David Hochstein, Stephan Partos, Josef Hassid, Josef Wolfsthal, Ginette Neveu, Emanuel Feuermann, and most recently, Jacqueline du Pré and Michael Rabin.

Renardy began violin lessons at age five, but his early training is obscure. After his arrival in the United States he studied with Theodore Pashkus in New York. Following his Vienna debut at age thirteen, he won great acclaim for his Italian debut in Merano in 1933, playing the Paganini Concerto No. 1 and the Schubert A-major Sonata. In 1937 he toured some of the midwestern American states and in 1938 made a successful Town Hall debut. In a 1939 Carnegie Hall debut he scored a triumph by playing all 24 of Paganini's caprices in the second half of his program, after having played Nardini's E-minor Concerto, Dvořák's Sonatina, Op. 100 and Lalo's *Symphonie Espagnole*. Immediately hailed as a Paganini specialist, Renardy was the first to record all 24 caprices in 1940, before Ricci. To set the record straight, Ricci was the first to record them in their original solo form. Renardy used the skeletal Ferdinand David piano accompaniments, omitted nearly all of the repeats and made several cuts, most of them negligible. Nevertheless, it was a prodigious recording feat, which skyrocketed his reputation at the time. He rerecorded the caprices shortly before his death in 1953, the tragic result of an automobile accident near Santa Fe, New Mexico, while enroute to a concert. His pianist Walter Robert, who was driving, survived the crash, as did his Guarnerius violin. During World War II, Renardy had served in

COURTESY OF KENWAY LEE

Ossy Renardy

the American armed forces.

Renardy and Ricci have a major similarity in tonal texture. Both play with exceedingly vibrant finger intensity that tends to produce tautness of sound, though Ricci's tonal palette is wider in scope. One of the most impressive features of Renardy's Paganini is that he never made a fetish of stressing his vast technical prowess for mere vaudevillean effect, although his playing is always brilliant in character as well as disciplined in execution. He could play as rapidly as anyone, but shunned mindless speed and always respected the innate pulse of the music. The sheer neatness and flexibility of his performance is stunning. He does not play Paganini with the precipitous aggressiveness or explosive bow contact of Ricci, but his playing is devoid of the impurities sometimes occasioned by Ricci's devilish razzle-dazzle. His commitment to the music is consistently expressive.

Renardy's recordings number about 87, fifty of which comprise two sets of Paganini's caprices plus two caprices recorded for the third time with more complex piano accompaniments. In comparing Renardy's recording of Ernst's *Hungarian Airs* and Saint-Saëns' *Konzertstück* with those of Ricci, both are swashbuckling in delivery, but Ricci's sound is a bit more satisfying. The "live" performance of the Tchaikovsky concerto and his recording of the Brahms concerto with Munch and the Concertgebouw of Amsterdam (and many other performances that I heard) in-

Jaime Laredo

dicate that Renardy, for all his instrumental command, would not have joined the elite. Unfortunately the angularity of his rather monochromatic sound detracted from the poetic imagery and diversity of color demanded by distinguished performances of the romantic masterworks, and certainly was not suited to the subtleties of Mozart and Beethoven. Yet Renardy left his mark on the development of violin art, and at his best was an imposing violinist.

Jaime Laredo (b. 1941), born in Cochabamba, Bolivia, learned to read music at age four, and at six he received his first violin. His first teacher, Carlo Flamini urged the boy's parents to take him to the United States so that he could have the best training. The family moved to San Francisco where he studied with Antonio de Grassi and Frank Houser over a five-year period. At eight he played the Mendelssohn concerto in Sacramento. His parents then took him to Josef Gingold in Cleveland for further study, and later, upon Gingold's recommendation, be began work in 1955 with Galamian at the Curtis Institute. As early as 1956 he made a Latin American tour of ten concerts, and in 1959 played a Washington recital prior to his entry later that year in the Queen Elisabeth Competition in Brussels. Funded in part by the Bolivian government and various American contributions, his expenses for the Belgian competition were offset further by the sale of the family piano. Using a Stradivarius loaned by the John Phipps Foundation, Laredo was awarded first prize shortly before his eighteenth birthday by a jury which included David Oistrakh, Menuhin, Francescatti, Szigeti, Grumiaux and Galamian. He was followed by

Albert Markov (second prize) and Joseph Silverstein (third), eight and nine years his elder, respectively. He was the youngest at that time (and probably still is) to ever win the coveted award. The Bolivian government accorded him a hero's welcome and issued a stamp in his honor with his name la-re-do, cited in musical terms.

Like many another major competition laureate, Laredo found that forging a bonafide concert career was even more difficult. A New York recital he gave after the competition evoked mixed critical response. Yet I heard him play the Sibelius concerto the following year and found him to be a violinist of outstanding accomplishment and potential. His early recordings substantiate this appraisal. In 1961 he joined the Serkin Marlboro group, which emphasizes chamber music, and this partially succeeded in diverting his career from single-minded concentration on solo work.

After his marriage in 1960 to pianist Ruth Meckler, he began to stress sonata playing, though he continued his intermittent solo appearances. Replacing Charles Treger as first violinist of the Chamber Music Society of Lincoln Center in 1973, he increased his activities in that field and later created his own chamber music series in New York. When he and cellist Sharon Robinson were married in 1976, they formed a trio with pianist Joseph Kalichstein that has since achieved prominence. Currently Laredo is conductor-violinist with the Scottish Chamber Orchestra. During a recent tour I heard him with that ensemble in a Mozart concerto which he played with admirable refinement and polish. His successful recordings with that group continue to increase in number.

Laredo's early recordings (1959 - 1960) display him both in the virtuoso role and as a sonata interpreter. It is youthful playing, not fully mature in subtlety, but in Sarasate's *Carmen Fantasy* he exhibits exceptional facility and daring. His tone is bright, gleaming and ingratiating, abetted by a vibrato that is fast and close, though its range of color is not particularly wide. Brahms's Sonata No. 3, Op. 108, already indicates musicianship of a high order and warm expressivity. Like most violinists of his generation, his use of expressive slides and position changes is sparing, at times to the degree that one may feel that his overall playing is not fully in accord with his inherently fervid temperament. The dance movements in Bach's Solo Partita in E-major are exuberant, and the sound is alive and vibrant with no pretense at artificial interpretive posturing. One can note a certain diminution of spontaneity in his 1976 recordings of Bach's Six Sonatas for Violin and Harpsichord with Glenn Gould (playing piano), but Laredo's radiant musicality nevertheless shines through, especially in the faster movements, and his genial artistry shows substantial development.

I had the pleasure of meeting Laredo when we served as members of the jury at the 1982 (first) Quadrennial International Violin Competition of Indianapolis, and found him to be a reserved, affable man with a ready sense of humor, and utterly absorbed in his judicial responsibilities. Now in mid-career, his reputation continues to expand, and he is one of our leading American violinists.

By the late 1930s, invigorated by the emergence of Menuhin and Ricci, American-born violinists had become a real force in violin art. During the next several decades, the United States began to rival the Soviet Union in the production of superb string instrumentalists, a situation which continues to this day. Foreign-born American pedagogues played a principal role in their training, but following in the footsteps of Persinger, American-born pedagogues, too, have been making their mark in the foremost American conservatories and university music departments. The conflux of these two currents of American pedagogical expertise has transformed what was a backwater of violin art at the turn of the twentieth century into one of the two leading international centers of violin artistry and pedagogy. Whereas for so many decades talented Americans had gone to European centers for advanced training (i.e. "finishing"), gifted young people from countries the world over now travel to the United States.

Every so often some commentator refers to the "American School" of violin playing. I believe such a sobriquet is farfetched. What similar characteristics are there, for example, in the playing of Elmar Oliveira and Joseph Swenson that would unqualifiedly indentify them as protagonists of a definitive American School? Or Dylana Jenson and Ida Kavafian? Or David Nadien and Paul Zukovsky? Or Michael Rabin and James Buswell? Or Carroll Glenn and Eugene Fodor? Or for that matter, Menuhin and Ricci, both products of the same teacher in their youth? The truth is that American playing more than any other represents cosmopolitan violinistic attitudes, styles and methods. And this is vital for its continued good health and prosperity. Should one particular outlook gain control through acquisition and manipulation of monetary grants, sheer publicity, or any other monopolistic device, the totality of American violin art will be poorer. Such a danger always lurks in the byways of the music establishment.

With Stern's rise to stardom around the mid-1940s, a new era began to dawn in the Western violin world. The Soviets, of course, were dominated by David Oistrakh, and later joined by Kogan. And the late-blooming Henryk Szeryng (abetted by the influence of his friend, pianist Artur Rubinstein) and Arthur Grumiaux, both elegant, elite artists, deservedly achieved careers on the top level. But particularly in the United States, the ever-expanding Stern hegemony was to have a crucial effect upon the career aspirations of numerous outstanding American-born violinists for some four decades. And many a splendid violinist of soloist caliber was

Oscar Shumsky

forced to settle for less.

One of the most highly respected American-born violinists is **Oscar Shumsky**, born in Philadelphia in 1917, esteemed by such stellar colleagues as Oistrakh, Menuhin, Primrose and a host of fellow professionals everywhere. Starting the violin at age four, his first teacher was Max Senofsky (father of Berl). He then had lessons with Albert Meiff, after which he studied with the aged Auer, later completing his training with Zimbalist at the Curtis Institute. His adulation of Kreisler, further heightened by a youthful meeting with the Viennese giant during which Kreisler accompanied him at the piano, resulted in a special affinity for performing Kreisler compositions with exceptional charm and nobility. Shumsky taught at the Curtis Institute from 1961 to 1965, and was a member of the violin faculty at Juilliard from 1953 to 1978. Among his pupils are Ida Kavafian and Philip Setzer. He is an excellent violist and has performed concerts featuring both violin and viola on the same program. He is also one of a growing number of violinists who have taken up the baton. Once a member of Toscanini's famous NBC orchestra, he decided to leave after two and a half years under the Italian maestro's "hypnotic spell." "I had learned a tremendous amount, but felt it was time I began listening to my own inner voices." Shumsky is also a chamber music player of extraordinary caliber, and was first violinist of the Primrose String Quartet. In later years, he was the violinist in the noted Bach Aria group. His advice to students seeking a career is: "...instead of becoming a chronic contestant, adjust your sights to becoming a first-class instrumentalist and musician. There have never been too many of them. This has always been my creed."

Even at fifteen, when Shumsky performed the Elgar and Brahms concerti with the Philadelphia Orchestra, he seemed headed for a brilliant career as a soloist. His repertoire ultimately ran the gamut from Corelli to Hindemith's *Kammermusik* No. 4. He could play with tenderness as well as elegance. Yet it was Stern who gained the top position in the American scene, along with Menuhin and to a lesser degree the spectacular technician, Ricci, both of whom had attained international fame as young prodigies. Shumsky's press notices did not always reflect the practically unanimous enthusiasm of his professional colleagues. Nor did his playing seem to attract a mass audience. I recall Howard Taubman's critique of a New York recital in the 1940s that chastised Shumsky mercilessly. His solo career languished for several decades. It has only been since reaching his mid-sixties that Shumsky has begun to garner the international prominence as a soloist many believe he should have won forty years earlier—a phenomenon of sorts. His early recordings, mostly on minor labels, were "lost in the crowd." However, his recent recordings of the complete Mozart sonata cycle, the six solo sonatas and partitas of Bach, and a comprehensive panorama of Kreisler originals and transcriptions, have served to inject new life into his career as a soloist.

Admittedly, the two occasions on which I heard Shumsky in the 1980s were not nearly as impressive as his recordings. One was a somewhat undistinguished performance of the Beethoven concerto, not top-level either technically or musically; the other, a sparkling but impersonal rendering of a Haydn concerto. Neither was in the class of his taped "live" performance of Spohr's *Gesangsszene* and a crystalline, patrician version of the Corelli-Kreisler *La Folia*. Shumsky's music is neither characterized by impassioned drama nor a bravura "kamikaze" daredevil. Rather, it is large-scaled, tasteful, polished, and above all, *stylish* playing that seems all the more persuasive in the current era, when stylistic subtleties and spiritual grace are in such short supply. His tone is silken, wonderfully pliant and soft in texture, though good-sized in volume. His sound is not as sensuous or as highly individualized as that of the topmost romantic violinists, though it is invariably sweet and impeccably nuanced. Nor is his musical personality as marked as that of Heifetz, Menuhin or Stern. The Shumsky platform image might be described as unusually severe. He is capable of performing any type of music with éclat, but it is perhaps in Kreisler specialties, both classical and romantic, that his playing is most personalized. Shumsky's pristine sound has not the sensual rapid vibrato of a Kreisler, but he is a master of all the unique Kreisler subtleties and expressive devices which he applies not imitatively, but with meticulous discrimination and refinement. His Bach is crystal-clear in sound and bright in character, although some purists might resent his slight rhythmic liberties in the slower movements. The Mozart sonatas are buoyant and sensitively etched. In all, Shumsky is a superb artist and one of the finest America has produced.

Sidney Harth, born in Cleveland in 1925, began violin study at age four with Albert Sack, and at age nine went to Herman Rosen, an Auer pupil. From age fifteen to twenty-one, he studied with Joseph Knitzer, whom he considers his principal teacher, though he later spent two years with Piastro ("he taught me a lot about bow articulation and solo projection") and played once a week in Enesco's master class at the Mannes School of Music. He also had some lessons with Felix Eyle and Joseph Fuchs. In 1949 Harth won the Naumburg Competition, made his New York debut that same year and, in 1952, his debut in Paris.

While continuing to establish a solo career, he became concertmaster of the Louisville Orchestra (1953-1959), an ensemble strongly emphasizing contemporary works. Sponsored by the Louisville Orchestra Association, he competed in Poland's Wieniawski Competition in 1958, missing first prize by only three-quarters of a point. However, even as a second-place winner he was presented with the Wieniawski medal that previously had been awarded only to the pianist Wittold Malcuszynski and David Oistrakh. Harth states: "I am not one to indulge in 'sourgrapes.' Before entering such an affair, one should realize that political ramifications and overtones must inevitably play a part in the proceedings, and if one cannot be realistic about it, perhaps he should stay home" (from *The Way They Play*, Applebaum, Roth, Volume 5, p. 125).

Harth's publicity from the Poland competition accelerated his career considerably, and he has appeared as soloist with many major orchestras. He was concertmaster of the Chicago Symphony for three years under Reiner and for seven years was concertmaster of the Puerto Rico Musical Festival Orchestra under Casals. In 1963 Harth was appointed administrative head of the Department of Music at the Carnegie-Mellon University in Pittsburgh, where he founded a string quartet and conducted the Carnegie College Community Orchestra. Meanwhile he continued to strive for conducting assignments.

In 1973, attracted by the opportunity to serve as associate conductor with Zubin Mehta, he became concertmaster of the Los Angeles Philharmonic. I heard him regularly for five years as concertmaster, conductor and soloist. Now deeply immersed in conducting, Harth strove to juggle the three activities, a Herculean task with which a full-time soloist would not have to contend. Though his efforts as a conductor were sincere and respectable, they in no way rivaled his talents as a violinist. This is the case with most fine violinists who hanker to conduct the major symphonic repertoire. Top-level conducting is an art in itself that requires many long years of apprenticeship, intellectual mastery of a multitude of scores and vast podium experience undistracted by the daily practice grind demanded by a great violinist in the current era of an ever-widening repertoire. Under such pressure, the performance of any violinist, no matter how skilled, tends to become inconsistent, though the artist himself is often oblivious to the fact.

At his best, Harth is a violinist of international stature with broad expressive powers, just a bit below the highest echelon. Actually, he has no violinistic shortcomings whatsoever. His technical resources are vast, though he is an all-around musician rather than a gymnastic specialist. While his vibrato is not of the most rapid variety, it is meticulously controlled. Thus his tone is multifaceted as well as sweet and warm, if not uniquely individual. The scope of his playing is large, as is the man himself. His knowledge and use of expressive devices (i.e. slides, etc.) is extensive. Among his concerto performances that I heard were stunning renditions of the Elgar and Walton, a colorful Sibelius, a sensitive Mozart, a rather spotty Tchaikovsky and a Beethoven riddled with rhythmic aberrations and diverse loose ends. His concertmaster solos were seldom less than impressive in all genres of music. Outstanding among his recordings are stylish, sensitive interpretations of sonatas by Brahms (Nos. 1 and 3), Fauré, and Schubert, Op. 162; exciting viruoso performances of the solo Ben-Haim and Ysaÿe No. 3 sonatas; and a commanding reading of a splendid Concert Suite by Herbert Elwell. Since leaving Los Angeles in 1978, when Mehta took over the New York podium (the incoming Giulini wished to select his own associate conductors), Harth has undertaken various assignments, but at this writing has neither secured a major orchestra podium appointment nor accepted a steady concertmaster post.

Berl Senofsky, whose parents were both violinists, was born in Philadelphia in 1925. After initial lessons with his father, he studied with Persinger, Stassevich and, later, with Galamian at Juilliard. Following a three-year period of military service he became assistant concertmaster of the Cleveland Orchestra, and in 1946 received the Naumburg Award, which led to his New York debut that year.

In 1955 Senofsky was the first American ever to win the Queen Elisabeth Competition in Brussels, surpassing such prominent violinists as the gymnastics-oriented Russian Julian Sitkovetsky (second); his brilliant countryman Viktor Pikaisen (fifth); and the Argentine Alberto Lysy (sixth). His victory secured, Senofsky made some solo appearances with major orchestras, culminating in 1958 with the New York Philharmonic and the Boston Symphony. But, strangely, his career sputtered, despite a recording of the Brahms concerto that was first-class in every respect.

Berl Senofsky

Young Americans who think it is tremendously difficult to pursue a career in their own country in the 1980s (and it is!), are fortunate that they were not vying for fame in the 1930s, 1940s or 1950s when opportunities, sponsorship, and public interest were at a disgracefully low ebb.

I heard Senofsky during the late 1950s in the Brahms concerto at a time when it was said that he was experiencing domestic difficulties. His performance tended to be spotty and not overly inspired, certainly considerably inferior to his recording. However, it was apparent that he is a tonalist of stature, with an intensely rapid vibrato (a bit too rapid at times) coloring the type of sound that immediately titillates the ear. Some years later I had occasion to verify this opinion at a concert featuring his trio, in which the vibrant beauty of his tone dominated the admirable collaborations of the pianist and cellist. And his recording of the Fauré and Debussy sonatas with the virtuoso partnership of Gary Graffman, while not models of Gallic subtlety, are perspicuously clean, vital, energetic, tasteful and refreshingly appealing. A recent tape verifies that at sixty he retains full command of his virtuosity and tonal resources. Senofsky, highly respected by fellow professionals, is currently chairman of the string department and a professor at the Peabody Institute in Baltimore. He was founder and organizer of the American Artists International Foundation, a juror at the Tchaikovsky, Queen Elisabeth and Montreal International Competitions and decorated as an "Officer of the Order of

Leopold" by the King of Belgium.

Aaron Rosand, born in 1927 in Indiana, studied with Leon Sametini in Chicago, a former pupil of Ysaÿe and Ševčik who once commanded a pedagogical authority in that city somewhat analogous to that of Kneisel in New York. Later Rosand worked with Zimbalist at the Curtis Institute. He made his New York debut in 1948 and has been battling to achieve star status ever since, generally with more success abroad than in his own country.

After many years of greatly admiring Rosand's recordings, I had occasion to hear him in concert. Frankly, it was disappointing. In Tartini's *Devil's Trill* Sonata (with orchestral support), his playing was neat, overcautious and low-keyed in an interpretation that seldom delved beneath the surface of the music, though the trill-tremolos of the Kreisler cadenza were brilliant. The ensuing Paganini Concerto No. 1 (A first movement cadenza, mostly by Wilhelmj, had the climactic fingered-octave scales omitted) was more convincing, but indicated that for all his considerable dexterity, he is not a devil-may-care gymnast of the type that thrives on Paganini's satanic theme-and-variation intricacies. The *Adagio* was warmly affectionate, if not dramatic, and the G string of his Guarnerius (formerly Kochanski's) occasionally sang fervently; the finale, with the double harmonics omitted, lacked the kind of daring that can render Paganini's music truly spectacular.

However, Rosand has long since proved himself one of the leading American violinists of his generation. The scope of his playing can be described as medium-scaled; his tone is velvety, sweet and soft-grained, and his vibrato speed ranges from moderate to rather slow. Like many violinists trained in that period, Rosand is a master of expressive devices (slides and position changes) and employs them with extraordinary suavity and impeccable taste. In works best suited to his ardent temperament, he is a stylist par excellence. His recording of Saint-Saëns' *Introduction and Rondo Capriccioso*, wisely avoiding the mindless racing of so many of his younger colleagues, captures the Gallic piquance of the work with exceptional grace. In many of his recordings, made mostly with minor league orchestras, one can pinpoint phrases of compelling beauty, whether in the *Canzonetta* of the Tchaikovsky concerto or in the piquant lyricism of the Saint-Saëns Concerto No. 3.

Rosand has made a significant contribution to romantic violin music by seeking out and resuscitating nearly forgotten but worthy concerti by Joachim (*Hungarian*), José White, Hubay No. 3, Arensky, Ernst, Godard (*Romantique*) and other works of this genre. His warm-hearted recordings of Sarasate's Spanish specialties are instilled with an Iberian zest that is lacking in all too many contemporary renditions of this work. His facility sparkles. Rosand recordings exude refinement and sophistication.

David Nadien

David Nadien, born in New York in 1928, studied with Adolpho Betti and Galamian. He made his solo debut with the New York Philharmonic at fourteen, and has since appeared over thirty times as soloist with that orchestra under such conductors as Bernstein, Mitropoulos, Maazel, Steinberg, and Ozawa, and with several other major American and Canadian symphonies, receiving critical praise. He has been highly successful as a recitalist in the most renowned New York concert halls and their counterparts in metropolitan centers throughout the United States and Canada. Best known in the East, Nadien was concertmaster of the New York Philharmonic from 1966 through 1970, at which time he resigned to resume a full-time career as a teacher and solo performer. Throughout the country he is greatly admired by professional colleagues, who recognize him as one of the leading American violinists of the day. For several years he has been in charge of string workshops at the Stratford Music Festival in Ontario, Canada, and at Wolftrap in Washington, D.C. In addition to his nationwide telecasts, his playing is known to millions, anonymously, through innumerable solo excerpts in commercial phonograph and film recordings. He is, in fact, apart from his other achievements, one of the few finest "commercial" players among thoroughly schooled violinists to ever record in that field.

Nadien's expressive powers are prodigious, and his sound is supremely intense, propelled by an "impulse" fingertip vibrato. It stamps him as a tonalist of extraordinary stature, even among stellar violinists. His recordings include the sonatas of Franck and Debussy; Vivaldi's *The Four Seasons*," the Prokofiev Duo (with Ricci); a lengthy list of shorter virtuoso showpieces by Sarasate and Wieniawski; tonally oriented favorites: *On Wings of Song, Humoresque* and others, played with surpassing grace, sophistication and ravishing sound; and the violin solos in symphonic works of Tchaikovsky and Richard Strauss with Bernstein and the New York Philharmonic.

There are those who may find his vibrato excessive and not sufficiently diversified in his recordings (with David Hancock) of the Franck and Debussy sonatas. But one would be hard pressed to find more than a small group of younger generation violinists, including many overpublicized, post-1965 international competition winners, who can even approach his mastery in heartwarming vignettes. Elgar's *Salut d'Amour* as performed by Nadien may well bring a tear to the eye of the most stone-hearted listener.

Enormously respected by his professional colleagues, **Joseph Silverstein**, born in Detroit in 1932, had violin lessons with his father, a string teacher in the public schools, from age three to age twelve and a half. From 1946 to 1950 he studied at the Curtis Institute with Vida Reynolds and Zimbalist. He also worked for several years with Gingold, whom he calls "an immensely exciting, inspirational personality," and briefly with Mischakoff and Demetrius Dounis.

In 1959 Silverstein took third prize in the Queen Elisabeth Competition, and the following year won the Naumburg prize, which earned him a New York Town Hall recital and other appearances. Apparently not one to rely on the unpredictabilities and vicissitudes involved in building a solo career, he opted for symphonic work. After stints in the Denver, Houston and Philadelphia Orchestras, he joined the Boston Symphony as a section player in 1955, and in 1962 became its concertmaster. At the onset of the 1971 - 1972 season, the post of Assistant Conductor was added to his duties. His violins include a 1773 J.B. Guadagnini once owned by Grumiaux, and more recently he acquired the 1742 "Camilla Urso" Guarnerius del Gesù.

Through the years, Silverstein has achieved nationwide prominence by means of his many impressive televised appearances as soloist with the Boston Symphony. His listed repertoire includes more than 30 major concerti, ranging from Haydn to Schoenberg. He has toured Europe as first violinist and director of the Boston Chamber Players, a group which boasts several outstanding recordings, and was leader of the Symphony String Quartet. Included in his activities have been teaching assignments at the Berkshire Music Center in Tanglewood and at Yale University. However, his ultimate goal has been to establish himself as chief con-

Joseph Silverstein

ductor of a major symphony, and in addition to his podium efforts in Boston, he has appeared as conductor of various important orchestras. I heard him conduct the Los Angeles Philharmonic as a neophyte in 1973. It was an unsuccessful effort. But Silverstein has gained considerable experience since then, and recently retired as Boston's concertmaster to become Musical Director of the Utah Symphony.

As a violinist, Silverstein has no instrumental weaknesses. His facility is prodigious, and his tone, meticulously colored by a vibrato capable of several speeds, is rich and capacious. Especially convincing in twentieth-century music, he can toss off the immensely difficult Schoenberg concerto immaculately, and his recordings of the Bartók No. 2 and Stravinsky concerti, and Bartók's Solo Sonata invite comparison with any. In a recording of Bach's G-minor Solo Sonata, his approach is respectfully disciplined, his sound, romantically vibrant. Marginally less impressive are his performances of romantic concerti, though they are certainly first-class in every violinistic respect. In classical compositions he plays buoyantly and with crisp, "live" sound, though I once heard him in a Handel sonata that was quite charmless. Silverstein has an extremely analytical musical intelligence, and his romantic and classical playing, judging by Olympian standards, lacks the ultimate in spontaneity and imagination. Still overall he ranks very high among the elite American-born violinists.

A tragic figure among American violinists was New York-born **Michael Rabin**, (originally Rabinowitz, 1936 - 1972). In the quarter-century between the birth of Stern and that of Perlman, Rabin was one of the most elite talents to emerge anywhere in the world. He initially had lessons with his violinist-father, who played for many years in the New York Philharmonic, and at age nine he became a pupil of Galamian, who ultimately considered Rabin his greatest pupil. At eleven he made his first public appearance, and two years later won first prize in a contest sponsored by the National Federation of Music Clubs. In 1950, at fourteen, he established himself as a genuine prodigy, publicly performing such technically difficult works as the Vieuxtemps Concerto No. 4 in A-minor and the Wieniawski Concerto No. 1 in F-sharp minor, and brilliantly recorded eleven of Paganini's caprices. The following year he made his debut with the New York Philharmonic as soloist in 45-minute performances occurring four times a day, and later that year was guest soloist with the orchestra both at Carnegie Hall and in Philadelphia with Mitropoulos. Fortunately, unlike so many gifted American-born violinists of his generation, Rabin's success as a youthful prodigy guaranteed him the opportunity to attain a solo career without having to do commercial or symphonic work for economic survival. Nor was he forced to ply the treacherous international competition circuit.

I first heard Rabin in a 1954 radio broadcast playing the Glazunov concerto with the New York Philharmonic. It was obvious immediately that here was a young man of extraordinary promise whose violinistic attributes were practically flawless. Several years later when he was about twenty-three, I attended a comprehensive recital that, despite his burgeoning reputation, attracted only a tiny audience. In top form, Rabin exhibited all the qualities of a rare virtuoso. His Bach sonata was splendidly etched; his Fauré sonata sang sweetly and fluently; his Elgar *La Capricieuse* sported a staccato faster than that of the young Heifetz, though the lyric passages were somewhat less graceful; his Paganini caprices were impeccable. On the purely violinistic level he compared to the young Kogan. His long, powerful fourth finger would make almost any violinist green with envy. All this was abetted by an instinctive suavity of phrasing and delivery recalling only the most elite among his colleagues. Yet I had a strong impression that he was still searching, musically, for a personal identity.

Rabin's tone was softer in texture than that of Heifetz, less vital and penetrating; his vibrato generally slower, although it was capable of the ultimate intensity in the high G and E string registers. He had total control of his vibrato, produced many shades of tonal color, and for the most part he avoided the "on-and-off" usage in a single melodic line that was to become so prevalent. His sound resembled more that of Perlman's,

Michael Rabin & his father

Michael Rabin

and his temperament was extremely warm and sensual. Heifetz's influence was strong in his general style. He used the Heifetz slides lavishly, but not in blatant imitation. Rabin was a master of expressive finger portamentos and kindred devices, and employed them tastefully. Tenderness, charm and a certain gentleness of character pervaded much of his playing, along with his tremendous virtuoso flair and daring. In his prime years his performance consistently exuded youthfulness of spirit.

For all his wonderful attributes, Rabin's playing did not communicate the overwhelming personal aura and individuality of Heifetz, Menuhin, Oistrakh or Stern, either in sound or stylization. And when around 1960 be began to suffer from instability and illness, the quality of his performances declined sharply. Later he made a comeback during which time I heard him in a rather technically spotty, uninspired rendition of the Tchaikovsky concerto, and a clean, energetic interpretation of the Brahms concerto that lacked, however, any comprehensive sense of profundity. The fabulous boy virtuoso never had the opportunity to develop into the mature artist and man. His return to the concert platform was short-lived. Rumors of drug dependency, debilitating illness and a variety of personal pressures persisted. The official explanation for his unexpected death denied that it was self-induced, attributing it to an accidental fall.

Rabin left over 60 recorded works, major and minor, some of them recorded more than once. Among them are Paganini's 24 caprices, made in his early twenties, that collectively are fully equal to or even possibly surpass any recorded before or since, and transcendental discs of the concerti by Wieniawski, No. 1, Paganini, No. 1 (Flesch cadenza), Glazunov, Bruch's *Scottish Fantasy*; as well as of Ysaÿe's Solo Sonatas No. 3 and No. 4. It is interesting to note that in his recording of Bach's formidable Solo Sonata No. 5 in C-major, the playing is beautifully polished and his vibrato usage is more attuned to the spirit of Bach's era than that of several older, stellar, romantic-oriented violinists whose Bach recordings have received the effusive praise of critics and commentators. This suggests that had his development been able to continue without interruption, he might have transcended the limitations of mere violinistic bravura and romance, and matured into an artist capable of performing masterworks demanding musical introspection of the highest order. Sadly, we will never know.

The Bach recording certainly merits rerelease. Discs of many medium-length and shorter pieces, such as Saint-Saëns' *Introduction and Rondo Capriccioso*, Sarasate's *Zigeunerweisen*, the Dinicu-Heifetz *Hora Staccato*, and the devilish Scriabin-Szigeti *Étude in Thirds*, are performed on an exalted level. With the exception of Perlman and possibly Zukerman, I do not know of any younger generation (post-1945) violinist who can play

Erick Friedman

the Chopin-Wilhelmj Nocturne, Op. 27, with a tenderness and beauty of tone comparable to Rabin's.

Erick Friedman was born in Newark, New Jersey in 1939. His first violin lessons were with Samuel Applebaum, from age six to ten, after which he studied with Galamian until he was sixteen. Towards the end of this period he was also coached once or twice by Milstein. At seventeen he began study with Heifetz, an association that lasted between two and three years. Since 1956, when he made his Carnegie Hall debut as a recitalist, Friedman has appeared as recitalist and soloist with leading orchestras in this country and in many parts of the world. He has held the Mischa Elman chair at the Manhattan School of Music in New York, and is currently a professor and chairman of the string department at Southern Methodist University in Dallas. His recordings number around 35 and include the concerti of Paganini, No. 1, Tchaikovsky, Prokofiev, No. 1, Bartók, No. 2 and Mendelssohn, the Franck and Debussy sonatas, and numerous medium-length and short showpieces, all on the RCA label. His recording of Bach's Double Concerto with Heifetz is the only instance in which Heifetz deigned to record one-on-one with another violinist.

Friedman's story is unusual, and a vivid example of the more perni-cious aspects of the competition syndrome. By his early twenties he seemed well along the way to a promising career, with a list of recordings second only to that of Rabin—an extraordinary accomplishment for an

American in the Stern era. A contract with the eminent impressario Sol Hurok was pending, but never came to pass, presumably because of powerful inimical pressures. Compounding his ill fortune, in an effort to accelerate his career Friedman took the well-intentioned advice of David Oistrakh, and, apparently tempted by the prospect of a Cliburn-like avalanche of international publicity, decided to compete in the 1966 Tchaikovsky Competition at Moscow. There, a "loner" in an atmosphere of "wheeling and dealing," he could do no better than to tie for sixth place. It was a cruel blow that temporarily sidetracked his career. However, after a sabbatical during which time he concentrated on scholastic subjects, he continued his violinistic pursuits and, at this juncture, performs 50 to 60 concerts a year while fulfilling his responsibilities as a teacher. Standing about six feet three inches tall, handsome of feature and figure, Friedman when bearded is positively Lincolnesque, and always presents an imposing platform image.

In his early career, Friedman epitomized Heifetz's influence perhaps more directly than any other violinist. Whereas Kogan played strongly in the Heifetz manner, Friedman's entire musical personality was practically an extension of the Heifetz muse. As he matured he shed the most obvious reverberations of this influence, though he still profitably employs expressive position changes and the subtle horizontal devices (that are neither slides nor portamentos) that recall those of Heifetz. The soprano character of his sound, the nature and application of his vibrato, his articulation in both hands and his stylistic inclinations as heard in those early recordings, link him to Heifetz to a startling degree. He has the equipment of a daring, top-level romantic virtuoso. While the body of his vibrant tone is somewhat lean, his overall delivery is almost invariably suave. If one is willing to overlook these similarities, the recordings are exceptionally brilliant in every violinistic respect.

A 1980 live concert disc of the Bartók Concerto No. 2 reveals Friedman to be an artist of important stature. If not exactly a striking, individualistic musical personality in his own right, he has become "his own man," though still readily recognizable as Heifetz's disciple. His pellucid, intelligently wrought recordings of the Beethoven String Trio cycle with violinist Emanuel Vardi and cellist Jascha Silberstein, rank with the finest performances of this music. The several times that I heard Friedman play in his forties confirm the quality of these recordings.

Eugene Fodor, born in Colorado in 1950, started violin lessons at age seven. At eleven he made his debut with the Denver Symphony, of which his teacher, Hans Wippler, was concertmaster. As a youth, he played duo violin recitals with his older brother John, who is now a member of that orchestra. Following his high school graduation in 1967, Fodor's study began in earnest when he received a scholarship to Juilliard and became a pupil of Galamian. Subsequently he studied with Harry Farbman, Josef Gingold and finally at the University of Southern California for nearly a year with Heifetz, two days a week, each lesson lasting several hours.

I heard Fodor in the Glazunov concerto when he was about seventeen, but his playing, while manifesting virtuoso promise, was raw and that of a student. Working assiduously, he soon won the moderately prestigious Merriweather Post Competition in 1972. He leaped into the international limelight when he tied for second place with two Russians, Rueben Agaronian and Rusida Gvasalia in the 1974 Tchaikovsky Competition in Moscow, a contest in which no first prize was awarded. The epitome of the all-American boy from the wide-open spaces, handsome, poised and glib, Fodor, then twenty-four, came home to a hero's welcome. The publicity tub-thumpers found themselves with an ideal product to sell. Sponsors, mostly of minor league concert presentations throughout the country, eagerly snapped up his services. He played for President Ford at the White House and Mayor Beame in New York. RCA quickly arranged several Fodor recordings. Television talk-shows vied for his presence. Now all he had to do was to win the hearts of the metropolitan music critics and cognoscenti.

Here he made a decision that was both naive and unintelligent. Apparently in an effort to counteract the current trend of violin recitals which are almost always overweight chamber music affairs featuring three or four sonatas, containing little or no crowd-pleasing virtuoso fare for balance, Fodor went to the opposite extreme. In his 1974 Fisher Hall debut he offered a program starting with Sarasate's *Caprice Basque* and ending with Paganini's *Nel cor più non mi sento* Variations, and included Tchaikovsky's *Valse Scherzo* and *Sérénade Mélancolique*, Wieniawski's *Légende* and Beethoven's *Romance* No. 2 in F-major. Such an act of defiance towards the critics was like waving a red flag in front of bulls. Had Fodor played like Heifetz he still would have been in for a drubbing. He was immediately deprecated as a "lightweight" not deserving of top-level contention, and failed to receive an invitation to appear as soloist with the New York Philharmonic.

In later major appearances Fodor attempted to placate his tormentors by programming some sonatas, but the harm had been done. To give the critics their due, his performance, for all its flashy virtuosity, reflected considerable artistic juvenility, and was not always consistent even in the favored portion of his repertoire. It was playing calculated to delight unsophisticated audiences.

In contrast to young Friedman, Fodor's violinistic approach is not cast in the style of their teacher, Heifetz, though occasionally there are certain similarities, particularly in articulation and aggressiveness. His tone is of medium sonority, rather spare in texture but capable of extreme vibrant intensity. However, in flowing lyric phrases his vibrato can project a feeling of tautness. It is playing invariably oriented toward brilliance and bravura utterance. Fodor's temperament is tempestuous but not innately sensuous. An important violinistic talent, his basic shortcomings are vested in the man himself, in the areas of aesthetics and general culture, as has been the case with innumerable highly accomplished performers throughout the history of violin art. For some time he played on a borrowed Guarnerius del Gesù, but he has also performed many concerts on contemporary Peresson instruments.

Fodor's recordings reflect the best elements of his performance, except for an album of Kreisler pieces for which he is not equipped, as is the case with nearly all members of his generation in terms of communicating charm and elegance. His disc of the Paganini Concerto No. 1 is dashing and flamboyant, highlighted by a rapid stiff-arm staccato as spectacular as any I have ever heard. His *Nel cor più non mi sento* Variations compares favorably with any other performance in flair and excitement. The concerti of Tchaikovsky, Mendelssohn, Glazunov, Khachaturian and sundry shorter showpieces are all brilliantly negotiated, but below the highest artistic standards. Made in his mid-twenties the interpretations still contain vestiges of the gifted student who has not yet attained profundity of spirit and rounded musicianship. Now in his mid-thirties, Fodor is still striving to make the transition from precocious adolescence to maturity, from splashy instrumentalism to full-fledged artistry.

Like Fodor, **Elmar Oliveira's** road to fame and fortune came via Moscow. Both had an older violinist-brother named John, and the elder Oliveira (now a violinist in the Houston Symphony) was Elmar's first teacher when he began studying at the comparatively late age of nine. Son of a Portugese carpenter, he was born in Waterbury, Connecticut, in 1950. At eleven he played his first recital. Later he studied for three years with Ariana Bronne and then for eight years with her father, Raphael Bronstein, a disciple of the Auer Russian school, at the Manhattan School of Music. At fourteen he won the Hartford Symphony Scholarship Competition, and made his official solo debut with that orchestra. His 1966 victory in the New York Philharmonic Young People's Concerto Competition earned him a solo appearance with the prestigious group. A 1973 New York recital debut brought mixed reviews. Performing on the borrowed 1708 "Empress of Russia" Stradivarius, he was cited for his facility in Paganini caprices, his "masterly" Bach, his lack of elegance in Vitali and his insufficient drama in Beethoven. His playing in general was characterized as small-scaled and restrained. In 1975 he achieved national recognition through the G.B. Dealy Award, giving him two solo stints with the Dallas Symphony. The highly coveted Naumburg String Competition First Prize provided two Alice Tully recitals in New York.

I heard his tape of short pieces taken from a live concert of this period. Evaluating the performance by the highest standards it was stylistically immature and tonally undistinguished. However, a tape of the Glazunov concerto made under inferior live concert conditions, with orchestra, revealed much expressiveness and inner warmth, plus a tone that was songful and solid, if not opulent. It was playing of unusual promise. Despite his contest successes, engagements were not very plentiful. Oliveira easily could have gravitated ultimately to the commercial recording jungle, as had so many gifted American-born violinists before him.

A man of unlimited self-confidence and determination, enormously fortified by his longtime close friend Sandra Robbins, he decided somewhat belatedly to enter the 1978 Tchaikovsky Competition. Oliveira shared first prize with the less-talented Russian Ilya Grubert. A strange manner of selection presented dual awards to the first four places. Had the written point scores of the individual jurors been placed into a computer and the judges forbidden to discuss the performances with anyone during the competition, as at the 1982 Indianapolis Competition, such a ridiculous outcome as eight co-winners of four prizes could scarcely have occurred mathematically. Oliveira's gold medal, the first for an American violinist in Moscow, together with that of cellist Nathaniel Rosen, created a temporary American euphoria. The pair were invited to the White House; engagements began to pour in.

Oliveira's first New York concert after his return from Moscow met with critical reservations as to the quality of his tone and the degree of his musical personality. Another recital four months later at Carnegie Hall, more successful, still met with some adverse criticism. Nevertheless, in the following years his career, in contrast to Fodor's, has been on the rise. This is both understandable and deserved.

Oliveira's tone is not one of unique personalization, nor is it of rich, lustrous vibrance. At times it can be taut and lacking in variety of color. But it is clean-cut, penetrating and polished, and especially effective on the E string. What places him above a sizable legion of admirable but essentially "faceless" violinists of his generation is a fiercely impassioned personal involvement, a sense of spontaneity, and expressive powers that communicate directly to the listener. Whereas so many play with machine-like efficiency, Oliveira has studied the subtle expressive devices of Kreisler and Heifetz from their old recordings, and liberally and tastefully applies slides and position changes in his lyric playing. This adds an extra dimension to his performance. No longer can anyone rightly characterize his playing as "reserved." In fact, he now often goes to the opposite extreme, and one wishes for an occasional slackening of his drive, a bit more self-discipline and serenity. At thirty-five he has yet to reach full maturity.

Unlike the great majority of violinists whose recordings flatter their playing, Oliveira's do not fully reflect the impact of his live concerts. I refer specifically to his Franck and Saint-Saëns sonatas. Perhaps future recordings will offset the imbalance. Unfortunately RCA-Victor did not accord him the comparatively extensive recording roster it gave Fodor and Friedman. Be that as it may, Oliveira at his best can produce many an exciting moment. And there can be little doubt that his career will continue to burgeon and his audiences grow.

The list of American violinists who have led or are leading solo careers, some in conjunction with other violinistic functions, continues and is long and honorable. The amount of attention given them varies individually, but all are known to professional colleagues as violinists whose accomplishments merit respect and admiration. More than a few, for a diversity of reasons, have not won the measure of sustained exposure as soloists they deserve. The following roster is not intended to be encyclopedic, but merely representative of the tremendous reservoir of violin talent in America.

Julian Olevsky (1927 - 1985), son of a violinist, was born in Germany, and began violin study at age seven. When his family emigrated to Argentina two years later, he came under the tutelage of Alexander Petschnikoff. He made his Buenos Aires debut at ten, toured widely as a youthful prodigy, and later concertized throughout the world. Arriving in the United States at twenty, he later became a citizen.

Olevsky's 60 recordings include concerti by Brahms, Bruch, Mendelssohn, Lalo and Wieniawski, the Bach solo sonata cycle, the 12 concerti of Vivaldi's *Il Cimento dell'Armonia e dell Invenzione*, fifteen sonatas by Handel and eight by Scarlatti. They show him to be a brilliant virtuoso, a fine tonalist with glowing temperament, and a tasteful musician and stylist, confirming the excellent impression I received when I heard him in concert during the 1950s. His 1955 disc of Kreisler's short numbers was rereleased in 1974 by Westminster Records under the waggish title, *Putting On the Fritz*. They are easily comparable in stylistic panache to the best three or four disc compilations of this music recorded in the last quarter of a century.

Sidney Weiss, born in Chicago in 1928, studied in that city with Joseph Gorner and Paul Stassevitch. His first major position was with the Cleveland Orchestra, in which he played for ten years. Later he played in the first violin section of the Los Angeles Philharmonic, and in 1968 became a co-concertmaster of the Chicago Symphony under Carlo Maria Giulini, a post he held through 1972. From 1973 to 1979 he was concertmaster of the Orchestre National de Monte Carlo. When Giulini became music director of the Los Angeles Philharmonic, he selected Weiss as his concertmaster

Sidney Weiss

in preference to several well-known violinists interested in the position. As of this writing he is still occupying the chair, and has frequently been soloist with the orchestra in concerti of Beethoven, Brahms, Prokofiev, Sibelius, the Vivaldi *Four Seasons* (the latter with without the music), and other major works, winning critical acclaim. For many years Weiss and his pianist-wife Jeanne, have performed successfully as a duo in sonata and concerto appearances. The Weiss repertoire is extensive. As a hobby he makes violins of such high quality that he sometimes plays them in public performances.

One of those violinists who has brought himself up from the ranks, Weiss is greatly underpublicized in relation to the caliber of his performance. With an intensely vibrant sound, a smartly controlled vibrato, excellent facility, cogent musicianship, a fervent temperament and mastery of suave digital expressive devices, he ranks among the leading American concertmaster-soloists.

To date, **Charles Treger** is the only American to win first prize in the Poznan Wieniawski Competition (1962). Born in Detroit in 1935, Treger studied with Hugo Kortschak, Szymon Goldberg and Adolf Busch (though his romantic-oriented playing reveals no trace of Busch's austere, old-fashioned, Germanic style). At sixteen he was soloist with the Detroit Symphony, and at twenty gave a New York recital in the Metropolitan Museum which was enthusiastically received. Appointed head of the University of Iowa string department, little known nationally, his Wieniawski victory came as a bolt from the blue, and resulted in the usual initial spate of concerts. The U.S. State Department, taking advantage of the situation to publicize American culture, sent him to fourteen countries. He also appeared as soloist with the Pittsburgh Symphony.

In 1969 Treger was offered the post of first violinist with the Lincoln Center Chamber Music Society, and relocated in New York. In 1972, apparently seeking to regain a solo career that was clearly in decline, he gave a series of three concerts in New York titled *The Romantic Revival* that received positive reviews, but not the kind from which great careers are made. In 1973 Treger retired from the Lincoln Center group. Forming a duo with the pianist André Watts that lasted for several seasons, Treger's public image was considerably enhanced. I heard one of the concerts and was impressed with his strong musical attributes, even though the highly individualistic Watts virtuosity is not ideal for team playing. As of this writing the partnership is not operational, possibly permanently dissolved. In 1985, Treger was named Musical Director of the Meadowmount School of Music, succeeding Galamian in the post.

On hearing Treger's recordings of the Moszkowski, Szymanowski No. 2 and Joachim *Hungarian* concerti, it is obvious that his Poznan triumph was no fluke. While the consistency of his medium-scaled playing varies, he displays a neatly facile technique, an ardent tone with a rather wide vibrato, and persuasive expressive powers. In all, here is yet another gifted American violinist, perhaps not of the highest international rank, but of admirable stature. And like so many worthy colleagues, he is sadly underpublicized.

Charles Castleman, born in 1941, made his first major appearance at age seven as soloist with Arthur Fiedler and the Boston Pops. Following successful youthful recitals, plus network radio and television shows, he made a debut at age twelve with the New York Philharmonic. He first studied with Emmanuel Ondricek and lists Josef Gingold and David Oistrakh as his "coaches." A graduate of Harvard and the Curtis Institute, which he attended simultaneously, he is now Professor of Violin at the Eastman School of Music in Rochester, New York. Castleman has also been soloist with the orchestras of Moscow, Chicago, Brussels, Philadelphia, San Francisco and, in 1981, the St. Louis Symphony, with which he gave the world premiere of the David Amram concerto, commissioned for him by the Ford Foundation.

In 1981, Castleman played the six Ysaÿe Solo Sonatas in Alice Tully Hall, the first New York performance of the complete cycle. With his recording of this cycle, Castleman joins a select international group of violinists who have recorded these works in their entirety. His interpretations exude flair and virtuosity. One might wish for a more heightened sense of poetry, but he does project a good measure of the freewheeling

Paul Zukovsky

style for which Ysaÿe was noted.

It would be nearly impossible to name an American-born violinist more dedicated to the cause of twentieth-century music than **Paul Zukovsky**, born in Brooklyn in 1943. Son of the author-poet Louis Zukovsky, he studied with Galamian from age seven. At thirteen he made a Carnegie Hall recital debut as a prodigy, and at seventeen his programs began to reflect his interest in contemporary compositions. He holds a bachelor's and a master's degree from Juilliard, where he won the Loeb Prize in 1963, followed by the Albert Spalding Prize at the Berkshire Music Center in 1965 and various laurels at the Paganini, Thibaud and Enesco international competitions. His activities have included faculty positions as a professor of violin at several major universities and conservatories.

Since there are about as few contemporary violin compositions that achieve repertorial permanence as there are full-fledged artists (as opposed to mere violinists) emerging from violin competitions, some observers would dispute the efficacy of devoting the overwhelming portion of one's career to the performance of new violin works. Yet this task must be undertaken! Many an admirable violinist who is not of topmost soloist rank finds himself partially limited to learning and performing contemporary works in order to obtain engagements. Still, an historic survey would indicate that stellar violinists have at one time or another performed and even commissioned new works (Sarasate, Ysaÿe, Kreisler,

Heifetz, Oistrakh, Stern, Perlman et al.).

Composers who ignore the inherent singing propensities of the violin, and insist upon using and abusing it for unorthodox, sensationalist purposes, are apt to find their works automatically consigned to oblivion. However, it is vital to remember that concerti such as Prokofiev's No. 1 and Bartók's No. 2, which three or four decades ago were considered impossibly avant-garde by many listeners, are now part of the standard repertoire. One must be forbearing and careful in judging new violin works. Only time can judge the true worth of a composition, and, for that matter, of an artist.

It is only natural that contemporary composers and their publicists tend to overrate a violinist like Zukovsky inasmuch as he is a champion of their products. But conversely, violin traditionalists will be just as likely to downgrade him, choosing to emphasize his negative attributes and overlook the service he is rendering to the cause of violin art. True, Zukovsky's tone is commonplace and generally one-dimensional in terms of beauty. And while he plays with great vigor and daring, his emotional communication is slender. But his facility is tremendous, registering at times with almost computerlike efficiency. Works such as the Roger Sessions concerto, Hindemith's *Kammermusik* No. 4, Penderecki's *Capriccio* and Elliot Carter's Duo for Violin and Piano are exceptional digital challenges, as are many of the works in Zukovsky's *Music for a 20th-Century Violinist*, representing 14 composers from Babbitt to Wolpe. He has recorded all of these except the Hindemith, along with the William Schuman concerto, the Ives sonatas, the overlong but provocative *A Mitzvah for the Dead* for violin and tape by Michael Sahl, and J.K. Randall's *Lyric* Variations for violin and computer.

As if to prove his worth as a legitimate virtuoso, Zukovsky has recorded Paganini's 24 Caprices, but in an unorthodox individual manner which drastically slows down the lyric segments as well as some of the technical passages, while still maintaining propulsive bravura tempi in many of the rapid sections. The results are debatable; the natural flow of the music is vitiated, melodic phrases become ponderous and dull, and the innate heroic brilliance that exemplifies Paganini is too often rendered academic. Caprice No. 4 takes 11 minutes and 39 seconds with repeats, No. 8, 9 minutes and 51 seconds. His playing of Caprice No. 6 in *ponticello* is quite bizarre. However, one cannot deny Zukovsky's ability to play as rapidly and cleanly as anyone.

Hearing him in concert, it was easy to ascertain why he chose the contemporary path. It required only a few bars of the *Adagio* from Bach's E-major concerto to realize that his awkward, stiff vibrato and his earthbound musicality were not calculated to produce transcendental artistry. But the *Kammermusik* No. 4 that followed was extremely impressive in

James Oliver Buswell IV

lightning-like, glistening passagework. In his best element, Zukovsky is a violinist to be respected.

Born in Fort Wayne, Indiana, in 1946, **James Oliver Buswell IV** is the son of an anthropologist father and a pianist-organist mother. At age five he began to play both piano and violin, and at seven was a violin soloist in the New York Philharmonic Children's Concerts. A year later he performed in similar concerts in Chicago and Fort Wayne. His teachers were Joseph Knitzer at the Eastman School, Paul Stassevitch at De Paul University and, starting in 1959, Galamian at Juillard. As a Harvard student he majored in fifteenth-century Italian art. But the violin was his destiny. He won first prize in the Merriweather Post contest in Washington, which led to a solo appearance with the National Symphony. In 1965 he played the Mendelssohn concerto in New York with the visiting Pittsburgh Orchestra under Steinberg, and the Stravinsky concerto with Bernstein and the New York Philharmonic. I heard him in the Stravinsky and was quite taken with his clean-cut, vigorous performance. However, one should not make serious artistic judgments on the basis of the Stravinsky concerto alone, no matter how well played.

In 1969 he was soloist with the Los Angeles Philharmonic in Mozart's Concerto No. 4 in D-major. His publicists had him decked out in top-hat, tails, cape and cane, in a sort of "blue-blood" image. One critic captioned his review with "The IV Buswell & the IV Mozart," and archly char-

acterized him as a branch off the Anglo-Saxon violinistic tree that produced Maude Powell, Albert Sammons and Albert Spalding. He displayed
a small, sweet tone of smooth texture and clean intonation. But while the
Rondo projected a measure of ebullience, the performance generated little
suavity or sophistication of style. Nor did the rather scrappy accompaniment of Frühbeck de Burgos facilitate matters.

Sometime later he dropped the "IV" from his publicity along with the
stuffed shirt image, and began his artistic growth in earnest. One of his
best-known recordings is Bach's Six Sonatas for Violin and Harpsichord,
with the eminent harpsichordist Fernando Valenti. The interpretations
are only partially convincing. The faster movements generally project the
verve of an uninhibited twentieth-century violinist. But in the slow movements, apparently in an attempt to blend with the inherent monochromatic sound of the harpsichord, Bushwell turns his vibrato on and off to
no specific purpose, except possibly to court authenticity, but the results
are aurally and spiritually arid. In contrast, his recording of Vaughan
Williams' boisterous and songful *Concerto Accademico* is bright and
buoyant.

Buswell has matured musically to a greater degree than many of his
colleagues born in the 1945 - 1955 period, and has become a well-known
figure at music festivals. He has been an artist-member of the Chamber
Music Society of Lincoln Center since 1976, and its only principal violinist. A professor at the vaunted Indiana University School of Music, he
is also founder-conductor of the Indiana University Chamber Orchestra.

In a recent performance of the Brahms Double Concerto with the redoubtable cellist Lynn Harrell, Buswell demonstrated that he is now a
formidable artist. He collaborated with his august partner on equal terms,
with a strong, vibrant sound, incisive attack, secure intonation, warm
temperament and thoughtful phrasing—the playing of a man who would
appear to possess broad cultural interests.

Glenn Dicterow, born in Los Angeles in 1948, is the son of Harold
Dicterow, long-time principal of the Los Angeles Philharmonic second
violin section, and Irina, an artist. He began violin at age eight with his
father and later studied with Manuel Compinsky, Naoum Blinder, and at
Juilliard, Galamian. Dicterow first came to my attention when he had
scarcely turned sixteen in a program that included the Sonatas No. 3 of
Leclair, Brahms and Ysaÿe. the Bruch Concerto No. 1 and Wieniawski's
Polonaise No. 1. At the time, I felt that among players of his age group, he
ranked just after Perlman and Zukerman. His technique was practically
infallible, his tone glowingly vibrant and smartly varied, his musicianship unusually disciplined for his age, and his interpretations charged
with a sense of spontaneity. My column was the first to give his potential
career serious consideration, and since then I have viewed his progress

with special interest.

About two years later he went to New York for further study, and in 1970 competed in Moscow's Tchaikovsky Competition. He took fifth prize behind Spivakov in a contest won by Kremer—neither of whom, in my opinion, is as well endowed with natural tonal lustre or sheer communicative power. There were the usual grumblings about the bias of East European jurors, and Dicterow, like Friedman before him, was sorely disappointed. He returned to Los Angeles, and in a "coming home" concert shared with pianist Horacio Gutierrez (who had won second prize in his category), played the Tchaikovsky concerto with Mehta and the Los Angeles Philharmonic.

It was not a night of glory for Dicterow. He played accurately and in a disciplined manner, but the wings of his temperament had been clipped and his expressive fire cooled. He had fallen into the "on-and-off" vibrato syndrome, though not to a pernicious degree (a habit he still retains). Whether this was the fault of unwise guidance from domineering Eastern advisors, or due to his own devices, is not possible to ascertain. Perhaps both were involved. Since top managers are more interested in "winners" and publicity-generating defectors than in fifth-prize laureates, his future as a soloist was not bright.

Fortunately, Zubin Mehta took an interest in Dicterow and recruited him for the Los Angeles Philharmonic, and after a period of orchestral experience, moved him to the nominal position of concertmaster alternating with Harth, who was the principal concertmaster. During this period Dicterow's natural talents began to revive, and his appearances with the orchestra, which included concerti of Saint-Saëns, Prokofiev, Vieuxtemps and Mendelssohn, among others, reasserted his stature as a soloist. His recordings of Wieniawski's *Polonaise* No. 1 and *Scherzo-Tarantelle* with the orchestra compare with the finest performances of these showpieces. With Harth's departure from the Los Angeles scene and Giulini's selection of Weiss as his concertmaster, Mehta brought Dicterow to New York where he is currently enjoying outstanding success as concertmaster of the Philharmonic. His Eastern solo stints in the concerti of Brahms, Shostakovich No. 1, Vieuxtemps and Prokofiev have won extraordinary acclaim. In his playing of Mozart, Dicterow does not project the ultimate grace and spiritual repose, but in romantic and contemporary works his rich sound and aggressive musicality rank him among the very finest American concertmaster-soloists.

Ida Kavafian was born around 1953 in Istanbul of Armenian parents, and came to America as a child. She studied with Mischakoff for three years, Galamian for two and Shumsky for four. In 1974 she won the Loeb Prize at Juilliard, and since then has been active as the violinist in the noted Tashi chamber group initiated by pianist Peter Serkin, which has concertized widely and boasts numerous recordings. Concurrently she has been striving to establish a career as a soloist.

At twenty-nine, in the interest of furthering her solo status, she entered the 1982 International Violin Competition of Indianapolis, and was awarded second prize. As a juror I could see immediately that she was among the most polished and experienced players of the forty-four participants. She had made noticeable progress from the time I heard he in recital about a year prior to the competition.

Like so many younger generation players, she excelled in twentieth-century music; her brilliant performances of the Bartók Solo Sonata, Ravel's sonata and Prokofiev's Concerto No. 1 stamped her as a virtuoso of uncommon accomplishment. Yet her solo Bach was overly stoic, her Mozart *Andante* from Concerto No. 4 wanting in subtlety and her Saint-Saëns *Introduction and Rondo Capriccioso* somehow lacking in sentiment and affection. A year later, in another recital, my opinion of her Bach and Mozart was reaffirmed but she had obviously made further strides. A performance of Ysaÿe's Solo Sonata No. 6 was dazzling, and her fingered octave passages were delivered with a dash and surety superior to any I have heard by a small-handed person. Superb by any standards, her Ravel sonata and *Tzigane* were intense in G string sound, stunning in facility and alert to the dictates of style. Her post-eighteenth-century music-making had gained in emotional projection though she still cannot be characterized as a movingly romantic player. But even if Kavafian does not win your heart, she can be an exciting violinist and one to admire. No doubt if she were a foreign defector her opportunities for a solo career would be greatly enhanced.

I have heard her sister **Ani Kavafian**, born around 1948, only on a disc of Kreisler favorites. They are played with clean agility, graceful phrasing, cool sound and limited sensuality. One cannot presume to make a serious evaluation of her artistry on such meager evidence. She enjoys a fine reputation as a chamber music performer and all-round musician.

Winner of the 1985 Queen Elisabeth Violin Competition in Brussels, **Nai-Yuan Hu,** born in Taiwan about 1961, now resides in the United States. A pupil of the late Broadus Erle for five years and of Silverstein for about one year, Hu ultimately became a confirmed disciple of Gingold. I first heard him in the 1982 International Violin Competition of Indianapolis. After making no more than a fair impression in the *Adagio* from Mozart's Concerto No. 5 and the *Adagio and Fugue* from Bach's C-major Solo Sonata, Hu literally "brought the house down" in a blazing performance of Sarasate's *Carmen Fantasy* that was the personification of sensuousness and subtle expressive devices. Paganini's Caprices No. 11 and No. 21 had been tossed off previously with flair and aplomb, plus extraordinary stiff-arm and flying staccatos. Later he offered a rich-toned expressive rendition of Fauré's Sonata No. 1 and an impassioned, idiomatic Bartók Concerto No. 2, almost impeccable in execution. His vibrato ran the gamut of speeds. Only experience and a measure of polish separated him from stellar artists. Here was a romantic-oriented talent of major stature. He launched into Saint-Saëns' *Introduction and Rondo Capriccioso*, and after a reasonably acceptable *Introduction*, he unaccountably ripped off the *Rondo* with mindless speed and graceless style. It was enough to reduce his award to fifth place. However, given discipline and maturity, a violinist of this vast violinistic and temperamental equipment can scarcely fail to make his mark in the world. Abetted by his magnificent performance of the Elgar concerto in Brussels, Hu has taken a great step up the ladder to fame. If he can perform the masterworks of Beethoven, Mozart and Brahms with comparable artistry, he has the potential to attain the uppermost ranks. He is also an assistant teacher to Gingold at Indiana University. It will be interesting to note the progress of his career.

Other younger-generation violinists deserve mention. **Andres Cardenes,** a Gingold pupil and 1982 Tchaikovsky Competition third prize laureate, promises to become an outstanding concertmaster-soloist. I heard **Stephanie Chase**, a Sally Thomas pupil (also a 1982 Tchaikovsky Competition third prize laureate), in a sensitive performance of Mozart's Concerto No. 5 and a recital which included a workaday Beethoven Sonata in C-minor and a scintillating Prokofiev No. 2. At her best, Chase is a violinist of considerable communicative talents. **Peter Zazofsky,** born in Boston in 1954 is the son of George Zazofsky, a former assistant concertmaster of the Boston Symphony. First taught by his father and later by Silverstein, Galamian and DeLay, Zazofsky has won laurels at many competitions. His citations include the Leventritt Award, bronze medal in Poland's Wieniawski Competition and second prize at the 1980 Queen Elisabeth Competiton. A recording of Bartók's Concerto No. 2 presents him as a player of technical brilliance and positive expressive powers, though neither his sound nor his musicality is strongly personalized. **Joseph Swensen**, born in 1960, a pupil of DeLay, is exceptional neither as a tonalist nor as a stylist at this writing, but his conscientious command of the instrument is prodigious. His recording of Ernst's *Last Rose of Summer* and *Erlking* compares favorably with those of similar showpieces played by such Soviet gymnasts as Kremer and Julian Sitkovetsky.

Approaching the forefront by leaps and bound is **Joshua Bell**, born in 1967, a Gingold disciple. One of the most outstanding natural talents since Perlman and Zukerman, Bell first received major acclaim as soloist with the Philadelphia Orchestra at age fourteen, and at eighteen is practically a veteran of the concert stage. He is also enrolled in a full scholastic program at Indiana University. On the basis of his successes to

Joshua Bell

date, it is possible that Bell may rise to stellar rank without recourse to the international competition circuit. His concert schedule is already substantial.

An exciting performer with great intensity of spirit as well as sound, Bell also has an ear for diversity. When he was sixteen I heard him perform the Tchaikovsky concerto with stunning virtuosity. His poise, polish and sophistication were beyond his years. Some months later, in recital, he played a Handel sonata with uncommon charm, Beethoven's *Kreutzer* sonata with a degree of introspection rare for his age, and a dazzling Ysaÿe Sonata No. 6. Bell is well along the way to becoming a master of stylistic variety, and is a violinist of daring and enterprise. It is hoped that he will divest himself of some distracting knee-bends. Here is a career to watch!

Daniel Majeske, concertmaster of the Cleveland Orchestra, has made an admirable recording of Paganini's caprices. **Rafael Druian's** sonata recordings register stylistic piquance. **Charles Libove** and his pianist-wife Nina Lugovoy, constitute a duo of impressive stature. And while this volume is not designed to explore chamber music playing in any comprehensive manner, one can scarcely refrain from mentioning such leading American violinists in the field as Robert Mann, Alexander Schneider, Arnold Steinhardt, John Dalley, Earl Carlyss, Isidore Cohen, Daniel Guilet and Donald Weilerstein.

Note: For further discussion of women violinists, see the chapter Women and the Violin in *Master Violinists in Performance*, Henry Roth, Paganiniana Publications.

A future volume by Henry Roth will include in-depth evaluations of Szeryng, Ricci, Grumiaux, Perlman and Zukerman, plus surveys of Israeli, Italian, French, Korean, Japanese, Chinese and leading Middle-European violinists.

It will also trace the career development of many current generation players already mentioned, and examine the rising crop of violinists.

CHAPTER NINE

Violin Art in China

A NUMBER OF OBSERVERS have noted the amazing ability of individual Chinese string players to imbibe and communicate the Western musical ethos. Such artists as cellist Yo-Yo Ma and violinist Cho-Liang Lin have already won international honors; Nai-Yuan Hu won the 1985 Queen Elisabeth Competition; and several other players of Chinese descent are in the process of developing important careers. Until the present time all of the most internationally eminent Chinese string soloists were born outside of mainland China. However, my recent invitation to the People's Republic of China, which gave me the opportunity to hear and work with many of their outstanding young violin talents, has convinced me that this country is on the threshold of international violin prominence.

Violin art in China is comparatively young. The nation's oldest institute of higher musical education is the Shanghai Conservatory, founded in 1927. The Central Conservatory at Beijing was not established until 1950, the year after the victorious revolution. Today the nation boasts nine music conservatories led by those of Shanghai and Beijing. The latter two, as is to be expected, maintain a spirit of friendly competition. Their student bodies consist of an elementary school, ages nine to twelve, an intermediate school, ages thirteen to seventeen, an undergraduate school, ages eighteen to twenty-two, and graduate school, ages twenty-three to twenty-five. There are also special classes for older players, particularly professionals who come from various parts of the country to refurbish their skills. The study of English is avidly pursued, and I was told that each professor, associate professor and lecturer must now pass a rudimentary English examination before appointment.

Although the levels of leadership are clearly defined, the faculties cooperate and work in a collective manner, far more so than their Western counterparts. A good number of the senior professors received top-level training in Moscow, Leningrad, Budapest, Bucharest and Prague before

1960. And some of the teachers and students have studied in the West.

As in the Soviet Union, there is emphasis on solo performance, but in recent years chamber music training and playing are becoming an integral part of conservatory curriculum. At Beijing's Central Conservatory, students are obliged to take two chamber music classes per week of two hours each for three years, and three sessions per week of orchestra rehearsal. Although many virtuosic works such as Wieniawski's Concerto No. 1 in F-sharp minor and the *Original Variations*, Op. 15, and the Ysaÿe sonatas, among others, are more or less staples of their repertoire, the masterworks of Bach, Beethoven, Mozart and Brahms are receiving their rightful share of attention. A number of young Chinese violinists have already gained some initial experience in major international competitions with their foreign contemporaries. In view of the obvious competence of Chinese violin professors, I found their willingness and, indeed, eagerness to accept constructive Western recommendations remarkably selfless. One can scarcely overstate their enthusiasm in receiving new violinistic and musical ideas, and concepts that were often divergent from their own. The pupils avidly soaked up every suggestion, despite the difficulties of communicating through an interpreter. My own contribution consisted of a series of lectures on *The Development of Violin Art in the Twentieth Century* (all to capacity audiences), and lengthy master classes at both the Shanghai and Beijing Central Conservatories. Lecture attendance was not obligatory at either conservatory. To my delight, my trepidation as to the fate of my lectures because of possible translation problems proved baseless, thanks to the splendid cooperation and expertise of interpreters Gu Lian-Li in Shanghai and Situ Hua-Cheng in Beijing.

Any objective evaluation of the present status of Chinese violin playing must take into consideration the havoc wrought by the mindless Cultural Revolution, 1966-1976. Players in their twenties, who might now be competing with their peers internationally, had been cut off from study in their critical formative years. During this sad decade, lessons were suspended, instruments and books destroyed, professors and students reviled and even physically abused. Fortunately the large library of records and tapes at the Shanghai Conservatory were for the most part successfully protected from the marauding "Red Guards." The rapid recovery in only a comparatively few years by the Chinese is incredible, and testifies to the resiliency of their basic music education apparatus. Surprisingly, there are some admirable violinists in the twenty to twenty-five-year age bracket. However, the intermediate students, now teenagers, who were too young to be affected by the political aberrations of that period, represent the heart of China's violinistic potential in terms of future international competition.

Those teachers and students who read English keep abreast of international violin news and developments through *The Strad* and other foreign publications. Each institution has comprehensive music, book, record and tape libraries, and up-to-date equipment. The students and teachers listen carefully to recordings of Heifetz, Oistrakh and the other great violinists. Like their counterparts everywhere, small practice rooms abound on the campuses, emitting a cacophony of diverse sounds, vocal and instrumental.

The violin is extremely popular in China. There is a total of 140 violin students in the nine to twenty-two-year-old group at the Beijing Central Conservatory and a comparative number at the Shanghai Conservatory, representing the nation's finest violin talent.

In addition, Beijing has some 300 pupils in special pre-elementary classes for the four to six-year-olds. It is estimated that in a few years there may be as many as ten thousand violin students throughout the nation. Positions await conservatory graduates as orchestra players and teachers, while job security is universal. In fact, some professors enjoy full salaries although they have only three or four pupils. Average pay for workers in China at this writing is about forty yuan a month (a yuan is around forty American cents). Symphony orchestra musicians earn sixty to eighty yuan, a full professor at the conservatories, one hundred. This is still little enough in terms of buying power. But a feeling of elation gripped the Beijing Central Conservatory just prior to our departure because the government was in the process of making sweeping reforms and economic improvements among all classes of intellectual workers.

Our first stop was the Shanghai Conservatory, a huge sprawling campus with a conglomeration of new and old buildings. It services 800 students, including those studying Chinese traditional instruments, and employs 400 teachers divided between musical and academic subjects. Violin students receive two one-hour private lessons a week (though I was told the burgeoning intermediate group usually is given one and a half hour lessons). Several fathers and mothers who are on the violin faculty are either their children's nominal teacher or give guidance at home in daily practice.

The school abounds in violin talent, I heard twenty-six players from all categories. Among them were Wang Xiao-Dong, just turning fifteen, a pupil of Zhang Shi-Xiang, initially taught by his father. Wang, already winner of honors at the Menuhin competition for juniors in London, played Prokofiev's Concerto No. 2, Bach's Partita No. 1, Brahms's Sonata No. 3, Mozart's Concerto No. 1 and Szymanowski's *Romance*. His playing is marked by a natural instinct for expressive phrasing, splendid facility, a sense of discipline, an ability to adapt to stylistic diversity and a full, round tone. His vibrato is a bit slow in intensely romantic episodes, but if he continues to develop properly, his potential is outstanding.

Gu Wei-Fang, twenty-two, pupil of Zheng Shi-Sheng (chairman of the string department), played Wieniawski's Concerto No. 1 with exceptional agility and vibrant bravura aggressiveness, and tossed off the difficult Saint-Saëns-Ysaÿe *Valse Caprice* with stunning virtuosity. His Chausson *Poème* wanted more subtlety and imagination, but his Mozart Concerto No. 5 was smoothly wrought and intermittently graceful. His sound is brilliant but tends to be one-dimensional. Judging by the highest current major competition standards, his work is still somewhat uneven and needs maturing.

Qian Zhou, fifteen, pupil of Zhou Bin-You (wife of Professor Zheng), winner of the first prize in her age group in the 1984 all-China Competition, displayed a fiery temperament in Vieuxtemps' Concerto No. 4 and Saint-Saëns' *Havanaise*. After being alerted to the difference between blatant passion and controlled visceral intensity, she played the concerto's *Andante Religioso* with surpassing beauty. Qian needs much more self-discipline, training and experience, but has the capacity to go far. Zhang Le, another Zhang Shi-Xiang pupil, handled Wieniawski's Concerto No. 1 with dexterity and fervor, and Beethoven's Sonata No. 7 with intelligence and a measure of drama, if a bit heavy-handedly. He is a very strong player who, when he gains more polish, we may be hearing more of.

The Zheng pupil Hu Yi, twenty years old, played Ravel's *Tzigane* with formidable technique and tonal intensity, then proceeded to a thoughtful, well-ordered Beethoven *Spring* Sonata. Her playing needs to gain in subtle inflection; her violinistic mien is somewhat over-serious and could profit from an occasional "smile" in light-hearted passages. Zhuo Gun, eighteen, pupil of Shen Gua-En, offered musical probity and a sweet tone in Beethoven's Sonata No. 7, and played Paganini's Caprice No. 24 with flair and solid, if not quite impeccable technique. His projection is large-scaled; here is a promising talent. Li Wei-Gang, twenty-one, pupil of Li Ke-Qiang (his father), exhibited good equipment, drive and a strong vibrant sound in Brahm's Sonata No. 3. He still has difficulty in slowing down his generally rapid vibrato to conform to the spirit of Bach's solo sonatas. (I found this to be a problem with several talented pupils at both conservatories). If Li can surmount this obstacle and continues his development, he, too, can be a contender.

Five other teenage girls indicated superior talent. Zheng Chin, fourteen, pupil of Zhou Bin-You, played Mozart's Concerto No. 3 warmly and buoyantly, and Sarasate's *Introduction and Tarantelle* with facile fingers. Shen Sang, fourteen, pupil of You Rou-Bin, generated some fervid G string sound and solid technical command in Wieniawski's Concerto No. 2, and stylistic enterprise in *Morning at Mountain Top*, a catchy Chinese-idiom vignette, cleverly constructed, that would make a charming encore on any program. Zhang Yao, fifteen, another You Rou-Bin pupil, played Lalo's *Symphonie Espagnole* with glowing sound, brio and a budding sense of style. Wang Bin, sixteen, a Zhou Bin-You pupil, daringly hit the initial high E and A phrase endings in the opening of Dvořák's Concerto in A-minor with electric vibrance. Though she had a tendency to rush, her playing was scrupulously clean and warm. Qi Ming, seventeen, pupil of Li Ke-Qiang, gave an exuberant and reasonably neat account of Paganini's Concerto No. 1. Among those pupils not named here, any one could suddenly blossom into a player of distinction. The same can be said of five or six youngsters in the nine to twelve-year-old category who gave rousing performances of concerti by de Beriot and Rode.

Jin Zhe, thirty-four, a Li pupil, concertmaster of an orchestra in Northern China, played Bruch's *Scottish Fantasy* with verve and competency.

Ding Zhi-Nuo, vice-chairman of the Department of Orchestral Instruments and one of several professors sent to study in Europe and America, appears to be the catalyst for chamber music playing at Shanghai. Formerly a violinist in the conservatory's all-woman string quartet which performed abroad, she has formed several student quartets. It is only in recent years that the invaluable contribution of chamber-group playing in strengthening musicianship and refining aesthetic sensibilities has begun to be fully appreciated here. Two Ding-coached quartets gave tidy, conscientious readings, one in Brahms and Mozart quartets, the other in those of Haydn and Barber. One of these Shanghai quartets won second prize at the 1985 International Competition in Portsmouth, England.

The Chinese-style main building of Beijing's Central Conservatory, once the birthplace of a prince, must certainly be one of the most picturesque of edifices consecrated to music education. The atmosphere, perhaps a bit more formal (as befits a capitol city) than the relaxed ambience of Shanghai, in no way affected the generous, sensitive hospitality of our hosts, which proved equal to the warmth of our reception in Shanghai. Of the Central Conservatory's 140 violin students, 100 are in the primary and intermediate groups, and 40 in the eighteen to twenty-two university classes. Each pupil receives two one-hour lessons a week; the teaching staff numbers thirty. Though our stay in Beijing was shorter than that in Shanghai, my lectures and master classes again enjoyed capacity attendance. Professor Han Li, the cosmopolitan English-speaking Chairman of the Violin Department, presented some of the institution's best pupils. We soon learned that Beijing, too, has its share of promising students.

Unfortunately, Jiang Yi-Wen, twenty, who competed at the 1982 Indianapolis Competition, was temporarily sidelined with a severe case of "violinist's neck." Not surprising, since he told me he practices eleven hours a day when preparing for a competition (which is a good deal of the time).

Chai Lian, sixteen, pupil of Wang Zhi-Long, easily surmounted the challenges of Sarasate's *Carmen Fantasy* with powerful fingers, though his vibrato was overrapid and his understanding of the Iberian idiom, rudimentary.

Conversely, Mong Hai-Ou, twenty-two, a Han Li pupil, played Beethoven's Sonata No. 7 with meticulous musicianship and thorough self-discipline; her tone, too, is sweet and congenial. She then turned to Vieuxtemps' Concerto No. 5, and in a reversal of musical character, instilled the work with bravura aggressiveness, ardent sound and firm digital command.

Kong Zhao-Hui, twenty-two, pupil of Sui Ke-Qiang, handily negotiated Ysaÿe's Sonata No. 3, but was not sufficiently conversant with the poetic nature of the opening page. Pin De-Zheng, twenty, another Sui pupil, gave workmanlike performances of Ysaÿe's Sonata No. 6 and the Bach *Chaconne*. Zhao Qian, twenty-one, pupil of Zhao Wei-Gian, her father, read through Ysaÿe's Sonata No. 1, rendered a Paganini caprice cleanly, and after she was instructed to chasten her vibrato, played the opening segment of the Glazunov concerto with rich tone.

Chao Bing, nineteen, a Sui pupil, medalist in the 1984 all-China Competition, exhibited good musicality and secure technique in the Brahms concerto. His interpretation is still in the process of developing, but he possesses strong potential.

The day before our departure, a lad of thirteen, who looked more like eleven, Guo Chang, pupil of Lin Yao-Ji, played in my final master class. His violin actually seemed too large for him. He launched into Smetana's *From My Homeland* with the sound, spontaneity and expressive powers of a mature stellar romanticist, then played Wieniawski's Polonaise No. 1 with blazing temperament. His tiny hands seemed to encounter little difficulty in the various batteries of thirds, tenths and fingered octaves. I have long since learned not to make hard-and-fast predictions about precocious juveniles. All too many have come to naught. However, little Guo is a rare world-class talent. Nurtured properly, he could have a brilliant future.

In the realm of sheer talent, China would seem to have an ever-increasing supply. Their continuing violinistic contacts with the West will no doubt spur improvement in such matters as broadening their range of tonal color, better relating vibrato speed and usage to the type of music they are performing, alerting them to new vistas of interpretive and stylistic subtleties, and above all, gaining in overall polish and sophistication. Obviously the arbiters of their violinistic destinies are well aware of these shortcomings, and take every opportunity to eradicate them. A number of young violinists are now studying abroad.

In dire need of improvement is the piano accompaniment situation, which is utilitarian rather than artistic. This militates seriously against the overall quality of performances. It is to be hoped that the Chinese will begin to recognize that piano collaboration is an art, and take measures to train pianists in this important field.

Practically all Chinese students play on Chinese-made instruments. These are surprisingly good in sound and response, but in no way comparable to the fine vintage violins many Western youngsters either own or can borrow for competitions and concerts. This represents a major problem. How can the Chinese overcome this handicap in international contests? Their country, pulling itself up by the proverbial bootstraps, cannot afford to buy top-quality instruments for their collective string players at current inflated prices. Recently a wealthy Chinese businessman living abroad donated over twelve million dollars to help develop Chinese athletes for world competition. Will some similiar philanthropic gesture result in procuring fine instruments for mainland China?

Will the Chinese cultural establishment, so eager for international recognition, overemphasize the value of contest medals like their counterparts in other countries? Will they realize that medals won by musically-limited, soon-forgotten soloists can be no substitute for artists thoroughly grounded in every phase of the repertory?

In 1986, China plans to enter the field of international competitions, the same year the Moscow Tchaikovsky Competition takes place, and practically at the same time as the Indianapolis International Competition. However, the Chinese have wisely decided to limit their contest to two age groups, i.e. twelve to sixteen and seventeen to twenty. Meanwhile, the world of violin art should take note—a new giant is looming on the scene.

This article was published originally in the April 1985 issue of *The Strad*. A short time later, Wang Xiao-Dong of the Shanghai Conservatory and Guo Chang of the Central Conservatory of Music in Beijing, cited in the article, won first prizes in their respective age groups in the 1985 Menuhin Competition for young violinists.

BIBLIOGRAPHY

Applebaum, Samuel and Sada, *The Way They Play*, Vols. 2 (1973) and 3 (1975), Paganiniana Publications, Inc., Neptune City, New Jersey.

Applebaum, Samuel and Roth, Henry, *The Way They Play*, Vols. 5 and 6 (1978), Vol. 7 (1980), Vol. 10 (1981), Paganiniana Publications, Inc., Neptune City, New Jersey.

Auer, Leopold, *My Long Life in Music*, Frederick A. Stokes Company, New York, 1923, 1925.

Bachmann, Alberto, *An Encyclopedia of the Violin*, Da Capo Press, New York, 1966, 1977.

Chotzinoff, Samuel, *Days at the Morn*, Harper & Row.

Creighton, James, *The Discopaedia of the Violin*, James Creighton, 1974, University of Toronto Press, Toronto and Buffalo.

Davenport, Marcia, *Too Strong for Fantasy*, Charles Scribner's Sons, New York, 1967.

Finck, Henry T., *My Adventures in the Golden Age of Music*. This 1971 Da Capo edition is an unabridged re-publication of the first edition published in New York and London in 1926 by Funk & Wagnalls Company.

Flesch, Carl, Memoirs of *Carl Flesch*, translated by Hans Keller, Rockliff Publishing Corporation, Great Britain, 1957.

Gingold, Josef, *Private Notes* (unpublished).

Lahee, Henry, C., *Famous Violinists of Today and Yesterday*, L.C. Page and Company, Boston, 1899.

Lochner, Louis, *Fritz Kreisler*, Macmillan Publishing Co., Inc., New York, 1951.

Martens, Frederick H., *Violin Mastery*, published by Frederick A. Stokes Co., New York 1919.

Martin, George, *The Damrosch Dynasty*, Houghton Mifflin Co., Boston, 1983.

McBrodie, Fawn, *Thomas Jefferson, An Intimate History*, W.W. Norton & Co., New York, 1974.

Persinger, Louis, *Why the Violin?* Cor Publishing Co., Massapequa, New York, 1957, 1965.

Piatigorsky, Gregor, *Cellist*, Doubleday, Garden City, New York, 1965.

Plaskin, Glenn, *Horowitz, a Biography*, William Morrow and Company, Inc., New York, 1983.

Primrose, William, *Walk on the North Side, Memoirs of a Violist*, Brigham Young University Press, Provo, Utah, 1978.

Saleski, Gdal, *Musicians of a Wandering Race*, Bloch Publishing Company, New York, 1949.

Schwartz, Boris, *Great Masters of the Violin*, Simon and Schuster, New York, 1983.

Soroker, Yakov, *David Oistrakh*, Lexicon Publishing House, Jerusalem, 1982.

Spalding, Albert, *Rise to Follow*, Henry Holt and Company, Inc., New York, 1943.

Thomas, Theodore, *A Musical Autobiography*, edited by George P. Upton, Da Capo Press, New York, 1964; original 2-volume work publishing by A.C. McClurg & Co., Chicago, 1908.

INDEX